SPINDRIFT

Spindrift

Stories from the Sea Services

Dan, Robert, and Paul Gillcrist

Schiffer Military/Aviation History
Atglen, PA

ACKNOWLEDGMENTS

Our principal debt of gratitude goes to all of those colorful characters whose escapades are chronicled here. However, they are too numerous to mention, and to single out a few would be unfair to those ignored.

Nevertheless, the encouragement and humility of Don Colyer (USMC), in generously allowing himself to be portrayed as the villain or hero in many of these sea stories is appreciated. An ever greater gift was the enjoyment, once again, of his company after thirty-five years.

The chapter entitled *"HMS Leopard,"* was "cleared" through Midshipman John Joss, Royal Navy (Retired) for accuracy. His editorial comments, imposed so rigorously, made the product much more readable.

Of all the contributors to this effort, the most important was Steve Millikin, Captain, USN (Retired). Steve volunteered to do all of the initial editing of this book *pro bono*, an enormous effort for which he considered a bottle of Chivas Regal "adequate compensation." His editing skills, honed over seven years as editor of "Hook" magazine, has added immeasurably to the credibility of this work.

Steve's input was merciless...but essential! We will be forever grateful for his input...rendered so unstintingly.

Book Design by Ian Robertson.

Printed in the United States of America.
ISBN: 0-7643-0590-5

We are interested in hearing from authors with book ideas on related topics.

Published by Schiffer Publishing Ltd.
77 Lower Valley Road
Atglen, PA 19310
Phone: (610) 593-1777
FAX: (610) 593-2002
E-mail: Schifferbk@aol.com
Please write for a free catalog.
This book may be purchased from the publisher.
Please include $3.95 postage.
Try your bookstore first.

Contents

Foreword

"...any man who may be asked in this century what he did to make his life worthwhile, I think can respond with a good deal of pride and satisfaction: 'I served in the United States Navy'"
- President John F. Kennedy, 1917-1963

Rarely, if ever, do we attend a gathering of old shipmates wherein someone doesn't ask something like, "do you remember the time when old...?" What follows that query is always a recounting of a sea story.

Of course, the passage of time, and the number of times that particular story has been told, are both inversely proportional to the accuracy with which the account compares to the actual event. And, after so much time has elapsed, and after so many recountings, we suspect that a story makes an effortless transition to the apochryphal.

All of the stories contained in the pages of this book are based upon true events. We make no boasts, however, about their accuracy; and suspect that at least some of them are truly apochryphal. Nevertheless, the cumulative effect of their recountings (one more time), may give the reader the sense of a fraternal organization of people, many of whom are genuine characters; but all of whom are dedicated to protecting our way of life.

Should any of our readers take issue with the details in any of these stories, we stand ready to admit to the effects of the passage of some 40 plus years and the "maturing" of our memories.

It isn't clear to us why the U.S. Navy and Marine Corps seem to have so many more characters than, say, the other military services. But we believe that to be the case.

There has always been the thread of suspicion in our minds that the reason lies in the notion of proximity. People on board Navy ships live "cheek-by-jowl" to one another. But the analogy doesn't end there. Shipboard people live close to everything...from the sublime to the ridiculous...life included. For example, on any man-of-war people work, eat and sleep within a few feet of enough munitions, that a chance ignition could turn everyone on board to dust.

Also close at hand are engineering power plants that generate superheated steam hot enough to incinerate everyone on board in a few seconds. Also a few feet away from those same bunks are enormous sewage holding tanks, a jail, a chapel, an armory, bathrooms, messing spaces, incredibly lethal weapons and all the other accoutrements of a military organization.

Small wonder, then, that a sense of community exists on a ship that is far more tightly knit than that found, for example, on a garden-variety army base.

The difference may also lie in the fact that the crew of a warship is always steaming in harm's way! One small error by even the least important member of the crew can send a ship to the bottom in an astonishingly short time. Rescue is never a certainty at sea.

The sea is always the relentless, unforgiving enemy.

Robert Gillcrist, Corporal, U.S. Marine Corps   (Marine Corps insignia)

Dan Gillcrist, Torpedoman Second Class, U.S. Navy (Silver dolphins)

Paul Gillcrist, Rear Admiral, U.S. Navy (Retired)   (Gold wings)

PART I:
The Bubbleheads

"He goes a great voyage that goes to the bottom of the sea."
- George Herbert: "Jacula Prudentum" 1651

The different communities in the Navy refer to one another often in quaint terms. The aviation community, for example, has always referred to the submariners as "Bubbleheads." It doubtless had something to do with the rudimentary roll indicator (much like a carpenter's level) which used to be a primary instrument for determining level operations.

The operational imperative for "running silent" never seemed to transfer itself to other aspects of submariners' naval careers. They have been vocal, dedicated, outspoken, and selfless for the most part. The fact that submariners occupied the office of Chief of Naval Operations for an unprecedented fourteen years from 1982 to 1996 speaks volumes for the "silent service."

Chapter 1:
The Scientist and the NR-1

"Sunset and evening star,
And one clear call for me!
And may there be no moaning of the bar,
When I put out to sea."
- Alfred, Lord Tennyson: "Crossing The Bar"

The deep, booming voice of the Commander in Chief, Atlantic Command, came out of the telephone headset so loud that I gave an involuntary flinch. "Those fellas are doing it again!," the voice said. I instinctively knew better than to ask either of the two questions which were being begged by his opening salvo: Who are "those fellas," and what are they doing? It should become obvious if only I could keep him talking.

"Yes, sir," was all I could think of saying (not a bad answer for the Director of Operations of the Atlantic Command).

"They are towing NR-1 to the Norwegian Sea again, in spite of what happened the last time they tried it." Now, I knew that the CinC was talking about the submariners. Being relatively new on the job, I had only a faint understanding of what the highly classified mission of NR-1 really was. But I remembered that it was the Navy's research and development, nuclear-powered submarine, and that it did classified things in the Norwegian Sea. The things that it did way up there was to blunt the threat posed by the submarine forces of the Soviet Union to the free world...and specifically to the United States and our Navy. By now I was frantically signaling for one of my staff in the outer office to come in to my office. He was a submariner, and I knew he would be able to help. He came in and glanced at the note I had hastily scribbled on a pad of paper. It said, "NR-1, WTF???" What the f— was going on with NR-1?, was the meaning which my submariner assistant understood immediately. He scribbled a note on the pad as follows: "The tow rig failed and it broke loose last spring. We almost lost the boat and the crew...hairy!!! The CinC was pi—ed!. SubLant plans to tow it north next week." Now, I understood.

"Admiral. I'm going to watch the progress of that whole operation like a hawk," was all I could think of responding.

Summary of Features

Missions

- Search
- Large and small object recovery
- Geological survey
- Oceanographic research
- Installation and maintenance of underwater equipment

Search Capabilities

- Side looking sonar
  - 600-ft (180-m) search width with 1-ft (30-cm) resolution or
  - 2400-ft (730-m) search width with 4-ft (1.2-m) resolution
- Forward looking sonar (CTFM)
  - 3- to 1500-yard (3- to 1370-m) range
  - Range resolution: 1 to 30 yards (1 to 27 m) depending on range scale selected
  - Lateral coverage: automatic wide sweep, 190°; sector narrow sweep, 60°

PRINCIPAL CHARACTERISTICS

Length overall	137 ft (41.8 m)
Pressure hull length	96 ft 1 in. (29.3 m)
Diameter	12 ft 6 in. (3.8 m)
Maximum beam (at stern stabilizers)	15 ft 10 in. (4.8 m)
Maximum navigational draft	15 ft 1 in. (4.6 m)
Box keel depth	4 ft (1.2 m)
Design operating depth	2375 ft (724 m)
Displacement submerged	372 tons
Speed, surfaced/submerged	4.6/3.6 knots
Endurance, nominal	210 man-days
maximum	315 man-days

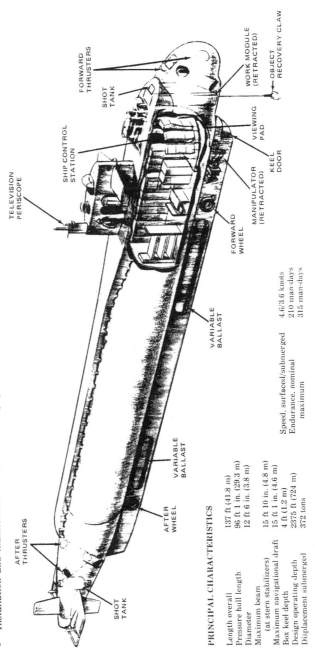

AFTER THRUSTERS

AFTER WHEEL

VARIABLE BALLAST

SHOT TANK

TELEVISION PERISCOPE

SHIP CONTROL STATION

VARIABLE BALLAST

FORWARD WHEEL

MANIPULATOR (RETRACTED)

KEEL DOOR

VIEWING PAD

FORWARD THRUSTERS

SHOT TANK

WORK MODULE (RETRACTED)

OBJECT RECOVERY CLAW

"You had better, Paul, because I am going to watch you like a hawk!" He hung up the hot line telephone without waiting for a response. I was a little annoyed because the submariners (they don't call them the silent service for no reason) had not told me about this. Had they given me a "heads up" it would have helped a bit. I would have asked for a briefing on the whole subject, and surely the disastrous events of the previous spring would have come to light.

By the time of my next conversation with the CinC I knew considerably more about NR-1 and the coming operation with her. She was a one-of-a-kind ship (that always meant operational problems), 137 feet in length, with a beam of 15 feet 10 inches, a draft of 5 feet surfaced, and she displaced 372 tons fully loaded. She normally deployed with a crew of 11, which included one to four "observers" (scientists). She had a single screw and both bow and stern thrusters, and could make only about five knots surfaced and four knots submerged. She had been built and launched in 1969.

Details of her capabilities were highly classified, but I knew we had to tow her to her operating area because she could only hold a 30 day supply of food and consumables. For a number of reasons we always towed her manned and submerged. The crew was always hand-picked and highly talented, and were all called "pilots." The on-board scientist this trip was to be a famous ocean engineer, a PhD in ocean engineering.

The good doctor will best be known by naval historians as the brilliant scientist who produced that magnificent map of the underseas surface of our planet. In conjunction with the National Geographic Society, he created a full-color map showing the intimate geodetic details of the Earth's surface that was covered by water as well as the dry land. The model made the planet look as if the oceans were not present. The various sea mounts are shown, as are the deeper portions of the oceans. The deeper the area, the darker the shade of blue. The Marianas Trench, for example, the deepest spot on the planet, is a deep cobalt color. I kept a four-by-six foot replica of his famous chart on the wall of my office for years until I finally gave it to my son.

But the good doctor will forever be etched in my memory for an entirely different reason. The famous scientist died on board the U.S. Navy's nuclear powered research submarine NR-1 while it was on that special deployment to the Norwegian Sea. But I am getting ahead of the story.

The ominous warning given to me by the CinC that afternoon stayed with me. He was vastly more experienced than was I. When he said something, it warranted careful watching. I took the warning literally. Therefore, it should have come as no surprise to me when my submariner representative walked into my office with a worried look on his face. I knew before he even opened his mouth that there was "trouble in River City," and it had to do with NR-1!

"The scientist died last night!" he told me. At first it didn't sink in. I hadn't even considered that anyone could die on a submarine of natural causes. All sorts of dire disasters had occurred to me, but not the natural death of one of its crew.

In my job as the Assistant Chief of Staff for Operations (J-3), I had dealt almost on a weekly basis with medical emergencies on our deployed submarines. Since we didn't keep too much medical talent aboard, it was a matter of getting the ship or the patient to a doctor. If the submarine was not on patrol, we would normally divert the ship to a facility…be it afloat or ashore. If, however, the ship was on a patrol and therefore could not be diverted, we went through all sorts of extraordinary means to get the patient transported to a medical facility. The most frequent scenario seemed always to occur at three o'clock in the morning. It was a message from an SSBN (ballistic missile submarine) saying that one of her crewmen was gravely ill and required immediate medical transfer. We went through this so often that it was an almost automatic drill.

First, we would notify the Joint Chiefs of Staff in Washington, D.C., that we were going to have to pull an SSBN off the line. Then we would plan for a shift of nuclear targets to other deployed SSBNs. It was almost like the game of musical chairs. Literally hundreds of nuclear targets were shifted around, from SSBN to SSBN until we had the ship with the medical problem "covered." Then we would pull her off the line, arrange a rendezvous with a ship or helicopter (depending on the severity of the emergency), and transfer the stricken crewman to a medical facility. Rarely did we try to replace the crewman with another…and never did we try to get the crewman back to his deployed ship while it was on patrol.

The business of launching a CH-53 helicopter, along with an aerial tanker, running it out to some remote spot in the Northern Atlantic to rendezvous with an SSBN which we had

just pulled off the line, was complicated. Of course, we tried always to do it under cover of darkness. Then the problem of getting a sick crewman from the submarine into the helicopter was even more difficult. Submarines behave like predatory sharks when they are submerged…sleek, silent, swift, and deadly. However, when they are on the surface in any kind of moderately rough seas, they wallow, pitch, roll, heave, and yaw in an atrocious manner. To get an injured man, strapped into a Stokes litter, from the deck of a submarine into a helicopter was an agonizing exercise.

Once the stricken man was safely aboard the helicopter, our carefully orchestrated evolution went into reverse. We ordered the submarine to return to its nuclear deterrent patrol. To do that we had to exercise traffic control over the patrol areas to avoid what we called "confliction." Once the submarine was back in its assigned patrol area, we had to reschedule the nuclear targets all over again, from SSBN to SSBN until things returned to "normal." When this was all completed, we would report back to the Joint Chiefs of Staff that the evolution was completed. The whole evolution could take anywhere from three to twenty hours, depending on where the assets happened to be.

Of course, NR-1 wasn't an SSBN, but its business was interconnected with their mission. So as soon as I learned of the scientist's untimely death, I set in motion the mechanism for dealing not only with a death at sea, but the death at sea of a 350-pound male aboard a tiny nuclear-powered research submarine operating in a very sensitive area of the world. Retrieving this man's remains was definitely not going to be a "cake walk," I knew. But I had no idea how complicated it was going to be.

Almost as important as getting the man's remains to his family was the urgent need for keeping the CinC informed of progress. So, my treks every four hours or so to his office (or to his house at night) began in earnest. Our first effort was made under cover of darkness by the CH-53 helicopter just south of Keflavik, Iceland. Sea conditions were "ugly," and NR-1's wallowings would have made the transfer of an ambulatory patient difficult…but for a 350-pound corpse it became an impossibility. The swells were 20 feet high and irregular in their cycle. Surface winds were 35 knots gusting to 50. I had made it clear to my submariner staffers that I would kill one of them if they "lost" our scientist over the side in their transfer attempts. After an agonizingly strenuous effort, the transfer crewmen got the poor man's body, strapped into the Stokes litter, up the ladder, through the hatch and onto the slippery deck of the submarine. The CH-53 had great difficulty hovering in such strong and capricious winds. Time and again the crew attempted the hook-up to the helicopter's electric hoist. Frigid green water cascaded over the poor crewmen as they struggled frantically to keep their feet and, at the same time, keep their precious cargo from being torn out of their grips. I was being kept appraised of progress and was literally holding my breath…praying that no harm would befall those brave sailors in that icy nightmare. We all knew that if one of them went over the side, he was gone. There was little chance of a successful rescue under those hideous conditions. Finally, unable to stand the suspense any longer, I called a halt to the operation and directed the helicopter to return to base to await further instructions. NR-1 was directed to take our scientist below, submerge and continue its movement north. I was now searching for a calm spot in the lee of Iceland where the sea conditions were more favorable for a transfer operation.

The following day we received a message from the captain of the towing ship that they had located a calm area to the leeward of the island of Butir off the southeast coast of Iceland. We immediately set in motion the necessary forces for a CH-53 helicopter pick up, and this time we were successful. There are two things I remember about this hazardous operation.

The first is the seemingly endless trips I made from the command center to the CinC's office on the second floor of the building next door. Usually I took pride in bringing him good news about fleet operations on a regular basis. So, most of my reports to him had been made under pleasant circumstances. Never in my wildest dreams had I imagined such an uninterrupted series of "bad news" briefings. Underlying all of the stern glances, glowering, scowling, and endless unanswerable questions, I have always suspected that he found the bizarre circumstances of the affair a little bit amusing.

This leads to my second consideration. Knowing the average United States Navy bluejacket to be a little cynical and irreverent about the "system," I can only imagine what some of those poor lads were thinking and muttering among themselves during the first rescue attempt. With ice cold sea water pouring down the open hatch in the main deck and the submarine wallowing sickeningly about all three axes, they must have struggled mightily to get that Stokes litter up the ladder, through the hatch and onto the windswept deck...all 350 pounds of it! But, once on deck, they must have had an equally daunting job keeping that enormous cargo from slipping out of their frozen hands and over the side, possibly carrying them along with it. The most daunting thing of all, however, must have been, after half an hour of trying to get the litter hooked up to the sling from the hovering helicopter, to be told that the rescue was canceled and then having to get the precious cargo back down the ladder.

Of course, none of us would argue that the death was not a terrible tragedy for the deceased doctor's family. Nonetheless, there is a certain amount of irony about the whole affair that brings a smile to my face whenever I hear anyone mention NR-1!

Chapter 2:
Free Ascent

"Those who do not do battle for their country do not know
with what ease they accept their citizenship in America"
- Dean Brelis - "The Face of South Vietnam"

When I left the Naval Academy Prep School (NAPS), the yeoman asked what Navy school I wanted to attend, since at that point, I had no particular skill. I told him that I wanted to go to UDT (Underwater Demolition Team) training. The yeoman said that to do this, I would have to extend my four-year commitment by several more. I had only been in the Navy six months at this point, and the prospect of a 50 percent addition on my hitch was not very appealing. One of my roommates at NAPS was Jim Stuart, a submariner who had told me all sorts of stories which made me want to be a submariner also. So sub school was my next choice. The yeoman told me, "You just can't go to sub school, you need to know something...have some skill, like radioman or engineman." I thought for a moment how I could improve my chances of getting into sub school. What did all subs have in common? Hmmmm...torpedoes! I told my choice and off I went to Newport, R.I., for two months of torpedo school.

It quickly became apparent that the underlying process at sub school, apart from learning, was to screen people. We took lots of tests and were even interviewed, individually, by a psychiatrist. Surely there have been lots of jokes over the years to the effect of having one's head examined for volunteering for sub duty. Nevertheless, the testing is rigorous for very good reasons. I was told once that, in addition to claustrophobia and not being "well adjusted," "extreme ugliness" (I'm not making this up) was a cause for being screened, although we had a sonarman on *Barbero* who, in my opinion, put this rule to a real test. Apart from written testing and the interview, there were two "training" events which were undoubtedly for screening purposes.

The first was an atmospheric chamber where they crowded us in closely and opened an air valve to put in a fairly high pressure. We were told not to speak, which I thought was odd, until I spoke softly to the guy beside me and my voice sounded like Minnie Mouse, and everyone began to laugh. Since they also sounded like Minnie, only laughing, the situation nearly got out of control.

All my life I have had trouble with nasal breathing and clearing my eustachian tubes, something I was certainly not going to volunteer to the people at the school. So, this test was bad for me since I soon got behind the curve as the pressure quickly rose and I could not equalize both sides of my ear drums. It was very painful, but I knew that if I said anything, I'd be screened. Later, I blew my nose and got a handkerchief full of blood and tiny blood vessels.

The second and much more exciting "training" was the escape tank. Both Pearl Harbor and New London had towers over 100 feet tall and 20 feet in diameter, each with 100 feet of water in them. Welded onto the sides of these columns were authentic sub escape chambers at 18 feet depth, 50 feet depth and one at the bottom of the tank. These chambers all had a door which opened into the tank. I don't think they used the 100 foot chamber, since its use would not make the training experience much better and would significantly increase the risks.

Prior to going to the tank we had a number of classes that covered exactly what we were going to be doing and the physics involved relating mainly to our lungs. We then put on bathing suits and life jackets and climbed the tower to do a free ascent, first from the 18 foot and then the 50 foot chambers. "Free ascent" was an escape system which did not involve either breathing or a breathing apparatus, which prompted me to wonder how, exactly, this was going to work. But the system was sound, and it worked well—here is how.

A lung full of air at 50 feet depth is probably something like the volume of a 55gallon drum of air at the surface. You would have lots of air (oxygen) to supply the body, except it occupies a small space due to the pressure at that depth. If you kept your mouth shut and began your ascent, you'd be in trouble since the pressure of the surrounding water would decrease as you rose and the air in your lungs would expand, rupturing them. So, we were taught to completely exhale the air in our lungs before we began our ascent.

Now, exhaling all our air was quite a hurdle for the class. We all looked at one another as if to say, "Hold on, hold on, let me get this straight. You expect me to take one deep breath, step into the tank five stories below the surface without a breathing apparatus and then *blow all my air out, are you crazy?*" But it works well, and is based upon the fact that you really *can't* blow all the air out of your lungs because 20 percent "residual air" remains. This residual air expands as you rise, continually filling your lungs as the surrounding water pressure decreases. This of course works only if you continue to exhale all the way up. If you stop blowing bubbles (the divers watch you like a hawk) they will grab you and stuff you back into the chamber because you would certainly rupture your lungs. Since "ruptured lungs" did not have a good ring to it, I managed to get through both ascents. It was actually sort of fun the second time.

There was a subtle "test" which was part of the ascent. We all climbed into the chamber that, like the ones on subs, had lots of piping and valves and a small, dim light. The chamber is five feet in diameter and no more than seven feet tall, and there were at least five or six of us stuffed in there. The door was closed and dogged, and the instructor opened the flood valve that allowed water from the tank to roar in *very* fast. The water quickly rose up to my chest, compressing the air in the chamber to a fifth of what it had been seconds before, and in the process heating the air quite a bit, sort of a dieseling effect.

At this point the pressure of the water and air in the chamber became equal to the main tank, which allowed us to open the door into the tank. In turn, we each hyperventilated and ducked out the door, holding our breath, to be met by two divers who held on to us. They looked us over carefully for panic, and when they were satisfied that we had our wits about us, they poked us in the stomach as a signal to exhale *all our air!* Once we complied, they let us rise to the surface. I still remember saying to myself, "Now, Dan, thousands of guys have done this and you are better than most of them, so don't screw up and embarrass your brothers." I am certain that if you had *any* claustrophobic tendencies whatsoever, you could not do the "flooding the chamber" thing, *no way!*

Sub school was really an awakening for me because the subject matter was taught in a completely different manner from what I had been used to in the Catholic boys high school I had attended not long before. It was probably the best school I ever attended. I learned a tremendous amount. I retained what I learned, what I learned was very useful to me, and I enjoyed the experience.

Brother Spann, my high school physics teacher, was smart and a very good man, but to me he failed to excite us about a very interesting subject—most of my teachers were like this back then. It was, let's call it, "academic." It was presented without an "objective" and a purpose other than to pass the subject. Up until sub school, my education was like taking anatomy in med school without a cadaver. For me, the Navy's way of teaching was far better and more effective than the prior attempts using the classic methods.

In sub school we began with the "object," a diesel submarine in which we all would live and work. The instructors taught each system on the boat so that we had a sense of both the individual and the aggregate. Each system's components were taught in great detail. Knowing, for instance, there were a number of hydraulic systems that opened vents, moved the rudder and bow planes and so on, was not enough. Personally, by then, I was dying to find out how the system worked. I never had this feeling in any school until then.

At one time I had the notion that when I finished college, after my tour in the Navy, I would teach high school physics and base the entire course on teaching about a diesel sub. I am convinced that students would have fun and learn more. I left the Navy with a great admiration for its ability to teach effectively and quickly.

A good example was the teaching of hydraulics. In the very early boats there were rods that penetrated the bulkheads to the particular compartment where you wanted, for example, a main vent to open. This method was flawed since these bulkhead holes were opportunities for leaking, not to mention the mechanics of the thing. Subsequently, the bow planes, for instance, had a hydraulic pump near the planes, fixed to the torpedo room overhead which provided the power to move them. The man on the bow planes, aft in the control room, would move the wheel to the down position which sent pressure through a closed loop of hydraulic lines to this motor, tilting the internal rotating plate fixed with pistons, so that hydraulic fluid was forced to the proper side of the planes. The power to accomplish this was local, but the control was remote. Hydraulic systems operated the periscopes, the rudder, the bow and stern planes, the main vents, the snorkel, the sonar dome, the winches, and the torpedo tube outer doors.

Every system on the boat was taught along with its components. It is essential that each member of the crew of a submarine know how everything worked. If a hydraulic pump had a problem, an auxiliaryman would fix it. The rest of us could not repair it, but we all knew the symptoms of a malfunction and we all knew how to secure the pump to get it off the line, we also knew how to move the rudder or planes another way so we could continue. I believe this characteristic was unique to submarines—we were specialists with respect to sonar, engines or, in my own case, torpedoes, but we were also specialists concerning submarines. I found each system very interesting.

High Pressure Air System
An important power source aboard, its most important use was to expel the water from the main ballast tanks, to surface. It also propelled the torpedoes from tubes, blew sanitary tanks, started the diesel engines and other tasks. There were air lines virtually everywhere. For example, each compartment had a high pressure valve which, if the compartment flooded, we could open and quickly bleed air into the room. When the air pressure in the room finally equaled that of the surrounding sea water, the flooding would stop if the leak was low enough. The compartment would be pretty uncomfortable, but certainly a whole lot better than the alternative.

Electrical System
Electricity was used for propulsion and to run the "household," so to speak. Diesel engines did not directly turn the screws on subs, but powered electric generators that supplied the big electric motors that turned the screws. The windings of the armatures were actually on the propeller shafts, two motors on each shaft, and no mechanical linkage at all. It was an excellent design and the reason diesel boats were so quiet while running submerged. The generators also recharged the batteries. There were 256 tons of lead-acid batteries on my boat.

Trim System
Not only did we attempt to achieve neutral buoyancy when we were submerged, but we also had to deal with the distribution of weight, which constantly changed, throughout the boat. If we fired a one-ton torpedo, blew Sanitary #1 or if half the crew went to the forward battery to eat or watch a movie, the trim would change. It took surprisingly little to unbalance the boat when it was submerged. The solution was the placement inside the pressure hull of tanks in the bow, the stern, and on the port and starboard sides, connected with piping through a manifold in the control room. If we were heavy aft, as indicated by the

"bubble," (a calibrated, curved, glass tube filled with oil, except for a bubble of air) the diving officer would order 500 pounds to be pumped out of the after trim tank and into the bow trim tank. If we had a list, he would compensate between the port and starboard trim tanks. We constantly fine tuned the trim of the boat.

Fuel Oil System

Fuel oil was stored outside the pressure hull and used as ballast. As we burned fuel, sea water replaced it, so the tank was always full and would not crush when we dove. Subs carried very large amounts of fuel. Having it stored with sea water necessitated purification prior to burning. This was done with a purifier (just like a milk separator on a farm) located in the engine room.

Sanitary System

There were several internal tanks to collect waste water from the galley and the heads. When they became full, we put enough air pressure in the top of the tank to exceed the sea water pressure outside the hull and opened a valve at the bottom of the tank, expelling everything into the sea.

There were other minor systems throughout the boat, but these were the principal ones. Interestingly, most of these systems were cross connected which, under emergency circumstances, had proven useful in the past. If the boat were damaged, we could always devise another path to get fuel to the engine room or air to a cut off compartment. We had an old and vulgar saying in the submarine service, "We can blow shit through the ship's whistle."

While we learned an awful lot in sub school, it was only the beginning. It often took sailors another year to get "qualified," which was compulsory. Only then could we proudly wear our service's insignia - D O L P H I N S.

Chapter 3:
"...Things that go bump in the night"

*"If I had been censured every time I have run my ship...into
great danger, I should long ago have been out of the service,
and never in the House of Peers."*

- Lord Nelson: Letter to the Admiralty 1805

The skipper of a modern submarine reminds me of a blind man in so many ways.
Except when he is at periscope depth or on the surface, he has to rely for intelligence on
only one of his senses, hearing. His situational awareness is based on what his acoustics
systems tell him about the outside world and his relationship to it.

My own experience with submarines stems from three sources. The first was two indoctrination visits in 1973 and 1974 to a U.S. Navy nuclear-powered attack submarine (an
attack boat) and a ballistic missile submarine (a Boomer). Since both of them were tied up
at the pier, it wasn't much of an indoctrination. My second experience came in 1977-1979
when I served a tour of duty as Assistant Chief of Staff (Operations) at CinCLantFleet
headquarters. There I learned a great deal under the tutelage of Admiral Ike Kidd, aided by
his very knowledgeable submarine staff officers. I ran Task Force 84 operations for two
years. What an experience! Finally, in 1980, as a flag officer I went to sea in the attack boat,
U.S.S. *Plunger* (SSN-595), out of Ballast Point, on Point Loma, San Diego. That one day
trip was the icing on the cake! I loved it!

My mentors in Norfolk went to great pains to explain to me how and why submarines
operate the way they do. They also went to great pains to explain how to find submarines.
There was an entire shop at CinCLant dedicated to operating the enormous land-based air
anti-submarine warfare operation carried out daily and worldwide by what we call the VP
community. This community of patrol plane operators were equipped with 30 active and 15
reserve P-3 Orion squadrons, a community of 12,000 people dedicated to finding and track-
ing Soviet submarines worldwide. Called the N-35 shop, it generated the directives to all
deployed VP squadrons on an hourly basis for the aggressive prosecution of deployed Soviet submarines.

Operating out of such wide-spread and remote bases like Keflavik, Iceland; Sigonella, Sicily; Lajes, Azores; Argentia, Newfoundland; Bermuda and Rota, Spain, these dedicated men and women provided an enormous contribution to our Cold War effort to contain the submarine forces of the Soviet Union. But they were only a part of the whole effort.

There was a sign on the wall behind my desk at CinCLant headquarters. It read:

"ASW IS 99 PERCENT INTELLIGENCE AND INTELLIGENCE IS 99 PERCENT BULLSHIT!"

Notwithstanding this light-hearted attempt at humor, the intelligence community's contribution to the overall ASW effort was enormous. They had their own cast of talented experts; acousticians, electronic signals analysts, human intelligence analysts, naval fleet operational intelligence analysts, and finally, scientific and technical intelligence analysts. These incredibly talented individuals worked around the clock worldwide to fuse the many disparate sources of intelligence to present a cogent picture of the Soviet submarine force posture. I hesitate to postulate what the dollars were involved in the total program. It would, doubtless, boggle the mind. But, it was a necessary adjunct of the Cold War.

But in the event of an all-out shooting war, the single most important element of our ASW posture would be the efforts of the U.S. Navy's attack submarine force to kill not only the Soviet boomers (SLBMs), but also their attack submarines. That would indeed be a daunting task, not only because of the overwhelming superiority in numbers, but also because of the large difference in submarine performance characteristics; the result of the huge difference in submarine design philosophy between the two navies.

The United States Navy built Cadillacs and the Soviet Navy built Lamborghinis! That is as good an analogy as I can come up with for the moment...and the Cadillacs won! True, the Soviet attack submarines could go faster and dive deeper than their U.S. counterparts...but the U.S. Navy attack submarines were quieter...and that, in the end, proved the determining factor. The quieter submarines proved to be more lethal.

One could almost draw an aviation parallel between the Mig-25 and the F-14. The MiG-25 could go higher and faster, but the F-14 could kill better! Again, this is the result of a substantial difference in design philosophy.

I spent a large portion of each day at CinCLant headquarters on ASW matters, from the daily morning status briefings to the operational aspects of the various ongoing ASW programs being executed in the CinCLant sphere of influence. The huge display panels on the walls of the command center showed where every submarine was from the North to the South Poles, and from the Indian Ocean to the eastern shore of the United States. It showed our submarines and those of the Soviets, the British and French, and any others of interest. The accuracy of the positions varied from precise to estimates...but they were all there. The efforts spent to track them depended on the level of interest and threat that each of them posed.

The Soviet boomers (the Yankee class) received top billing as far as level of effort was concerned. The locating criteria we assigned to them as soon as they entered the "shooter's box," was close enough to initiate an immediate attack. The shooter's box was their patrol area off the East Coast of the United States. The box resembled, in size and shape, a reverse map of the state of California located in the middle of the Atlantic Ocean. That level-of-effort criterion was of course understandable considering that, on short notice, they could launch a devastating attack on dozens of major targets and cities in the United States.

The size, shape and location of the shooter's box was determined by a historical replication of Yankee patrols. Their departure from home port and transit to the patrol area were characterized by certain maneuvering parameters. Once they were on patrol, they reverted to different parameters regarding speed, depth, and frequency of reporting. On the return to home port the parameters for transit were replicated. A historical replay of patrol tracks ever since the beginning of the Cold War showed what we came to call the "shooter's box."

The Yankee was the Soviet Union's main battery during the Cold War...and it was what my patrol plane operators called a "mean machine." It was over 462 feet in length, displaced over ten thousand tons, and was equipped with sixteen vertically launched ballistic missile tubes. Each missile could be configured with two re-entry vehicles, each with a maximum yield of 5.0 megatons for a total throw weight of 160 megatons for each Yankee vessel. She had a maximum submerged speed of 26.5 knots and an operating depth of greater than 1,500 feet, and carried a crew of 120 officers and men. An unusual feature of the Yankee was her twin screws that generated 55,000 shaft horsepower each. The Yankee was truly an incredible war machine, and posed a formidable challenge to U.S. ASW forces.

The behavior and posture of all deployed submarines in the Atlantic became a preoccupation of mine as I came to realize that there were discrete behavior signatures associated with, for example, the ways that the Soviets, French, British, and U.S. submarines operated. I had even developed a chronology of some of the more bizarre submarine events I had observed.

Soviet SSBN Yankee II class, Norwegian Sea, 1994. (Official U.S. Navy Photo)

There was the U.S. attack boat transiting back from a Mediterranean patrol which plowed right into a sea mount that no one knew was there. Fortunately, no serious damage was done to the submarine, but reconstruction of the incident back at the repair shipyard revealed that the errant commanding officer was traveling far in excess of the speed permitted for a routine transit or dictated by good judgment.

Then there was the attack boat skipper who was in the middle of an extremely delicate trail operation when the Yankee he was trailing suddenly and inexplicably came to "all engines stop." The sonar operator in the trailing boat didn't interpret the action of the Yankee quickly enough, and there was a finite amount of time (perhaps 30 or 40 seconds) before the skipper also rang for "all engines stop." That interval developed a slight closure rate between trailer and "trailee." There, in the depths of the North Atlantic, the two behemoths slowly drifted together. The skipper of the trailer didn't dare try to stop by reversing power…that would be a dead give-away to the now-silent Soviet submarine. So, the Americans held their breaths as the boats slowly came closer and closer together. Finally, the bow of the American sub made contact with the stern of the Soviet boat with a loud clang.

One can only imagine the consternation of the skipper of the Yankee when the realization came over him that not only was he being followed, but the trailer had actually bumped into him. Of course, the Soviet skipper rang up "all engines ahead full," and the Yankee disappeared in a flurry of wake turbulence and noise. The skipper of the American boat was equally chagrined. Not only had he given away his presence, but after all his days of effort, had actually been so clumsy as to run into his prey.

The clang which occurred upon contact must have frozen the blood of all three hundred seamen, deep in the cold, dark North Atlantic. It must also have chilled all of the acoustics experts whose ears were glued to the listening posts in the North Atlantic ocean. As soon as I heard of it, it froze my blood, and I was seated at a comfortable desk more than a thousand miles from the event.

But the one event which comes to mind as best characterizing the dangers of "routine" submarine patrol operations occurred one evening, late at night in the western approaches to the Straits of Gibraltar. A U.S. attack submarine en route to a Mediterranean patrol was preparing to transit the Straits and had slowed down and come to best listening depth prior to surfacing. The purpose for surfacing was to get a final update before transiting the Straits.

As is appropriate for a submariner under these circumstances, the skipper drifted along for some time, listening carefully for the sounds of approaching shipping in all quadrants. Having determined that there was no one out there, the skipper came to periscope depth, put up his scope and searched the night horizon, in all quadrants, with his night scope. Their was nothing visible or audible in any quadrant, so the skipper gave the order to surface. That evolution had just begun. The watch crew were huddled in the base of the conning tower, ready to run topside and man their lookout stations as soon as the boat reached the surface.

RRRRRRIIIIIIIPPPPPPPP!!!!

Right at that critical moment there was a horrible ripping sound. The sound lasted several seconds…long enough for the skipper to give the emergency dive signal and to ring "General Quarters." Then there was silence…a long pregnant silence. Thirty minutes later, when the skipper returned to periscope depth and looked around, there was nothing to be seen. After coming to the surface he examined his own vessel and found nothing visibly damaged. Noting the event in his log, the skipper completed an otherwise routine transit of the Straits and resumed his patrol.

The following morning the skipper of an eastbound Polish freighter in the western Mediterranean was informed by one of his crew that there was an enormous gash in his hull just above the waterline. The hole was horizontal, over one hundred feet long and looked as though it had been made by a surgeon's scalpel. Naturally, the skipper of the freighter declared an emergency and limped into an Italian port for damage repair. Had it not been for the fact that the gash occurred above the waterline, experts said the ship would have capsized and sunk within a minute or so. Who had done this?

There were protests registered to the U.S. government, who refused to accept any responsibility pending a review of all deployed submarines who could possibly have been in the area. At CinCLant headquarters we began early…and we knew more exactly where our submarines were. The truth finally came out when the submarine skipper took a closer look at his fairwater plane, the wing-like surface which projects out horizontally from the conning tower. The trailing edge of the port fairwater plane had definitely made metal-to-metal contact with something big.

The outer trailing edge of the fairwater plane narrows to a fairly sharp edge…made of high yield steel. It performed exactly like a razor. Reconstruction of the accident established that both ships were headed toward the Straits of Gibraltar, the submarine cruising at five knots and in the process of surfacing; and the freighter approaching from astern at 20 knots. Because the freighter was astern of the submarine, the noise it was generating was obscured by the wake of the submarine. The freighter came alongside the submarine with a relative closure rate of 15 knots, and the sharp trailing edge of the fairwater plane made contact with the freighter's hull. No one on the freighter apparently heard a thing. The submarine heeled to starboard and the knife-edged fairwater plane came out of the hull of the freighter after doing its damage. The rest was history.

The U.S. Government admitted its culpability, and the repairs for the freighter were paid in full. Of course, there was a "come to Jesus" meeting at the fleet headquarters between the CinC and ComSubLant. Thereafter, strict new orders were issued as to how to clear one's baffles before surfacing. I do not remember what, if anything, happened to the submarine skipper.

One of the more interesting submarine events during my tour of duty at CinCLant occurred in the Pacific and was related to me by my counterpart in that ocean command, CinCPacFleet. It occurred to the U.S.S. *Salmon*, a diesel-powered attack submarine, as it was entering San Francisco Bay in the early 1970s. It was late at night, and there was an extremely dense fog blanketing the approaches to San Francisco Bay. As a consequence, the skipper was being understandably cautious and was proceeding at "slow bells," or about five knots.

He had placed a young sailor on the bow, as far forward as he could go, with a sound-powered telephone headset connected to main con. The young sailor was sitting on the forward capstan on the bow just forward of the sonar dome which, on this class of submarine, was mounted on top of the main deck. The sailor faced forward and reported that he could not see beyond about ten feet. It was a ghostly experience to be seated way out on the bow surrounded by fog and proceeding slowly but inexorably toward who knows what!

What the young sailor did not know was that the capstan had a small internal hydraulic leak which was causing it to turn, but at such a slow rate as to be unnoticeable to its rider. During the course of several minutes, the capstan rotated a full 180 degrees, which put the sailor facing aft, although he thought he was still facing forward. Sitting in such a dense fog bank he had no way of knowing. Now, our young bow lookout was facing aft, straining to see through the fog when the visibility cleared just enough for him to make out the huge shape of the sonar dome just a few feet away.

In absolute horror, the young man screamed into the sound-powered telephone set, "Oh, my God. We're going to hit!" To avoid being crushed to death in the imminent collision, he turned around and sprinted away into the fog. Of course, he thought he was running aft to safety when, in fact, he was running forward. His trajectory carried him over the bow and into the frigid water directly in front of the advancing submarine. Because of the limited visibility, it was a good thirty minutes before the submarine crew was able to fish him, soggy and suffering from hypothermia, out of the Pacific Ocean.

As I reflected on the hazards of "routine submarine operations," I remembered the quote from my high school English Literature class: "...from ghoulies and ghosties and long-leggity beasties, and things that go bump in the night." - Anonymous

Chapter 4:
U.S.S. Barbero SSG-317

"All ships were to some degree separate kingdoms with different customs and a different atmosphere: This was particularly true of those that were on detached service or much by themselves, far from their admirals and the rest of the fleet."
- Patrick O'Brien "Post Captain"

Since the following stories contain many references to various equipment and compartments on *Barbero*, I want to familiarize the reader with the basics of diesel electric submarines. First, the general characteristics concerning the "outside," or superstructure, of the boat. I'll next describe each compartment from forward aft.

General

There were two builders of WWII vintage diesel electric subs, Electric Boat Company in Groton, CT, and Portsmouth, a builder in Portsmouth, NH. There were a number of differences between the two boats, but few would be recognized by anyone but a submariner. So, for the purposes of this description, I'll be describing *Barbero*, which was built in 1943 by Electric Boat Company.

The boat was 311.6 feet long overall, had twin screws and the old-style sail. The sail is the structure located in the middle of the deck. It houses the conning tower, which is part of the pressure hull, and the main induction, through which air is sucked in by the diesels. The forward part of the sail is the bridge where the conning officer stands, and above him, in the sheers, stand the two lookouts on little platforms, with hand rails so they don't fall out. The hand rails are open forward so the lookouts can climb down fast in the event of a dive.

Just aft of the bridge is a wonderful place called the "cigarette deck," with two benches. In nice weather, off-watch sailors could go up there for what we humorously referred to as a "submarine shower" (more on showers later). The OOD had to be careful to monitor how many of the crew could be "up," so as not to leave someone up there if he had to dive in a hurry, an unpleasant experience to be sure.

The bow area of the forward deck has a bull nose through which lines pass, a winch called a "capstan," and an assortment of cleats for mooring. In addition, mounted flush with the deck and adjacent to the escape trunk to starboard, was a buoy the size of several 55 gallon drums. If we were ever stuck on the bottom, this buoy, with its spool of cable, would be released to float to the surface directly above us. Theoretically, an ASR (submarine rescue ship) would be able to locate the buoy and attach their rescue chamber to our buoy's cable. It would then winch itself down to the sub, seating right on top of our hatch and take us out six at a time....theoretically.

On *Barbero* we had a very large cylinder just aft of the sail which we called "the hangar," which I will include in the description of compartments. The stern, called the turtleback, tapered, creating a danger to the propellers when maneuvering, since the big screws extended to port and starboard beyond the sub's tapered stern. Big metal pipes were welded to the stern, horizontally, in the form of hoops, which extended beyond the screws, thus protecting them from hitting the pier.

The main deck was made of wooden slats with a 3/4-inch gap between them to be free flooding, but still provide something to walk on. Also, there was a track mounted flush into the decking which would keep us from being washed over the side. By snapping a toggle line into the track, we could walk the length of the deck in safety. Beneath this deck was a maze of vents, piping, line lockers, and the like.

THE PRESSURE HULL
The pressure hull was a long pipe 18 feet in diameter made of one-inch-thick steel. This cylinder has circular "I" beam ribs inside the hull about two feet apart that provide strength and serve to keep the hull a cylinder. This sounds obvious, but the moment the hull, under great sea pressure, got out of round, it would implode or collapse. Near the bow and stern, this cylinder tapered to somewhat less than 18 feet in diameter so that both the forward torpedo room and the after room, except for a well three feet deep, covered by deck plates, had only one level. All the others had two levels, just high enough to stand if you were not too tall.

This "pipe" was separated into compartments by bulkheads, each just as strong as the pressure hull and each with heavy, water-tight doors. It was very important that each bulk-head could withstand the same pressure as the hull, so that if one compartment flooded, the whole boat would not be lost. The inside of the hull was covered with sheets of cork glued onto the steel hull. This prevented condensation, which would otherwise be a constant prob-lem since the sea water surrounding the hull was almost always colder than the air inside the boat. The hull was just like a pitcher of iced tea, except the tea was on the outside and the condensation was on the inside.

Great design effort went into avoiding penetrations of the hull with fittings and pipes on the correct assumption that they would likely weaken it. Our particular "test depth" was 412 feet. On a few occasions we exceeded this number, accidentally, without too much fuss, since we were all convinced that a substantial safety margin was factored in by the Navy.

THE SADDLE TANKS

The pressure hull was surrounded by what amounts to another "pipe," completely subjected to the sea pressures the boat would encounter. This outside pipe is what we see near the water line as we view a sub. It consists of a series of tanks which wrap around the pressure hull. Most of these tanks are "ballast tanks," which are kept empty. The tanks float the boat and keep it on the surface. The non-ballast saddle tanks hold fuel oil.

At the tops of these tanks are large valves called "main vents," which are controlled hydraulically by the diving party in the control room. There are large holes at the bottom of the tanks. When the main vents are opened, the air trapped in the ballast tanks escapes out the vents and is replaced by sea water from below, and we quickly lose our buoyancy and begin to sink. ("Sink" is a word Navy people dislike—even with submariners, "dive" is preferred).

SAFETY TANK

The volume of this tank was approximately that of any one of our compartments. It was always kept full of sea water so that if one of our compartments ever flooded, we could blow safety tank, thus compensating for the weight of the flooded compartment. This, of course, had to be done very quickly to reverse the downward momentum of the boat before it reached crush depth.

U.S.S. Barbero (SSG-317), Northwestern Pacific, 1958. (Dan Gillcrist Collection)

U.S.S. Barbero in drydock at Yokosuka after the Kamchatka cruise, 1961. (Dan Gillcrist Collection)

FORWARD TORPEDO ROOM

There were six torpedo tubes in two vertical rows, which penetrated through the forward bulkhead of the room. About a third of the tube was in the room, and the rest was outside the pressure hull hidden in the superstructure of the bow area. Each tube was 21 inches in diameter and some 20 feet in length, and, of course, also had to be as strong as the hull since when we opened the outer doors to fire a torpedo, the tube would be exposed to the surrounding sea pressure just like the hull.

Under normal circumstances, we would go to sea with torpedoes in each tube, with two more strapped onto two of our three "skids," or torpedo cradles, kept in the well under the deck plates. We needed an empty skid so we could pull a torpedo out of the tubes for maintenance. We actually used the empty skid to store eggs and the like for the cooks.

The room was a sleeping compartment with about 36 bunks, called "racks." It actually slept more than 36, because junior sailors were forced to share bunks. One would go on watch and the other would sleep—thus our expression "hot bunking." The damn bunk never cooled off! Every little niche or space had a locker assigned to a sailor. Some of them were as small as 8 inches high 14 inches wide and a foot deep. This was supposed to hold his worldly belongings.

Just past the bunks going aft were the "head" to starboard and the sonar shack to port, neither much larger than a telephone booth or two. Next to the head was our garbage ejector. This was a mini torpedo tube a foot in diameter and about five feet long. We would put our garbage in mesh bags weighted with a few pieces of steel we would scrounge in the Navy yard and fire it out just like a torpedo. We went to this trouble only when we were submerged and wished to remain undetected—otherwise the trash was simply thrown over the side.

Life jackets were jammed into every opening not otherwise in use, and canisters of CO_2 absorbent were clipped everywhere on the overhead along with several oxygen bottles. On more that one occasion I found hung over sailors with bunks just under the oxygen bottles breathing the stuff to cure themselves in the morning. I guess the fact that this was very dangerous was a lesser of evils thing for them, to say nothing of the day when we might actually need the stuff to live, only to find the damn bottles empty!

FORWARD BATTERY

This compartment also served several purposes. The lower part housed half of the 256 tons of batteries, and the upper part was the galley and crew's mess. There was a crawl space above the cells large enough for the electricians to do their two regular maintenance functions, watering the cells and taking hydrometer readings of the electrolyte. You could always tell an electrician, even one from another boat, because his dungarees were full of holes from the battery acid. I should add that they would take great care not to have anything made of metal on them, such as the bunch of keys, and naturally, no dog tags. If they were not careful, they could end up as a large fuse.

Normally lead/acid batteries are not dangerous, except when they are on a sub. For one thing, when the batteries are charged they produce hydrogen gas, which is dangerous in a confined space unless carefully disposed of. The other danger was that, if for any of a dozen reasons, salt water entered the compartment and got into the batteries, chlorine gas would be produced which, of course, is lethal.

The mess area was the social center for the crew and where we ate our meals. There were tables and benches fixed to the deck. Each bench was really a long aluminum box with a cushioned lid. Space was so scarce that food was stored all around the boat. There was a very small galley no larger than six feet square, a scullery four feet by five feet at the most, and a combination walk-in freezer and refrigerator.

The mess was where we sat around to talk, drink lots of coffee, smoke lots of cigarettes, play cards, tell lies, and watch movies. It was the plaza, the village center. I am certain any old submariner has fond memories of the crew's mess. Ordinarily I would not bother to include something as insignificant as the one shower in this compartment, but it is an opening I simply can't pass up.

There were three or four stainless-steel showers half the size of a phone booth on the boat. We rarely used them because fresh water was scarce, so we used them to store food. Subs were notorious for the lack of bathing and for the complete absence of laundry facilities—we simply had none. One had to bring enough changes of clothes to last the entire cruise.

CONTROL ROOM

As the name suggests, what took place throughout the boat was "controlled" from this room. The boat's course, speed, depth, and trim were determined there. The main vents were opened from there to dive the boat. All the hull openings were displayed there by lights, "O" shaped for open and " - " for closed. Since it was a bad idea to dive with a hatch opened, the chief of the boat was in charge of this board as well as the main vents. Until the diving officer heard, "Straight board, sir!" from the chief, indicating that all the hatches were closed, he would not order the main vents to be opened.

The bow and stern planes were next to the chief of the boat and his vents and board, with the trim manifold just aft of the stern planes. The after part of the room was the radio shack five feet by perhaps ten feet and literally jammed with electronic stuff. The thing to remember is that as technology soared after WW II, the Navy kept adding new equipment to the old boats. The boats never got any bigger—the available space simply got smaller. So the boat we sailed in was a lot more crowded than it was in 1943 when launched. It had both more equipment and more sailors.

Below the control area was "the pump room" with pumps, lots of piping for the trim system, and an exposed bilge. This bilge is noteworthy because we would sometimes, in heavy weather, take a big slug of water through the conning tower hatch and down onto the people in the control room. Had it not been for grating on the deck we'd be sloshing about. Instead, the water went straight through to the bilge.

Above the control room was the conning tower—the focus of most submarine movies. This too was basically a big pipe perhaps 15 feet long and nine feet in diameter. The helm was at the forward end and the two periscopes (#1 and #2 scope) ran down the center. When on the surface, the OOD was "up" on the bridge, and while submerged he was in the control room. The conning tower was mostly used when we fired torpedoes and prepared to surface, since looking around through the periscopes was a good idea before we surfaced.

AFTER BATTERY

Like the forward battery, this compartment had several purposes and also held batteries below the deck plates. The "goat locker" was the berthing area for the four or five chiefs we had aboard. Because of their status, they deserved their own berthing area. Incidentally, everything in the Navy has a "locker." The definition of a locker in the Navy is any place where there is something!

The major portion of the after battery was devoted to the wardroom and the officer's state rooms. "Staterooms " conjures up vastly more elegance than really existed, as any sub officer would attest. Next to the wardroom was the tiny, separate kitchen for the officers, run by a steward. The Navy has a centuries old tradition separating officers and crew. I think in the area of chow, at least on *Barbero*, they got the short end of the stick. In fact, the officers responsible for supervision of the crew's mess often ate with us under the ruse of "being sure we were taken care of." Since the paperwork was generated by the officers there was a tiny "office" there run by a yeoman.

Unique to *Barbero* was another small room below deck in the compartment which housed the primitive guidance equipment we used to guide the flight of our two Regulus missiles. This room was my "Battle Stations Missile." One of my jobs was to flip the switch, "exploding" the bomb. LT McDonald, my boss, would often kid me about incinerating hundreds of thousands of people. I can't say I ever lost any sleep over the matter.

AUXILIARY ROOM
On every other sub this room was the forward engine room, the first of two. Since we had a hangar on the main deck and all sorts of requirements because of the missiles, this compartment was dedicated to the needed additional equipment. The two huge diesels that once were there had been removed. There were a few non-missile related pieces of equipment not worth discussing, except for one—the "evaporator." This was the machine that turned salt water into fresh water. It should be kept in mind that we used water for an additional purpose which other ships did not have. We used a great deal of distilled water for the batteries. Anyone with a bit of gray hair remembers the lead acid batteries in the old automobiles which had to be kept full of water. Well, our batteries were simply very big car batteries that consumed lots of distilled water that had to be made at sea.

Torpedoman Dan Gillcrist (cleaning fingernails) sitting in forward torpedo room hatch, U.S.S. Barbero, Pearl Harbor, 1961. (Dan Gillcrist Collection)

MISSLE HANGAR

Just aft of the sail on the main deck was a big steel cylinder with convex ends, the after end being the door to the hangar. Inside this chamber was the "bird cage" that had two Regulus 1 nuclear missiles attached, the lower one upright and ready to be pushed out of the hangar. The other hung upside down. We would rotate the cage 180 degrees to get the other missile ready to be "rammed" out. "Red birds" were for practice launches, they had landing gear so we could re-use them. The "Blue birds" had a nuclear warhead and, obviously, no landing gear. Everything else in the hangar was associated with launching missiles.

MAIN ENGINE ROOM

This compartment was our power plant. It contained two 1,600 horsepower diesel engines made by Fairbanks-Morse. They are the same size many locomotives use. I was once told that this was where the engines of subs being scrapped ended up. There was another much smaller engine we called the "auxiliary," that was used to charge the battery and supply the "household" requirements, while the two larger ones propelled the boat. The passageway aft went right between the main engines.

The engine room was always deafening underway—I don't know how the enginemen could stand the din and, oddly, they never wore noise attenuators of any kind as far as I could tell, probably a macho thing back in the fifties. I'm sure that their wives today think that these guys "just don't listen to them!"

As I mentioned earlier, the drive shafts of the two engines were not mechanically connected to the screws. Rather, they directly drove two electric generators—the only energy leaving the engine compartment was electricity.

MANEUVERING ROOM

If the engine room was the power plant, then the maneuvering room held the switches. There were very large knife switches moved by a series of levers manually thrown by the electricians on watch. This maneuvering room panel governed both how much electric power went to the main motors turning the screws and whether this electricity came from the generators or from the batteries. When the conning officer ordered, "All ahead two thirds," the helmsman turned a dial which repeated the order aft to the electricians on watch. They would then throw the appropriate levers and watch tachometers until the instruments indicated a certain number of turns associated with two-thirds speed. To them, everything was in "turns" (RPMs). If this lever throwing was not done properly and in careful sequence, "fireballs" would literally fly out of the cubicle! Think of the spark you get when you pull the plug of your toaster while its still on and muliply by a power of ten!

AFTER ROOM

In all the other old "fleet boats," this compartment was the after torpedo room. In our conversion to handle missiles, the torpedo tubes were eliminated, making this compartment crew's sleeping quarters. It was nothing but a lot of bunks and a head. All the "snipes" it seemed, lived in this compartment while the forward room was for the rest of us. Snipes were the rates associated with powering a ship. They were the denizens of the bowels of a ship, always greasy and always pale, clearly distinguishable from the electricians with the acid holes in their dungarees.

THE POSTMASTER GENERAL
WASHINGTON

June 1959

The First Official Missile Mail

Your receipt of this letter marks an historic milestone in the use of guided missiles for communications between the peoples of the earth.

It represents, too, the close cooperation of Secretary of Defense McElroy, the Department of Defense, and the Post Office Department in utilizing scientific advances for peaceful purposes.

A limited number of letters identical to this one were placed in the Regulus I Training Guided Missile on the guided missile submarine USS BARBERO (SSG-317) in this First Official Missile Mail experiment of the United States Post Office Department.

The missile was then flown at near the speed of sound from international waters of the Atlantic Ocean by the USS BARBERO while on a regular training mission.

After the Regulus I reached its destination, the Naval Auxiliary Air Station at Mayport, Florida, near Jacksonville, this letter was cancelled and forwarded to you as a significant philatelic souvenir.

The great progress being made in guided missilry will be utilized in every practical way in the delivery of the United States mail. You can be certain that the Post Office Department will continue to cooperate with the Defense Department to achieve this objective.

Arthur E. Summerfield

The Postmaster General

First ever Regulus missile mail certificate. (Dan Gillcrist Collection)

Chapter 5:
AUUUUUGGGGAAAHH!

"Take her down"
- Howard W. Gilmore
- Commanding Officer USS Growler (SS-215)
Posthumous Medal Of Honor recipient

The obvious distinction between submarines and surface ships is that subs are able to submerge and surface again. The process of both these activities is simple, but warrants a description, since the sections concerning subs make some references to diving, surfacing, and snorkeling, which might otherwise be hard to understand.

DIVING

Diesel boats are limited in the time they can stay submerged by the stored power in their batteries and the quality of the air inside the boat. On *Barbero*, as I recall, after a half day the air was foul as can be. Think of a really stuffy meeting room which makes you want to run screaming into the night, and you just begin to get the picture. So, in this section, I will also include a description of a clever German invention which allowed us to stay submerged and run our engines at the same time - *THE SNORKLE*

The diesel boats had a pressure hull in which we lived, partially wrapped with "main ballast tanks," which had a "main vent" on the top and a free flooding "hole" at the bottom, next to the keel. With the main vents on top closed and air "trapped" in the ballast tanks, there was sufficient buoyancy to keep the boat on the surface. When we chose to dive the boat, we simply opened all the main vents. The trapped air in the tanks would escape out the top, pushed out and replaced by the water entering from the bottom of the tanks. We quickly lost all of our buoyancy and began to sink. The boats were designed to be close to neutral buoyancy when all the ballast tanks were flooded, so that we did not expend a lot of energy trying to maintain a particular depth.

The sequence of a dive, for practice or otherwise, began with clearing the bridge of everyone. The OOD would shout, "CLEAR THE BRIDGE, CLEAR THE BRIDGE!" Once he was certain that everyone but him was below, he would announce, "DIVE, DIVE" over the 1MC and he'd hit the "AUUUGA" claxon two times. He would then scurry down the hatch, while the helmsman on watch pulled the conning tower hatch shut behind him with a four foot lanyard. The quartermaster then went up the ladder to dog down the hatch. The two lookouts who had just cleared the bridge became the bow and stern planesmen, the helmsman dropped into the control room and began steering from there, and the OOD became the diving officer. After the boat was underwater, all the main vents were closed again. An interesting exception to this was when there was a threat of being depth-charged during WWII—then they *opened* the main vents so that they would not trap gases from the explosions. If they didn't keep their wits about them they could, inadvertently, be surfacing in the middle of the attack!

As soon as the conning tower hatch was closed, the fixed amount of air inside the boat would, of course, begin to deteriorate, since 90 people were using up oxygen and adding CO_2. After several hours we all could tell the difference. If we planned to be submerged for some extended time, we would "snorkel." It worked like this:

The boat would maintain its depth at "periscope depth," which meant that our keel was about 60 feet beneath the surface. At this depth we would raise our snorkel mast fully. The snorkel consisted of a large pipe through which the engines sucked air and a shorter pipe through which the engine exhaust flowed. The pipe sucking air was kept a few feet above the surface, while the exhaust pipe was several feet under the surface. The exhaust had a defusion plate designed to minimize the appearance of smoke, since the whole purpose was to be able to run the diesels while remaining undetected. All that could be seen of the boat was the one pipe sticking up a few feet above the surface.

The snorkel head valve had several electrodes around it that shorted out when a wave connected them, triggering the valve to slam shut. When the wave receded, the valve would reopen. The main engines, of course, kept right on running in spite of all this, so we were continually having air sucked out of the boat and then restored. There was a trade off. We didn't want our ears popping all day, but on the other hand, we didn't want the snorkel too far out of the water, either. Snorkeling was not all that unpleasant, because we didn't do it continually while submerged. We did it maybe twice a day to charge the batteries and to restore our air supply in the boat. Once we snorkeled for 42 days straight without surfacing, and it was not too bad.

If we were ever forced to remain submerged for a long period either by an enemy on the surface or a disaster keeping us on the bottom, the threat of too much CO_2 in the air would probably be greater than lack of oxygen, since we normally had lots of compressed air stored in the many flasks up in the superstructure. The modern boats have lots of equipment to "scrub" the air and to add the right amount of oxygen, but we had none of that sort of thing. What we did have were cans of CO_2 absorbent. Fortunately, we never practiced with this stuff, but if necessary, we could open a lot of cans and spread them all over the place! The CO_2 in the boat would be taken up by the absorbent, supposedly. No wonder we never practiced!

SURFACING

Once the decision was made to surface, the diving officer would first bring the boat, gently, to periscope depth, climb the ladder into the conning tower, and order the #1 periscope raised. Then he would have a thorough 360 degree look to be certain there were no other ships about that we might run into during the surface. When he was comfortable that there was no danger, he started the sequence. He would announce, "PREPARE TO SURFACE," and hit the claxon alarm three times. First, the bow buoyancy tank was blown with high pressure air, giving us an up-angle on the boat, then the main ballast tanks were blown. As the air entering all these tanks began to expel the water out the bottoms of the tanks, the boat would begin to have positive buoyancy and rise. As soon as the conning tower hatch was out of the water, it was opened, the high pressure air blow was stopped, and a large, powerful blower was started to finish expelling the remaining water from the ballast tanks. The main engines were then started, and we were back in business on the surface.

Chapter 6:
"Crazy Ivan"

"He is not drunk who from the floor,
Can rise again and drink some more.
But, he is drunk who prostrate lies,
And who can neither drink nor rise".

- Old Navy sea chanty

During my tour as Assistant Chief of Staff, Operations at CinCLantFleet, I learned a great deal about something which had been heretofore totally foreign to me...submarine operations. It turned out to be one of the most fascinating parts of my assignment. One reason for this is that I had available to me a wealth of real submarine expertise in the form of dedicated, experienced submariners assigned to the staff.

One of the aspects which had been made clear to me by the CinC himself prior to my accepting the job was the proximity of my assigned government quarters...a beautiful, old two-story frame house directly across the street from the command center. There was a good reason for this. My job entailed frequent calls at all hours to go to the command center for important events...many of them submarine-related events. It came to be a routine circumstance to be called out of bed at 2:00 a.m. to slip on a pair of trousers and run across the street to respond to something unusual occurring in the vast domain of the Atlantic Command.

Of course the center, a large blockhouse-type building, was protected by some fairly sophisticated security measures, and access to it required high level security clearances...evidenced by identification cards which were color coded for various security levels. The very highest security levels were required by the submarine and satellite surveillance programs.

In the center of the building was the command center, an enormous three-story room with a series of maps on the side of the room opposite the second-level viewing booths assigned to the CinC and his senior staff members. The maps went from floor to ceiling, and were motorized so that they could be rolled back and forth to display a variety of geographic presentations of the CinCLant area of responsibility. This stretched from the South Pole to the North Pole, and was bounded on the west by the North and South American continents and on the east by Europe and Africa. Displayed on this series of charts were all CinCLantFleet ships and submarines, as well as the ships and submarines of other countries.

The sources of information for all of these vessels were many and varied. A principle input to the location of surface and subsurface contacts was the extensive organization of U.S. and NATO maritime patrol aircraft. These airplanes, stationed around the Atlantic littoral, flew around-the-clock patrol operations cataloging the location of surface ships and searching for submarines.

The search for submarines was a never-ending process involving nearly all aspects of maritime intelligence, as well as the active operation of every mechanism of anti-submarine warfare available to the Unified Command structure.

My anti-submarine warfare (ASW) experts were quick to educate me on submarine and anti-submarine operations. As a consequence, my ASW education entailed not only a thorough knowledge of U.S. submarine warfare operating procedures and capabilities, but those of other countries as well. We worried most, of course, about the threat represented by the submarine forces of the Soviet union.

Submarines on patrol depend upon their own silence for their very survival. They maintain a round-the-clock listening watch on various sensors, but especially their own sonar receivers. However, the one place they can't listen to is their rear aspect. Their screws blank out all sonar reception from a substantial cone of space behind them. So, it is standard operating procedure for any submarine on patrol to periodically execute something called "baffle clearing" turns. These are turning maneuvers which permit the turning submarine to listen to the area in the water that was directly behind them before they began the turn. The baffle clearing turn is a computer-generated maneuver which makes it virtually impossible for a trailing submarine to remain undetected.

We came to recognize the Russian baffle clearing turn as being almost identical to ours…and we called their turns "Crazy Ivan." But there was a real "Crazy Ivan" of whom none of us was aware until one early October morning in 1978.

"Captain, you had better get over here right away. There's something you should see." The message on the telephone hotline to my house was sufficiently cryptic and alarming to get me out of a warm bed, into my blue jeans, and out the door within one minute. Scampering across the 150 feet of lawn to the door of the command center, I wondered what in the world it could be this time. But I was also reasonably certain that the call was submarine related.

And it was! As I entered the floor of the command center there was a cluster of intelligence analysts standing there staring at the wall display and scratching their heads in group consternation. They were staring at the symbol of a Yankee class Soviet submarine-launched ballistic missile boat called CASE 005L. It was located about 200 miles northeast of Bermuda in the heart of the "shooter's box."

"What's the problem?" I asked the CinCLant duty officer as soon as he recognized my presence.

"We've got us a real Crazy Ivan, Captain," he answered. "Case 005L suddenly took off like a striped-assed ape headed due west, toward Washington, D.C."

"How fast?" I asked.

"Twenty-five knots!" came the reply.

"Jesus! Did you alert the JCS?" I asked, thoroughly astounded and alarmed. SLBMs, both ours and theirs, patrolled at speeds of about 4-6 knots…whatever speed was the slowest (and quietest), but still gave the skipper sufficient steerage way. Never in my limited experience had I ever heard of anyone doing this. It was tantamount to suicide, because it made the submarine clearly audible to anyone with a hydrophone listening within 1,500 miles! This guy must be nuts. "What does SOSUS say?" I pressed. Anytime a Soviet SLBM submarine in the shooter's box did anything out of the ordinary, the JCS wanted to be informed. More to the point, they wanted an explanation for the unusual behavior.

SOSUS was the system of underwater hydrophones we had implanted on the ocean floor all over the Atlantic littoral from the Norwegian Sea to the island of Barbados in the Caribbean Sea.

"They can't explain it, sir," came the response. "He must really be crazy!" I examined the plot on the wall chart. It told the story of the events of the last hour. Case 005L had been steaming along on a course of 310 degrees magnetic for over an hour at a speed estimated to be 25 knots. Then he slowed to patrol speed and all SOSUS contact ceased. Thirty minutes of silence had been broken and Case 005L was now stooging along at 25 knots, headed in the opposite direction… south southeast. What in the world was this wild man doing, I wondered.

"Put together your best submarine intelligence analysts, get with Lieutenant Commander Jon Coleman of the N-35 shop, and give me your best guess in one hour. Based upon that, I'll decide whether we ought to recommend to the CinC that we report this officially to the JCS. Meanwhile, I'd better call the CinC and give him a heads-up." Those were my instructions to my deputy for ASW operations.

By now it was 0200 and my telephone conversation with the sleepy-voiced CinC was not entirely pleasant. After I explained that I had given a small group an hour to come up with an explanation, the CinC asked the question I knew was coming. "Paul, what is your best guess…now?" I gave it my best shot but was not very comfortable with it.

"Admiral, I think the skipper is dead drunk." This was followed by a long silence. Then came the question I was dreading.

"Why?" Now it was my turn to be silent for a few seconds as I summoned up my mental faculties. I took a deep breath and told him.

"Admiral, there are only two possibilities as I see it. Either he is crazy or he is drunk." I paused for a moment to let that sink in, then pressed on. "If he had gone stark-raving mad, the executive officer and the political advisor would have overpowered him, locked him in his stateroom, and the executive officer would have assumed command of the submarine. This obviously hasn't happened, since they are still stooging along at 25 knots…as we speak." I continued trying to sound convincing.

"Admiral, we both know that drinking while on patrol is not an uncommon occurrence for Soviet ship captains. There have been enough occasions of this for the Soviet Navy to issue sharp corrective orders to put an end to the phenomenon…measures that, so far, have not been effective".

"Go on," the CinC said, sounding unconvinced. I continued feeling particularly unpersuasive.

"Well, Admiral," I continued. "If he were merely drunk…had too many vodkas after supper, the executive officer would have convinced him to turn in for the night. Then he would quietly have taken over in main con and slowed down immediately. This has not happened. So, therefore, I believe he is drunk and the XO has not yet convinced him to turn in for the night. The XO would not want to inform the POLAD (political advisor) if he were merely drunk…and the POLAD would probably not even be aware that the submarine was making all that noise." I ended my case rather lamely, then added. "We will know within another hour, Admiral, whether my assessment is correct or not. If he slows down soon, it will mean I was probably right. If he does not slow down, I will recommend to you that we alert the JCS." There was another pregnant silence followed by an enormous sigh.

"Okay, Paul," the CinC said resignedly. "We'll give it one hour. If he does not slow down by then, call me and we will go from there." Then he added, as an afterthought, "Oh, yes, Paul. Have the VP guys put a full-court press to pinpoint his location while he's still so noisy, just in case we have to go sink him!" The comment shocked me. But, of course, it was a very logical extension of the line of thought of the CinC. It made good sense.

One hour later, Case 005L slowed to normal patrol speed and was not heard from again that night…or any other night for the rest of his patrol, except for other detectable actions which need not be discussed here. I have often wondered whether the skipper's superiors ever heard about their captain's crazy maneuvers that night.

A short time later another similar incident occurred that convinced me that alcohol was a serious problem in the Soviet Union's submarine forces. This time the venue was the Mediterranean Sea, and the incident occurred in the middle of a major annual NATO maritime exercise code named National Week. Although a U.S. aircraft carrier battle group was the centerpiece of the exercise forces, the principal players in the incident were a squadron of five U.S. Navy frigates (equipped for antisubmarine warfare), a squadron of P-3C *Orion* maritime patrol aircraft, and a nuclear-powered attack submarine operating in direct support. Three of the frigates were configured with "tails" (towed sonar arrays), and the other two were equipped with the necessary suite of communications to coordinate the prosecution of submarines using all source data.

It was a highly sophisticated, high-tech team working aggressively to locate and track a Soviet Echo II class nuclear-powered submarine which was in transit from the Northern Fleet down through the North Atlantic, through the Straits of Gibraltar, and right into the middle of *National Week*. The submarine was localized outside the straits, tracked through Gibraltar and across the Mediterranean Sea to the exercise area. Every time the poor submarine skipper came to periscope depth for a look around there was his nemesis, a *Knox* class frigate named *Voge*. There is no doubt that *Voge's* continued presence, sitting right on top of him, must have maddened the skipper of the *Echo II* submarine. They were doing a great job of riding herd on the Soviet submarine and never gave her skipper a break.

Finally, the stress level must have gotten to the Soviet seaman, and he obviously snapped. He came to periscope depth right in the middle of the battle group, nearest to a the U.S. frigate, *Moinester,* identified her, then headed directly for *Voge*, which happened to be a few miles away, but clearly visible to the submarine. The Soviet submarine accelerated to 22 knots at periscope depth and produced an enormous surface wake pointed right at *Voge*. This was, of course, an unprecedented thing for any submarine to do. Her wake was clearly visible to anyone in the area, and the noise she produced could be heard for hundreds of miles. *Moinester* was quick to call *Voge* and warn her that the submarine was on a collision course at high speed.

Although the E*cho II* was behaving in a highly unconventional manner, the threat to *Voge* was apparent and unmistakable. The ship did the right thing—she turned to a course directly away from the suicide submarine, rang up flank speed and sounded General Quarters. Unfortunately, the engineering plant on V*oge* was just not up to the challenge. The Soviet submarine pulled up 600 yards on *Voge's* port beam, hesitated in that position for a few minutes, then began closing rapidly.

What followed is still hard to believe...the *Echo II* collided with the frigate at a point aft of the port beam, punching a large hole in the ship's hull below the waterline and knocking her single screw completely off its mountings. The fairwater plane of the submarine was then observed to swing away from the frigate, and the submarine rolled to port in a 70 degree roll as it disappeared below the surface. There were literally dozens of photographs taken by observers, many of them sailors on *Voge*, while others were taken by other ships and the P-3C *Orions* overhead.

News of the collision was relayed to the 6th Fleet commander, who immediately ordered one of the command and control ships, USS *Koelsch*, to send a message to Vice Admiral Akimov, the Soviet Mediterranean Squadron Commander. He informed the admiral that one of his frigates had been involved in a collision with one of Akimov's submarines; and that the status of the submarine was unknown. In due time Akimov's flagship arrived on the scene, located the submarine, and took it in tow. One of 6th Fleet's ships took *Voge* in tow and delivered her to Naples for extensive repair.

Of course, the political repercussions of the incident were enormous. Messages flew back and forth between various fleet headquarters, Washington, and Moscow until the furor died out. The fact that there were no human casualties had a great deal to do with the incident quickly passing from the center of action of the media.

Now, years later, after the end of the Cold War, I have often reflected upon the two "Crazy Ivans" and wondered what happened to them. Drinking was a problem rampant in the Soviet Navy. I have this expectation, some day, of asking one of my Russian friends who were intimately familiar with the Soviet Navy, "What ever happened to the 'Crazy Ivans'?"

Chapter 7:
The Crew

There were many pretty ingenious sailors on the boat. For that matter, this applies to the "yard birds," as well. There were numerous instances when a problem seemed insurmountable to most of us and someone would come up with some really clever solution. Here is a typical example:

Our only source of fresh water, apart from the tanks we filled prior to leaving on a cruise, was an evaporator in the maneuvering room. On a particularly long cruise, after predictably running out of the stored water, we began making our own. The evaporator was a heavy-duty machine run by a big electric motor bolted on top. The power was transferred with pulleys and five or six fan belts—like those in your car, except heavier. This machine ran through belts pretty often, so we always had a bunch of spares. When the first few belts frayed and had to be replaced, the auxilliaryman discovered that *ALL the spare* belts were the wrong size—too long! So, there we were in mid-Pacific and our only source for fresh water would not run.

Everyone was stumped until a sailor suggested that we simply put enough steel plates between where the flanges of the motor and the evaporator met, until the proper distance was achieved for the wrong belts to fit. The next step was to drill holes for the longer bolts, install the longer belts, and turn the damn thing on. Amazing! I don't know about you, but I thought that was damned clever, and it saved us from some very uncomfortable circumstances. The water situation was particularly critical for a sub with batteries that had to be watered all the time.

Saltier sailors have been playing jokes on newer guys for centuries. I recall once when I was the "new guy" and the lead torpedoman had snaked himself through the maze of piping between the starboard torpedo tubes and the tapering pressure hull. It took a long time to squeeze through the pipes. I was always uncomfortable whenever I did it myself, because if there ever was a fire or we began to flood, I'd be history, since it would take a good five or ten minutes to squeeze myself back out. However, this time I was the "gofer"—the one handing tools into the man all wrapped up in the piping.

"Hey, hand me a 15/16th box end wrench will you?" said my shipmate. I leapt over to the tool box and quickly went through it, only to find no wrench of that description.

"Hold on, we don't have one. I'll run back to borrow one from the pump room."

I took off, mindful of the this guy's discomfort. The people in the pump room did not have the tool either, so I went to the auxiliary room, only to be disappointed there as well. By this time I was really worried about my poor shipmate in the shape of a pretzel. The enginemen were sure to have a 15/16th box end wrench I thought, they had every tool you could imagine. But they didn't have this wrench. My last shot were the electricians in the maneuvering room. No dice! I could not believe it, not one 15/16th box end on the entire God damn boat! I tore back through the boat's narrow passageways to the forward room and reported the situation to "pretzelman."

"Sorry, I've looked everywhere and there isn't one on the boat," I told him.

"That's OK, give me anything, I just needed it to bang this pin into place."

Torpedo tubes are pretty large, 21 inches in diameter and 20 feet long. For the maintenance we had to perform inside the tubes we had a little dolly like the ones auto mechanics use under your car, except curved to the same radius as the tube. We could scoot back and forth in the tube lying on our backs on this thing.

A new sailor, anxious to help, volunteered to go into the tube one day. We told him that he had to watch closely to see that the firing mechanism moved properly. The way one-ton torpedoes are shot out of the tube is with a very large and sudden impulse of high-pressure air from a big storage flask next to the tubes. The air has to be introduced into the tube aft of the torpedo, and all at once, to be effective.

"Are you ready?" we all asked, smiling into the dark tube and seeing only his feet.

"I'm all set—go ahead," the muffled yell came back. WOOOSSSHHH!

After the blast of air, all we could hear was that dolly speeding towards the closed outer door, 15 feet forward. THUNK! his head stopped the forward motion. We could only hear since there was no light in there, and all we heard was that dolly slowly inching its way back towards us. He got as far back as the firing mechanism and shouted, "Better try it again. Everything happened so fast I didn't see the valve open."

I'm not certain that the expressions we often used on each other were universal for submariners at the time or particular to *Barbero*, but some of them were pretty colorful. Whenever anyone became a bit obnoxious, or they were getting on our nerves, one of us would say, "Hey, Haney, don't let that water tight door hit you in the ass on your way aft, you hear?" Vandergrif often used the word "HEAD'N" as in, "Now Gillcrist, I don't believe that that comes under the 'head'n' of your f—ing business." There was another I liked—"two blocked." If you recall, a block and tackle can only move something so far until both blocks meet. Anything which had gone as far as it was going to go was "two blocked."

"Gundecking" was basically lying. We applied it, for example, when we were referring to the logs we had to maintain for each torpedo. There were these stupid regulations, such as the one where we had to manually turn the propellers on each "fish" periodically—I think it was even daily. Of course, we saw this as utterly unnecessary and simply didn't do it. Once in awhile we'd break out the logs and catch up, just in case we got inspected. One of us would say, "Has anybody 'gundecked' those logs lately?"

After months in the Orient we called Honolulu "Honaruru," and my friend Jim Dresser always referred to the continental U.S.A. as the "Big Island"—just to irritate the "locals." When civilians want to be sure that you don't think they are stupid and uninformed, they say, "I didn't fall off the back of the (mellon, cabbage) truck this morning." Sailors say, "I didn't come in on the 'four to eight' watch."

Whenever we were on a serious cruise we did not drill at all. We simply stood our watches, so beyond sleeping and standing watches there was little to do. This was particularly true of me when I was on watch in the forward room, since it was a sleeping compartment and the lights were out. I'd just sit there, read by a little light, and wait for World War Three. One night I decided to make a set of Rorschach tests for the crew to take. You know, those ink blot figures the psychiatrists use? So I put ink in the center of ten pieces of paper, folded them in half and let them dry. Next, after I was relieved of the watch, I started aft to ask each of the crew what the images meant. I thought the way they worked was if 90 percent of the general population thought the ink blot was a bicycle peddle, and you thought it looked like a pumpkin, then *you were weird*—simple as that. What I found was that after 60 days at sea, all these red blooded, long isolated, young American sailors thought each of the pictures strongly resembled intimate female body parts! I quickly gave up on the project, completely suspect of all that psychology stuff and vowing to never, ever take "psych" courses when I went to college.

Johnson was a radioman first class who was tall and very skinny. His only form of nourishment, apparently, was coffee and cigarettes, which he constantly consumed. Oh, he'd make every meal, but it was entertainment to him, not an occasion of sustenance. Actually, everyone liked chow time; there was good food and always plenty of banter.

Our chief cook was named Reader. He was a good cook, very excitable, and a genuinely good man. The older crew liked to tease him, and for some reason we called him "the Greek." The Navy always posted a menu for every meal (not that you had any options). This was done throughout the Navy and *Barbero* was no exception.

What Johnson would do, since he rarely stood watches and was apparently never hungry, was to wait until third call for the meal and then be late even for that. I'd watch him step into the mess and go straight to the posted menu. Nobody ever read the menu except Johnson—what good would it do? After seeing what was on it, he'd sit down and scan the table to see what had already run out by this late time and, even though he had no intention of actually eating the peas or whatever it happened to be, he would say, "Reader, where are the peas? There are no peas on the table."

Chief Reader, "The Greek," cook on the U.S.S. Barbero 1957-1960. (Dan Gillcrist Collection)

Reader, having worked long and hard to produce the meal, particularly under lousy conditions, would predictably blow up, "God damnit, Johnson, you skinny son of a bitch, if you'd get here on time for a change there would be peas—we are out of peas and that's it." Johnson would reply, "God damnit, Greek, the menu says peas and when I signed on to this f—king Navy, I was guaranteed three meals a day and a place to sleep. You post the menu, it says P-E-A-S and by God I want mine...I'm entitled!"

Johnson just sat there ragging on poor Reader, drinking coffee and smoking. Reader was plenty smart and knew exactly what was going on, and played the game very convincingly. The rest of us would just laugh. It was like dinner theater, except on a sub at sea.

There was a chief named Wink on the boat whose rate was actually nuclear war heads, or something close to that. He was in charge of our Regulus missiles. I didn't know exactly what his rate was, because in the late 50s we did not go around, particularly overseas, advertising that we either had the "bomb," or knew anything about them. All he needed was to be walking around Japan with a mushroom cloud for a patch instead of whatever he wore on his arm! The Japanese were pretty touchy about the "bomb" back then—it was only 14 years since we dropped a couple on them.

In any event, we liked each other, Wink and I. He was smart, funny, and, for all I knew, he may not even have been in the Navy! It should be remembered that we had the first submarine-borne nuclear missiles. The time was 1959-1960, and the Japanese were very sensitive about Americans pulling into their ports with "the bomb." For all I knew, the chief could very well have been a civilian sent along on this particular trip to make sure we could fire the missiles if we had to. Our trip to Kamchatka, I believe, was the first time the United States put a sub with nuclear missles anywhere off the coast of the U.S.S.R.

This is not "Elvis sighting," and I would not have brought it up, except for another very strange thing which happened as we were getting underway for our trip to the Kamchatka Peninsula. (We, of course, had no idea where we were going on this cruise other than "WestPac.") We had stationed the maneuvering watch, had even singled up the lines, and were ready to bring in the brow, but the captain was waiting for something. Just then a truck pulled up to the brow and three sailors hopped out, grabbed their seabags, and came aboard. We immediately pulled in the brow and started to back down away from the pier. I thought it very odd, but subsequent events shed some light on the subject. After all, one does not show up six seconds before going on a cruise that would take them away for four or five months, with a limp, half-filled seabag. It turned out that their job was in the tiny missile guidance room in the after battery, which was off limits to us for this particular cruise.

Later in the cruise, one of them volunteered to give Japanese lessons each day in the crew's mess. Well, we quickly figured out that they were linguists and were listening to the Russians while we were off Kamchatka. The moment we pulled into Yokosuka after this 72 day trip and tied up, they were the first people off the boat. They got into a waiting truck and were gone even before we had the boat properly tied up. A week after this, one of the crew saw one of these guys in a bar in a Marine uniform! For most of us, the whole thing was a little too melodramatic.

Getting back to the nuclear weapons chief, or whatever he was, we had been at sea for a pretty long time and all of our fresh food had been long gone. It was probably a month and a half since we had any salad stuff to eat—everything was frozen or canned. We didn't even have any more onions or potatoes. I was sitting across from the chief eating my dinner when I said, "Know what I want more than anything else, what I'd probably kill for right now?" I could see it on the chief's face, he thought that I was going to name something carnal and vulgar after all this time aboard. I said, "A big green salad—I'd do anything for a salad right now. A whole head of iceberg lettuce covered with lumpy rochefort dressing. God damn, that would taste good." He looked a bit relieved and said, "Jesus, me too. I think about it all the time!" I am not convinced our priorities were shared by the entire crew at that point, but it is interesting what importance things take on when we have been deprived of them.

Monahan was an electrician first class who was smart and liked to tweak the officers, probably because he felt that he was as smart as they were but was still only an enlisted man. He would walk that thin line of insubordination which sailors, particularly submariners, often did. He'd always get away with it because he was good at this game, and because he really did know more than the officers about our electrical plant. He'd say things like, "Now Mr. Watkins, sir, Congress didn't make me an 'officer and a gentleman' and I didn't go to college, but I think you are mistaken about so and so." He was always irreverent and iconoclastic, and did not reserve this solely for the officers.

He loved to argue, and would take either side of any issue, since it was not the principle but rather the exercise that he liked. He should have been a lawyer. He would come out with some outrageous statement just to stir up the forward battery, like the day he declared that there were no virgin women—they had all "done it." I finally had had enough of this and said, "Monahan, you are so full of shit it's unbelievable! You don't know what the hell you're talking about. You're just a frustrated, fantasizing, irritable sailor with some 'thing' about women ...no virgins, my ass."

"So, aah Gillcrist, do you know any virgins?" he asked, sucking me into the trap.

"Of course I know some virgins, all four of my sisters are virgins!" I asserted.

"Jesus Christ, Gillcrist. How the f—k do you know your sisters are virgins? You are the most naive son-of-a-bitch I've ever met."

Well, he had a field day with that, as I hung in there and argued with him, fueled by the multitude of biases and bullshit I got out of twelve years of Catholic school, of course getting nowhere with him and looking foolish in the balance. He was completely in his element! You'd think we would have learned after a while.

Wally Vandergrif was a friend and fellow torpedoman. He bunked above me and we got along great. He was a "lifer," while I intended to get out of the Navy and go to college when my four years was up. Wally loved to sleep. Once he fell asleep standing up, draped over a Mk14 torpedo in the torpedo shop in Pearl, *while we worked on it!* Butch Miller (another torpedoman) and I decided to play a trick on him and see just how long he could actually sleep. This took place during a very long submerged period. Everyone was in on

Torpedoman Vandergrif (left), U.S.S. Barbero off Kamchatka, 1960. (Dan Gillcrist Collection)

this, and there was betting going on. We were always betting on something, "anchor pools" and the like.

It started when I relieved Vandergrif from the morning "8 to 12" watch in the forward room. He ate lunch and went to his bunk to sleep. Now, we had been snorkeling off the Kamchatka peninsula for several weeks by this time. There was no training and no drills of any kind to punctuate the day, and there was no way to know night from day except for the kind of food we were served—if it was bacon and eggs, it must be morning! Without days, nights, sunrises, and so on, one loses a sense of time orientation very quickly. It is a very strange existence indeed, common among submariners, but rare everywhere else.

At any rate, we did not wake Vandergrif for his next watch, the "8 to12" pm—rather, Miller and I shared his watch and let him sleep on. Everyone would come forward to see if he was still asleep, marvel, and verify their bets. It got to be the next morning before he awoke. Miller and I just stared at him as he sat on the edge of his bunk. He was even more groggy than he was when we woke him under normal circumstances, which amazed us since he had been asleep for about 17 hours! Anyway, he made a head call and went into the mess in the next compartment. *Everyone* was looking at him, wondering when he would realize what was going on. He stood there looking at the bacon and toast in bowls on the mess tables. "What is wrong with this picture?" we all assumed he was thinking. Finally, he knew something was up and we all broke into an uproar of laughter and explained the prank. He was probably grateful for the additional sleep, as if he needed it. Everyone settled their bets, and Wally ate breakfast—he was *very* hungry.

The Navy is so old that it uses a lot of anachronistic names for places, equipment, and the jobs people have. It is actually kind of nice and colorful. Some of the names, however, are for political correctness, like the cities calling garbage men sanitary engineers. One which comes to mind is COMMISARYMAN—it's short for "cook." The civilian sector is not the only one with the habit of obfuscation.

Vandergrif was reading my new set of orders, which began the process of mustering me out of the Navy after four years. I would leave the boat and go to Treasure Island in San Francisco Bay and do all sorts of things which took days. Vandergrif began to laugh hilariously, showing my set of orders to the other guys in the torpedo room. "What's so funny about my orders"? I asked. He pointed to a box on my brand new DD-214 entitled "RELATED CIVILIAN OCCUPATION," where the yeoman had entered "ASSEMBLER-SMALL PARTS," presumably for my future employer's benefit. Vandergrif and I, who had juggled one ton torpedoes around for three years, just looked at each other. Vandergrif said, "Gillcrist, the smallest parts you ever handled were a two-ton chain fall and a seven-pound maul, what the hell are those people thinking about? Small parts, my ass"! He thought that our "related civilian occupation" was more like moving a full dumpster by hand with another guy.

Vandergrif and I learned a lesson one day when we were modifying a rack for the boat. All of us learned continually due to the environment of the boat. We learned a lot of physics and chemistry—empirically. Most of us were high school graduates and most had no further aspirations for education, probably for economic reasons. I say this because there were very few sailors on *Barbero* who would have had a difficult time getting through a normal college. Most were plenty smart, if a bit rough around the edges.

I recall talking to my brother Bob, an engineering student, about the weather where I was then living and I referred to "sublimation," which is the transformation of water in the solid state (ice) directly to the gaseous state without melting, since the ambient temperature in Vermont, where I lived at the time, was close to zero degrees. Bob paused and said, "How the hell do you know about that?" His voice implied that since I had little scientific education, how would I have ever learned something so esoteric. My answer was that I knew lots of things and I really did. Part of it was my curiosity, but a lot was my Naval experience.

Getting back to Vandergrif and me with this rack—we found an old rack somewhere on the sub base and wanted to squeeze it into the forward room, since we were short. Racks were our bunks; they were a rectangular pipe welded once, at a joint somewhere on the rectangle, with wire and springs across the center upon which the mattress was laid. All of our racks already had hooks and chains, so we could "trice up" the bunks to get them out of our way when we worked in the room. However, this rack had no holes for the hooks. So, Vandergrif and I got out the big half-inch drill and started to drill the two holes we needed. He was on the drill and I was "holding the flashlight," so to speak. The lesson was about to be learned, mostly by Wally.

He was leaning on the drill with his face right over it, probably with his tongue sticking out the side of his mouth. The drill bit, I am sure, was dull, as usual. As the drill broke into the pipe the gasses trapped when the thing was welded, probably in WW II, shot straight up and, as they passed the sparking armature brushes of the drill, they exploded right in Vandergrif's face! He was hurt, and it was no minor burn. We both learned a bit of physics that day.

The cooks seemed to me to be the most colorful of the crew. I know this is a generalization, but they were very often amusing, almost as if they thought that entertaining us while we ate was part of their job description. One in particular, a first class commissaryman named Foster, comes to mind. I can picture the guy perfectly.

His "girlfriend" in Yokosuka was named Konna—a "business woman," if you get my drift. Foster was genuinely fond of her and spent all his available time with her and, no doubt, his available money, as well. While I was buying china and a camera in the PX, our cook was down in Black Market Alley with Konna. He talked to the crew hanging out in the mess about her, even after we had permanently left Yokosuka.

One morning, a week or two out of port, we were all eating breakfast when Foster, leaning out the half door to the galley, announced to our amazement and amusement that he had had a wet dream the night before! We all nearly choked on our food. He then thought for a moment and, in a voice of resignation said, "Well, I guess I'd better send old Konna some money as soon as we hit Pearl."

Before Foster, we had a rotund, red-faced Irishman from Boston named P.B. Spinney. He, too, was hilarious, which made up for any culinary shortcomings he may have had. It is curious to me to see so many funny men in the same rate. Why are so many cooks funny? Spinney, like Foster, apparently felt an obligation to provide entertainment during meals. He was an Irish Catholic and often spoke in a perfect immitation of an Irish brogue. One time in port, hanging out the gally's half door, he said to the hung-over crew at breakfast, "Say three Our Fathers, three Hail Marys and I'll see you at bingo Wednesday night."

Sometimes he would switch into his also perfect "ring announcer" routine with that deliberate and theatrical way they all seem to have, "...and his most worthy opponent, weighing in at 178 pounds, in the black trunks, recently acquitted of a felony charge, TOOONNNYYY PALOOOONE, Palone." Spinney was one funny son of a bitch!

I can't speak for the other boats, but I suspect that their meals were a form of entertainment like *Barbero's* were. Who knows? Maybe the selection process for submarine cooks included a sense of humor in order to make our uncomfortable existence easier.

The young junior cook baked fresh bread during the night when there were no competing meals to prepare in our tiny galley. He also needed the mess tables, since he could not do it all in the galley. So the entire process had to be at night. Like most cooks, this guy came from a different zip code and, as Shorty Freeman used to say, "He's got a full seabag all right, it just ain't stowed right."

Well, one night I watched as he did all those steps in preparing the dough—it was a whole lot of work. He ended up with two mess tables covered with baking tins full of rising dough. He stood back, covered up with flour and admired his night's work. The dough had risen properly, the ovens were pre-heated, he could visualize all those golden loaves and, no doubt, hear the nice comments he would receive from the crew in the morning. All was good in the world. That was until he heard a very unexpected announcement over the 1MC speaker near the galley, "Now hear this, commence snorkeling, commence snorkeling! Engine room start #1 and #2 main engines. Carry a zero float on the auxiliary. Commence snorkeling, commence snorkeling."

You could see his face turning white, even through the flour... "JESUS *H. CHRIST!*" and that was the least profane and just for starters. He began to curse loudly, directing the torrent toward the door leading into the control room where both the decision and its announcement were made. This was even before the huge diesels lit off and began sucking large quantities of air out of the boat, making his dough expand grotesquely. Like any self-respecting submariner, he knew what was about to happen and cursed even louder and with great originality (very uncommon on this boat). The snorkel head valve suddenly opened, restoring the pressure in the boat. The vacuum that made his dough expand grossly was no more and the bread all collapsed. His bread dough now resembled pita bread or rectangular tortillas. He ranted on about how his work was not appreciated, as he threw everything in the garbage pails and stormed aft, followed by a thin cloud of flour.

Whenever there was too little room at the piers, the subs would double up or even quadruple up—we called it "breasting out." Once we were the fourth boat in this little cluster—the inboardmost boat was tied up to the pier and the rest of us were tied to one another. We typically put our brows in a row so that we could walk to the pier in a straight line from one boat to the next. It happened that the second boat out in this cluster was being worked on one day, and they had to place their brow aft of the sail while the rest were all forward. The same cook from the "bread story" was on his way to throw out the garbage and, as usual, was operating out of the right side of his brain as he walked straight off the third boat and into the water between the boats. It made a hell of a noise as he and the garbage cans bounced off the tank tops and into the water. Miraculously, he was not killed either by bouncing off the tank tops, being crushed between the hulls, or by ingesting that nasty harbor water. Naturally, we all thought it was absolutely hilarious, as we tossed him a line. The head cook was not amused, however, at the loss of two expensive, specially welded, heavy-gauge stainless steel, U.S. Government property garbage pails, which he would now have to replace.

You had to be fairly careful when you were on the main deck in port, because for each two-inch wide piece of wooden decking, there was a 3/4 inch gap in the deck. Underneath were saddle tanks which sloped down to the waterline, so that if you dropped a quarter, it would nearly always go to the bottom of the harbor. My friend and fellow seaman at the time, Miguel Suarez, had the topside watch, but had no way of telling time since he had no wrist watch, (typical submariner), so he asked for mine. I had just purchased a diver's watch at the exchange, the first decent watch of my life. At any rate, instead of putting the watch on his wrist and having to adjust its metal band, he slipped it onto his belt.

I was his relief, and in two hours I showed up and took the duty web belt with the empty .45-cal. and signed the deck log. He started to leave and I said, "Hey, Suarez, how about my watch back?" He turned and pulled his belt out of the loops and my nearly new, stainless steel Zodiac diver's watch with its moveable bezel and glow-in-the-dark hands dropped straight through the crack in the decking. We both looked immediately over the port side only to see the watch slide down the tank tops and into the harbor. I thought, very briefly, about jumping in after the damn thing, but I knew that was stupid.

Miguel knew, since I had bragged about it, that the watch could withstand a depth of several hundred feet of sea water. He seemed pretty sanguine about my loss, mumbling something about the fact that the watch, while admittedly lost, was at least ok in the 50 feet of water in the harbor—after all, it was a "diver's watch" and had a test depth of several hundred feet, blah, blah, blah. It is, no doubt, still down there safe and waterproof. Some archeologist will probably find it three hundred years from now next to the two stainless steel garbage pails, and make up some bullshit story about how the three are somehow connected.

I don't recall any act of restitution on Miguel's part, although he may have compensated me in some way. But shipmates were special to one another—there was a lot of tolerance and generosity between them, particularly on a submarine. I think this has always been so. We always looked out for each other, whether ashore or aboard the boat.

Miguel was a handsome guy, very articulate and bright. He was Puerto Rican and proud of it. He had an accent just like Fernando Lamas, except he spoke a lot faster, but he was real cocky and very Latino, like that other Hispanic actor from the fifties, Gilbert Roland.

Somehow I always knew that Miguel wanted to be an actor, because he nearly always looked and sounded like he was acting. He always looked like he was checking himself out in the reflection of a storefront window. Many years later, I was watching a hilarious Woody Allen movie I had rented, about some Central American banana republic, and there was Miguel as a comical "Che" type, if you will forgive the oxymoron, in his green uniform. "Hey, Barbara, my old shipmate Miguel Suarez is in this movie!" He acted exac*tly* the same as he did on the boat! I guess he was a natural.

Our one-and-only Yeoman was a Philippino named Ibarra. He was quite bright and very small boned. He wore a Rolex Submariner watch that looked like an alarm clock on his tiny wrist. He was quite obsessive about cleanliness, which certainly set him apart from the rest of us! He would clean his teeth every day using a complete set of dental instruments, little round mirror and all! He was way, way too clean for the rest of us. No oil on his clothes, no acid burns in his dungarees, and I don't even think he smelled. He was really better off typing for the officers back in his little "office" rather than in the torpedo room with the "deck apes."

For some reason officers are not referred to as crew—they all had jobs, they lived aboard the boat just like us, and were crew in every sense of the word. I never figured it out. Another odd expression was "officers and men of the so-and-so"...what did that one mean, anyway? Admittedly, it was semantics, but it was odd to me, frankly, probably just more of that separation thing which goes back to the early British Navy. Nevertheless, I am going to include some officers in this section.

C - A - R , L -O -S , D - E - W

When I joined the Navy one of the forms asked if I had any relatives in the Navy. I filled in all four of my brothers' names, three of whom were officers. I gave it no more thought until I showed up on the *Barbero*'s barge tied up next to the boat in the Philadelphia Naval Shipyard.

Whenever we were in a yard, we were assigned a barge with a two-story building on it where we lived while the boat was being worked on. It was also a place where we could store our tools and things so the "yardbirds" could not steal the stuff. At any rate, when I arrived, seabag and orders in hand, I was sent in to see the captain—a LCDR named Carlos Dew. He took my orders, looked them over briefly and said, "Ahh, Gillcrist, I see you are from a Navy family." This was my first introduction into Navy politics, since I believe he knew, even before I got there, that my older brother John was senior to him.

Carlos Dew was easy to describe—tall, very good-looking, very distinguished, a deep southern and theatrical voice. All in all, he was a poster Naval officer. The problem was that he was a poor leader and highly political. He was very hard on the crew, and the officers, as well. In fact, he was the only captain I ever heard of who had officers painting the waterways of the boat for an important inspection we were about to undergo! We won the "E" as a result. The crew had a little song which they made up to the tune of television's Mickey Mouse Club theme song:

"Who breaks us from our present rate,
Who always turns us to,
C-A-R, L-O-S, D-E-W "
This was followed by several bawdy and profane verses that I choose to skip.

We were once on some exercise out of Norfolk where we were supposed to sneak in toward the East Coast and simulate shooting one of our missiles. I should have had a premonition when the captain had the quartermaster paper over our hull number on the sides of the sail, paint the paper grey, and then paint a bogus number in its place.

Now you have to understand that we were trying to deceive ships from our own port, and besides that, we certainly had the most recognizable sub in the entire Navy and probably the world! *Barbero* was an old fleet boat which, unlike nearly all the rest, was never converted to the streamlined sail, *and* we were the only boat on earth that had a big hangar just aft of the sail which looked like a barrage balloon! We could not possibly be confused with another boat, regardless of hull numbers. As we disappeared over the horizon they tore off the paper number. What a joke—we fooled no one.

Anyway, we were quickly "killed and sunk," and promptly kicked out of this particular exercise. The captain was mortified and really mad at us for, I suppose, making him look bad. I recall vividly his dropping down the ladder from the conning tower after hearing the news of our "sinking," and standing there in the control room. All talking stopped, and no one made eye contact with him. You could hear a pin drop. I was on the bow planes with my back to him as he looked slowly around the compartment and announced the following, "Well, I see at least the bow planes are in competent hands." He then went aft to his little compartment.

The only analogy I can make here would be a prison guard in some high security slammer saying out loud to a prisoner, "Thanks for the information." Christ! I was living inside of a pipe with 80 sailors in mid-ocean and the Prince of Darkness wants to be my friend!

After being "kicked out" of the exercise, we were departing the area when the captain got on the 1 MC and added to the Dew legend with the following, "Since we can no longer play in the exercise, we will move to another area and play with ourselves." Well, I need not tell you the response of the hardened veterans of *Barbero*, drinking coffee and smoking in the forward battery! It was near hysteria, and the laughter was clearly heard in the control room. The captain must have realized the gaff as he went aft, once more, to his compartment, no doubt to conjure up some sort of retaliation.

I recall heading back to Norfolk on a Friday afternoon and just outside the first buoy, on the way into port, we saw a destroyer also heading for the entrance to the channel. It was obvious the destroyer was going to beat us into the channel due to its speed. The captain read the hull number through his binoculars and called down to the quartermaster in the conning tower to ask for the name of the destroyer's skipper and some number designating Naval seniority. Quickly determining that he, Carlos Dew, was senior, he told the signalman with the light to send, "You may follow in my wake." I recall thinking how chicken-shit that was, knowing that the sailors on the destroyer could have been on their third beer had they not had to "follow in the wake" of the slowest sub in the fleet.

A pal of mine on *Barbero* named Jim Dresser was transferred to another sub, I think the nuclear powered *Sargo*, which was also in Pearl at the time. He was pretty excited until he discovered that Carlos Dew was also sent to *Sargo*.

Even on a small sub, most of us could sort of hide, like "Ensign Pulver," in the ship's laundry, because our jobs did not put us around the captain and the exec. Days would often go by without coming into contact with either the captain or the exec. But the quartermasters' turf was the conning tower, and their job included helping with the navigation. So, Dresser was sort of "sentenced" to his new boat.

He later told me about the time the crew of Sargo went to a lecture on the damage effects and characteristics of a nuclear blast. The audience included Carlos Dew in the back row smoking his ever-present pipe. Everyone was asking questions about the subject, "What does the blast do to this or that and how badly, etc." until Carlos Dew waved pontifically at the lecturer for his attention.

"Yes, commander, do you have a question?" asked the instructor.

Dew responded in his very deep, southern, and deliberate voice, reminiscent of Bella Lugosi in those Dracula movies, "What does it do to the BLOOOOOODDDDD?"

Well, everyone there, of course, started coughing, stifling giggles and biting their tongues. The only memorable thing to come out of the lecture was the coining of his new nickname - "THE COUNT."

From then on Dresser would cut little bats out of that shiny plastic electrical tape and stick them on the lenses of the periscopes. He even taped the lens of his flashlight and cut out a bat so the beam of light was a bat. When he went to wake up Carlos Dew to tell him that they had a contact or they wanted to eject garbage, he'd shine the bat in the man's face in the dark.

I can just see it,

"We have a contact, commander,"

"Very well, let me know if it gets any closer."

Apparently, he never got it. Incidentally, the phrase "Very well, let me know if it gets any closer" is the reflex response of a ship's officer who is completely asleep.

Several days after reporting to *Barbero*, the engineering officer, LT Murray, came up to me in the control room and asked, "How's Punchy?" I had no idea what he was talking about. He turned out to be a really good and able officer who was friends with my brother Paul while at the Naval Academy. Paul had been a boxer both at Gonzaga University and the Academy, and had managed to get his nose badly broken at Gonzaga. Since the family was quite large and of very humble means, none of us, particularly Paul, would dream of writing home for money. So, regrettably, the nose was fixed by the lowest bidder who, I suspect, was the boxing team's trainer with a couple butterfly bandages from the looks of it. But the nickname "Punchy" was a no-brainer.

Our executive officer was a LT James Watkins. I guess since he worked under Carlos Dew we should make allowances for his attitude and demeanor like we would for anyone suffering from Post Traumatic Syndrome. This is not a facetious statement, because I ran into him a couple of years ago at a special two-day event in Houston and found him to be delightful and completely different than I remember from our days aboard *Barbero* many years before. Incidentally, he ended up as Chief of Naval Operations. His first response at the cocktail party as I introduced myself as having been on *Barbero* with him was, "OH MY GOD...CARLOS DEW!"

James Watkins had been somewhat humorless and as serious as a heart attack aboard *Barbero*. He was very Catholic and intolerant of the frequent vulgarities uttered by us. I always thought that if you were going to be in the Navy, you'd better get a grip and get used to it, since the enlisted ranks were often very profane. However, I think he had a very tough job as XO on *Barbero*.

He had a habit of getting on the 1MC in the control room and going on and on about ship's matters. Perhaps it was some sort of release from the stress of being the XO under Dew, who knows? But he sure talked a lot on that 1MC. As he left the boat for his next assignment, some of us assembled in the control room and gave him a little gift put together by the radiomen. It was a 1MC mike with a two foot cable attached to a set of earphones, so he could listen to himself talk! We thought it was hilarious. Most of the officers I have known would have found it quite funny, also. He, however, was not at all amused, as I recall. I'm sure he threw it in the dumpster at the head of the pier on his way to his next assignment.

LT Jensen was an officer who was very comfortable around the crew. Whenever he was OOD and I was lookout, we had nice conversations up on the bridge, and he was never condescending to the crew. I think he played football at the Academy and, as happens to many athletes when they stop training, put on a little weight. Like any career officer in subs at the time, he wanted to get into the nuclear power program. I have no sense of how long the application process took, but we were in Yokosuka when Admiral Rickover's office summoned him for his requisite interview with the admiral. It was widely known that the admiral was damn picky about who he'd allow to run *HIS* nuclear subs, since they were, after all, *HIS* and not the Navy's in every sense of the word except legal title.

Our lieutenant left right away for the arduous trip, halfway around the world, back to Washington on military planes. He was cooling his heels in the admiral's outer office when he was called in, no doubt in a state of near terror due to the many awful stories floating around about what an SOB Rickover could be on these occasions. Rickover didn't look up from his work for an uncomfortable time while our well-traveled lieutenant stood at attention in front of his desk. LT Jensen didn't even get his name out of his mouth when the admiral barked, "Come baaaack when you lose thirty-five pounds." That was the end of the "interview!"

Chapter 8:
Watches

QUALIFICATION

When a new sailor or officer arrived aboard a submarine, he was expected to begin studying and working to earn his Dolphins—a process we call "qualification." It was clearly more difficult for the officers, since they had an additional level of responsibility apart from how and why things worked the way they did. They had to con the boat. This meant that they needed to know all the systems, understand navigation and maneuvering the boat, work the TDC (torpedo data computer) so they could hit a target with a torpedo, and finally know how to tactically fight the boat.

The enlisted men did not have to do any of these things directly. However, various of us helped on each of these responsibilities, depending on what his job was on the boat. For example, with respect to navigation and firing a torpedo, the quartermasters helped out. So, the officers would have to know, in addition to the things just mentioned, something of each of our jobs as well. They would probably not be able to do our individual jobs very well, but they needed to know enough for an understanding, for instance, of what it takes to load a torpedo in heavy weather.

My own qualification started with being assigned to LT Murray, an already-qualified officer who would keep me on track. His first assignment for me was to prepare drawings of all the boat's systems. The inside of the pressure hull is a maze of piping and wiring—it virtually covers the inside of the hull. I would start, for example, at the trim manifold next to the stern planes in the control room and follow the trim system's piping. I'd see where the pipes went through the bulkhead, climb out of the bilge, go into the next compartment and try to pick them up and then draw the entire system. This was done for each of the many systems so that when I took the "walk through the boat" examination at the end, I could identify a large portion of the piping, wiring, switches, and valves in the entire boat.

The other purpose of the walk through the boat was not only to determine whether we knew what everything was, but to find out if we knew what to do in various emergencies. The boat was simply packed with things which could either burn, leak, or explode just like many ships, except that potential mishaps were generally more lethal in a submarine. So, the questions on the "walk through" would be like these:

"Water starts flooding the compartment through that valve (pointing to it). What do you do?"

"That motor (pointing to it) is smoking, what are you going to do?"

"OK, Gillcrist, now start the main engines."

"Someone yells FIRE in the next compartment. What do you do?"

There were also lots of trick questions, such as, "How many square feet of surface area is there on the rudder?" or, "What is the smallest chain on the boat?" I happen to remember this answer—it is the tiny chain in the ship's main barometer. Forcing all of us to become qualified made the boat a far safer place.

In general, I believe that there is a relationship between the size of a ship, measured by the number of ship's company, of course, and this whole subject of overlapping skills and responsibilities. A plane captain in a squadron aboard a carrier probably does not even know where the fuel oil purifier is located. He may not even know there is one. It doesn't matter, since there is not the remotest chance that in some emergency he'd be in a position to turn the thing off or do whatever else was necessary. I believe that the smaller the ship, the more responsibilities overlap along with the increased likelihood that each member of the crew—including officers—has more than one job.

TOPSIDE WATCH

At sea, about one third of the crew stands the underway watches at any one time. We needed a helmsman, lookouts, guys on the bow and stern planes if we were submerged, and so on. The watches naturally changed a bit depending upon whether we were submerged or on the surface. But in port it was far simpler. Basically, we had an OOD with the "duty," who had overall responsibility for the boat. Also, there was a below decks watch and the "topside watch," responsible mainly for external safety. If we were about to be rammed by some sloppy merchant ship, no one below would be aware of it if it were not for the watch topside.

One of his responsibilities was to either slack off or tighten up the lines securing us to the pier as the tides came and went. I recall that on the Pacific side of the Panama Canal, the tides were from 10 to 12 feet, and watching the lines demanded constant attention so that we didn't tear bollards and cleats off their pier, or worse, snap one of our big nylon mooring lines—a very dangerous thing for anyone in the area!

On large ships ceremony was a big deal, but on *Barbero* ceremony was nearly non-existent because nobody ever visited us. I'll bet there was not one bosun's pipe on the boat. The "black shoe" people who ran the ports invariably moored us in some remote place for some reason. This was just fine with the crew, since we could play volleyball and have cookouts on the pier with our shirts off and not be harassed.

Torpedoman Gillcrist on lookout, U.S.S. Barbero, Carribbean, 1959. (Dan Gillcrist Collection)

BELOWDECKS WATCH

The other evening I did my usual walk through the house just before retiring for the night. We all do this, checking doors locked, lights in their night mode, everything turned off and secured. All of a sudden I heard an unfamiliar sound, and in a flash I recalled standing below decks watch on *Barbero*.

Below decks on a sub there were a lot of things which could (and often did) go wrong. The man on watch had to be "qualified." He'd wander completely through the boat every half hour or so, simply letting his senses take over. Stepping into a compartment, he would first listen for a sound which did not belong. It could be a very noisy compartment, but we knew all the "right noises" and could distinguish them from the ones that would indicate trouble. He would smell for trouble, as well. An overheated electric motor has a smell we all probably recognize; chlorine, fuel oil, etc., each have a signature odor. There were many odors in every compartment, and the trick was knowing which ones belonged and which did not. We were also aware of what I'll call "attitude." If the boat was a bit down by the bow or had a little list to port, we had to find out why. We were always alert and took this watch quite seriously.

BOW AND STERN PLANES

There were two wheels on the port side in the control room, one for the bow planes and one for the stern planes. They were manned by the two lookouts who, during a dive, would have just dropped down into the control room and were therefore available. Just above each of these positions a simple device helped them with up and down angles of the boat—they were long glass tubes curved downward at each end and perhaps 15 inches long. The tubes were full of oil except for a bubble of air, and were graduated with little marks indicating each degree off of the horizontal. At the extreme down angle end of this tube was a one inch dogleg up where the oil and air bubble were introduced when the device was made. The diving officer would call for ten degrees down angle on the bow planes, for example, and the sailor on the planes would use this instrument to guide him.

There was an expression peculiar to submariners—"losing the bubble." If the down angle were ever in the extreme, the little bubble of air would end up "lost" in the dogleg at the end of the tube. So, we would say things such as, "Jesus, Shorty, calm down. Don't lose the bubble over this." We often used the expression when referring to someone's mental state. "Remember old Miller over on the Archerfish? What the hell ever happened to him?" "Oh, he's out of the Navy on a 'medical'—I heard he lost the bubble on their last cruise."

FORWARD ROOM WATCH

Many of the watches at sea were passive and generally uneventful. The guy just stood there and waited until chow, his relief, or World War Three, whichever happened first. On the other hand, radiomen were constantly doing things during their watches, as were the helm and several others. In the forward room, which was a sleeping compartment, the watch had two responsibilities, to wake the oncoming watch who were sleeping there and to Blow

Sanitary #1 as needed. You may think this mundane job unworthy of discussion, but dispos-
ing of human waste products is essential and, as your gastroenteroligist will tell you, should
be done as often as possible. Believe it or not, on a submarine, this process is fraught with
danger!

Sanitary #1 was a large tank inside of the pressure hull that was topped by a pair of
stainless steel commodes. There was a lever on the side of each comode which controlled a
spool valve in the bottom, along with a sea water valve to help flush. When you finished
your business in the head, you had to open the door since you could not otherwise turn
around (well, you could turn around with the door closed, but you could not bend at the
waist because it was so small in there) and then you'd SLOWLY pull the lever to the spool
valve until the holes lined up and everything dropped into the tank.

When the tank was close to full, the man on watch would open a high pressure air valve
and put a pressure into the tank until it exceeded the pressure in the surrounding sea water.
Naturally, the deeper we were, the more air pressure was necessary. The watch was aided in
this by two adjacent pressure gauges—one for the sea and the other for the tank. Having put
a pressure in the tank, he then opened a large valve at the bottom of the tank and the air
pressure would expel everything into the sea. When he could hear air escaping into the sea,
he knew it was empty and would shut the big valve. This was only the first part of the
process—the "rewarding" part let's call it.

The second part was a problem—how to get the higher pressure, now left in the empty
tank, lowered to that pressure inside the boat so we could again begin using the head. As I
said, the deeper we were, the more air was necessary to blow the tank and, consequently, the
more air we had to dispose of to equalize the two pressures, i.e., that in the boat and that
inside the tank.

There was but one way to equalize—bleed the air in the now-empty, pressurized sanitary tank *into the goddamn boat*! At least Electric Boat Company installed a charcoal filter
in the venting line, although I doubt the filter was ever changed.

There was one other problem which was actually worse than this, although that is hard
to imagine, and it concerned snorkeling. When snorkeling, we ran these two huge diesel
engines that quickly sucked great volumes of air out of the boat. This air was, in turn, drawn
through the snorkel that stuck out of the water. This worked well until either a wave would
cover the snorkel or the diving party would inadvertently dip it beneath the surface. In both
events, the big head valve would slam shut with the engines still running, and create a
vacuum. This was hard on the ears when it occurred, and just as hard again when the situation corrected itself as the head valve reopened.

Each compartment in the boat had a very odd instrument for a submarine—an airplane
altimeter! In fact, they were very useful. Each time the snorkel head valve slammed shut
and air was sucked from the boat, we could look at the altimeter to see how bad it was
measured in altitude. In fact, the one mounted in the engine room was switched to shut
down the main engines when the pressure in the boat got to the equivalent of 6,000 feet.
Given the size of the diesels and the small volume inside the pressure hull, it didn't take

long to get to uncomfortable "altitudes." Imagine a mile-high building with an elevator that got you to the top in a few seconds.

However, the problem with the ears paled by comparison to what this cycling back and forth did to "old Sanitary #1." Every time the snorkel head valve shut, it created a pressure difference between the tank and the boat where the tank was at a higher pressure. If you did not keep your wits about you as you went to the head, you ran the risk while leaning over to flush the commode of vaporizing what was just left there all over you and the head. Of course this would not kill you, but you would wish it had.

Most western people, and certainly Americans, have come to expect gratification pretty quickly. The concept of some guy working on an oriental rug for a couple years or a Chinaman carving the faces of half the people in his province on a piece of wood is simply beyond our comprehension. There are two exceptions to this—prisoners doing time and sailors on very long cruises. They can relate to the idea that time doesn't matter.

Standing the forward room watch on our cruise to the Kamchatka Penninsula was, with the exception of a once-a-week cleanup, done in the dark. I rigged a No.10 can with a trailer light to fashion a discrete reading lamp that I clamped to the port mine table so at least we could read while on watch. Sitting in the dark was ridiculous. I had to do something, so I read a lot by my jury-rigged lamp. One of the many books inspired me to carve a sailboat. I switched into my "prisoner of war/Chinaman" mind set and started the first project of my life where time simply did not matter.

The only wood inside a sub, I quickly discovered, was in the oak handles of wire brushes. I cut off the handles with a hacksaw, glued them, and put this chunk in the enginemen's big metal vice for a day. Few people at first paid any attention to Gillcrist up there carving tiny chips out of a big, gnarly piece of oak. But, as time went by in this 42-day submerged period, the little hull began to take shape and people started to visit me each day to see how far I had progressed. Pretty soon the captain would walk forward each day to ask about the project and inspect the progress. Apparently I was not the only one with this "prisoner of war/Chinaman" attitude, because I was never once asked, "Aren't you done yet?" Nobody, particularly me, cared how long I took to finish the little sailboat. Ashore, all of us would have been our usual impatient selves, but faced with a "sentence" of 72 days at sea with nothing to do, we had an entirely different attitude.

Not that it matters to the point of this story, but the sailboat turned out to be beautiful, all waxed with lovely lines. I even hollowed out the bulbous keel and filled it with solder for authenticity. The whole crew loved it and felt a bit connected as a result of the sailboat.

HELM WATCH

The helm was controlled either in the conning tower or in the control room. When on the surface, we steered from the conning tower, and when submerged, from the control room. Neither location had a view, of course, as surface ships do, and we steered with the help of several indicators, the most important being the compass. If the course was 270, the helms-man constantly made small rudder adjustments to maintain that course until he was told

---

otherwise. When he was relieved and turned over the watch to the next man, he would inform him of the course and speed. There was also an indicator of the rudder's position relative to the boat's center line.

The Navy has lots of colorful and traditional language which, I am delighted to say, it has kept over the centuries. The dialogue between the officer of the deck and the helmsman has changed very little and lost little of its "color":

OOD: "Left full rudder."
Helmsman: "Left full rudder, aye."
Helmsman: "Rudder is left full."
OOD: "Very well. Come to 090."
Helmsman: "Come to 090, aye."
Helmsman: "Steady on course 090 "
OOD: "Very well."

If the helmsman was sleepy or inattentive and drifted off course, as soon as the OOD noticed from his compass repeater on the bridge, he would shout down the hatch,

"MIND YOUR HELM!"

"Mind your helm, aye" would be the sheepish reply.

I think this sort of communication was great, since it never left any doubt about whether or not the commands were heard and understood—after all, there are a lot of competing noises in a battle or a storm. All orders were responded to and repeated. Whenever we were entering or leaving port, a highly experienced man was put on the helm and, I might add, the best conning officer was on the bridge along with the captain. The Navy is touchy and unforgiving about careless people who bang up their ships and run them aground. Regrettably, the same can not be said of the world's merchant fleets and of some foreign navies.

Whenever a sub was extensively worked on in the yards, it would go to sea escorted by an ASR (submarine rescue ship) for "sea trials." This meant that the sub would first dive very carefully to periscope depth to see if it leaked. After all, some yard bird could have screwed up by failing to reinstall some hull fitting. The sub would then go a bit deeper as a further test, and so on, until it reached its test depth, which in our case was 412 feet. All the while the ASR waited on the surface in case there was trouble. Incidentally, whenever we did our sea trials, we would dive in water not too much deeper than our own test depth. I always thought the practice was very sound since, if the sub failed and sank, the ASR at least had a chance to help. If we did our tests in deep water and had a problem, it would be all over quickly.

When we left the Philadelphia Naval Shipyard on our sea trials, we steamed out to the Atlantic through Chesapeake Bay, accompanied by the ASR USS *Kittywake*. By the time my helm watch came up, it was the middle of the night and we were both running parallel, with the *Kittywake* several hundred yards to port. I was fighting sleep and nodding off at the helm, and in so doing, I unknowingly was putting a very slight pressure on the helm that very slowly moved the rudder to port. I was so tired that I failed to notice any of this. The OOD noticed our bow slowly swinging to port toward the *Kittywake* and yelled down the hatch, "Mind your helm." This of course woke me up from my stand-up nap, and I was pretty disoriented. I mistakenly put the helm hard over to port, which by this time was not much of a trip, since the rudder had been creeping to port for a while. The OOD by now was watching the submarine and its sleeping crew, for which he was responsible, heading straight for the K*ittywake* and *its* sleeping crew! He took over, screaming down the hatch, "RIGHT FULL RUDDER"!

"Right full rudder, aye," I said, completely embarrassed and ashamed of myself. All I could visualize was running 30 feet of our pointed bull nose into the vitals of poor Kittywake. I could just see the headlines;

"SUB SINKS ITS OWN RESCUE SHIP!"

"DYSLEXIC SAILOR NAMED GILLCRIST COMPELETLY RESPONSIBLE"

LOOKOUT WATCH

If you love the outdoors and quickly tire of small, sunless, smelly places, then lookout is your watch. You could always tell the lookouts from the rest of the crew. They were the tan, healthy looking ones with the sunglass marks on their noses and temples, while the rest of the crew looked as though they could use a month at summer camp. All of the interesting natural things like sunrises, sunsets, moonrises, water spouts, storms, marine life, and squalls were only visible to those topside at the time—the lookouts and the OOD. The poor guys below only saw these things when they came up for their "submarine showers" from time to time, so they missed most of it. Lookout sometimes had its tense moments, however.

Once in the mid-Pacific I was on lookout watch when I saw a contact that was clearly a sub. We always knew when there were going to be U.S. ships around us, so this contact startled me—it was clearly not American. I shouted, "Contact abeam to starboard, near the horizon, and it looks like a submarine, sir."

"CLEAR THE BRIDGE, CLEAR THE BRIDGE," shouted the heads-up OOD. We dove the boat for the first time in earnest and spent the next several hours listening on the sonar, keeping very quiet, exiting the area slowly and wondering, "Who are those guys?" We never found out. *Barbero's* mission was not to look for trouble but to avoid it, so we exited as discretely as we could manage.

I had many interesting things happen to me on lookout, mostly associated with nature. Fluorescent seas in our bow wave and wake, sunsets, whales and dolphins and all the rest, but our experiences with merchant ships at sea were disturbing.

From time to time we would pass merchant ships close enough to "glass" them fairly well. On an alarmingly high number of these encounters, I saw that no one was on the bridge! We were so vigilant that we had lookouts up, even during very heavy weather. Apparently these merchant ships had better things to do than watch where they were going—I was stunned to first learn of their carelessness.

Throughout my post Navy life I have watched the news only to see, time and time again, merchant ships running into bridges, each other, aground, and generally creating havoc. The stakes, with this sloppy seamanship, were raised considerably with the big tanker spills. Every time I see this kind of stuff I tell my wife Barbara the same thing, that this sort of thing would never happen in the Navy, or at least it is far less frequent. The difference, I believe, is both in the quality of the crews and how seriously Navy sailors and officers take their responsibilities. I've never been aboard a Navy ship where the crew did not take their jobs very seriously. I believe that this same trait exists with the Brits as well.

The first thing I thought of upon hearing the news about Three Mile Island was that I had never heard of a single U.S. Naval nuclear incident, even though they had hundreds of reactors operating since their beginnings in Hanford, WA, in the 50s. Why do the tankers run aground and why do we have reactor problems associated with the utilities? I believe that it must be attitude. Young men and women in the services—officers and enlisted—are inculcated with how important their jobs are to the success of their unit. As a consequence, I believe that they take their jobs a lot more seriously than their civilian counterparts. I dare say that if it were not for all those guys now working for the utilities who went through the Navy's nuclear power program, we would have a lot more problems.

One night on lookout I was up in the port shears, again fighting to stay awake. It was tropical, balmy, the middle of the night, and I finally gave in and just plain fell asleep, standing there on my little platform. My knees buckled and I began to fall out of the wide, open part of the railings through which we jumped when we cleared the bridge. The boat was on a port roll at that instant and I was past the pipe railing, over the water and in the air, with my feet still on the shears platform when I woke up! I grabbed the pipe railing and pulled myself back into the protection of the shears' rail with my heart pounding and adrenaline surging all over the place! I am confident that since the port roll put my port lookout platform well out over the water, that I wouldn't have bounced off of the tank tops, nor would I have gone through the screws—that was the good news. The bad news was that I wouldn't have made any noticeable noise and my absence would not have been noticed for an hour. Trying to find me in the dark two hours (and 35 miles) later would have been a challenge to say the least. I don't recall having trouble staying awake after that.

The other fascinating aspect was the sea's wonderful creatures! There always seemed to be dolphins playing in our bow waves. I once saw a whole pod of whales dive under the boat just off our starboard side. A little land bird lit in our sail near the shears while I was on watch one day. It was totally exhausted and stayed all day, regaining some of its strength. It was sad because we were far off shore and the bird did not have a chance. The other lookout and I tried to figure out how to capture the thing, but gave up on the project. In the mornings, the officers' steward would come to the bridge and ask permission to go down on the main deck to collect the flying fish which landed there during the night—fresh fish each morning for the officers. All sailors have these kinds of stories.

The oceans are a paradox. One moment it is a spectacularly wonderful and exhilarating place to be, and the next moment it is a terrifying and treacherous place swallowing up ships. It has always been this way, treating Odysseus and Bull Halsey alike.

Chapter 9:
"First, Do No Harm"

"I swear by Apollo the physician ... I will follow that system
of regimen which, according to my ability and judgement, I
consider for the benefit of my patients..."
- Hippocrates

It is reasonable to expect that small Naval vessels would not have a doctor aboard, because there surely is a limit to the doctor/sailor ratio. There is additional logic in the fact that most small vessels don't go very far to sea, nor for very long periods and, in addition, if they should go to sea, they would normally be part of a group of larger ships with doctors aboard. This policy makes good management sense, except when applied to submarines.

Subs are too small to have a doctor—they have under 100 officers and men. It would be like giving a doctor to each company in the Army. Impossible. However, subs, unlike most other small vessels, *do* in fact go to sea for long periods, and they almost always go alone. Subs are unique in the Navy with respect to medical care and, unless I miss my guess, this comes as a surprise to most people, even those in the Navy.

On *Barbero*, the medical world consisted of 'Doc' Hosea, a second class pharmacist mate and a locker full of bandages, drugs, iodine, and an apparently limitless supply of APCs—the Navy's version of aspirin. We were under the impression that APC stood for "all purpose cure." It seems so selfish of the Navy to have a single pill capable of curing all known illnesses and not sharing it with the rest of mankind!

If neither Doc's APCs nor his shots of penicillin cured what ailed you, you were in big trouble on *Barbero*. Actually, the boat was safe by comparison to, say, going on liberty with the enginemen. We would be at sea, many hundreds of miles from friendly shores, and we had Doc. Now, I really liked Doc, who was a personal friend of mine, but he was no Albert Schweitzer. He was a trained pharmacist mate with additional "independent duty training," but all he could practically do was bandage, hand out drugs, give shots, and maybe sew us up in a pinch.

Oddly, I never gave the medical situation a thought. We were all pretty healthy and most of us were fairly young and "bullet proof." So, the absence of a doctor was never an issue, in fact, I never once heard the crew discuss the subject. Nor did I ever sense any fear among the crew that if one of us became really sick, we could very well die and end up in the walk-in freezer with the food (providing there was room!) However, there were two episodes on *Barbero* where things got a bit out of control.

We went to Puerto Rico several times to fire practice Regulus missiles—Red Birds— and during our return to Norfolk from one of these cruises an illness suddenly broke out aboard the sub. I recall the first victim was at the helm when he simply collapsed. Then, in fairly rapid succession, crew began to collapse throughout the boat.

Doc told everyone in the after room to clear out and he turned it into a sick bay. So many became ill that we started to run out of people to stand watches. I remember going aft to see how things were going, and found Doc in the head staring at a dozen urine samples on the shelf under the mirror. I was shocked to see that each sample was more than half sediment! All I had until then was high school biology, but I knew that if half of your pee was solids, you were "in the hurt locker."

Poor Doc was in way over his head with sailors dropping like flies. The captain tried to figure out how to get a real doctor aboard, but a transfer in mid-winter off Cape Hatteras onto a sub whose deck was awash was not going to work. You can forget all that Tom Clancy stuff! As I recall we finally did get a real doctor, but it was not much before we got to the channel entering Norfolk. Doc did his very best and everyone recovered, but it really called attention to the exposure submariners had from the standpoint of medical care.

When you thought you were sick or when you were hurt, you simply looked for Doc. There was, as I have pointed out, no sick bay. Sick bay was wherever Doc happened to be! He'd sit you down anywhere and start to work. Forget privacy, medical ethics, and all that bedside manner stuff. If you had a varicocele of the left testicle, you told Doc with four or five guys sitting around listening and drinking coffee which, upon reflection, probably cut down on Doc's workload. I suspect some sailors would prefer to tough it out until they had a chance to go to a base hospital.

The second instance of an emergency happened in the Western Pacific southeast of Okinawa. We had an old chief with a big belly and a nose like W.C. Fields. He spent most of his time ashore drinking, and it showed. At any rate, he told Doc that he was feeling badly and described the symptoms. It turned out to be acute appendicitis. We were in real trouble because we were several days out of our destination—Okinawa.

The captain immediately consulted the charts and no doubt sent several messages, only to discover that there were no ships to help us and that the closest friendly place was an island named Chi Chi Jima, which was not all that close. So, we headed there as fast as we could, which was not too damn fast. I think the chief's appendix burst before we pulled into Chi Chi—however he lived. We left the poor guy on that God-forsaken island and got underway, and never saw him again.

The island was Japanese, had been bypassed during WWII, and as we pulled in we were rather dubious about this "medical facility" for our chief because the place was a shambles. The small harbor was still littered with rusting, half sunken Japanese ships. The bunkers for their big guns were all blown up and had not been altered since the smoke cleared from the satchel charges. The concrete main building, where we took the chief, was pockmarked all over from large caliber rounds. I thought at the time that life on Chi Chi toward the end of WWII certainly must have been anything but dull.

Evidently the island was in the path of a lot of carrier planes as they returned from raids to the northwest, and rather than land on the carriers with unexpended ordinance, the pilots would "hose down" the place with their bombs and machine guns. Years later, in a conversation with then Congressman George Bush discussing our military experiences, it turned out that he was one of those pilots. Unfortunately, he was shot down over the island and bailed out just offshore. The bypassed Japanese on the island were starving because they could not be resupplied, and so their efforts to capture him in their boats, I am afraid, were not "politically motivated." If it were not for the *Finback*, a sub on life guard duty in the area, that happened to be closer to him than the hungry Japanese, he would probably have ended up as sushi instead of President!

Modern nuclear subs still don't have doctors aboard, to my knowledge, but the circumstances for them are much better than on the diesel boats in the 50s. To begin with, we now have helicopters capable of flying long distances and refueling in mid-air. Also, I'm certain there are vastly better communications now between doctors ashore and the pharmacist mates aboard today's subs, enabling them to deliver a much higher level of medicine to the crews.

Chapter 10:
"Cat Futch"

" A fool there was and he made his prayer,
Even as you and I.
To a rag, a bone and a hank of hair,
The fool he called her his lady fair
We called her the lady who did not care,
Even as you and I. "

- Edgar Allen Poe: "The Harpy"

Mention the name Cat Futch to any U.S. Naval officer over 40 years old and you are guaranteed a powerful reaction. If the Naval officer happens to be a member of the surface warfare or aviation communities, the mention of the name will evoke warm smiles, perhaps a chuckle, or even a loud guffaw. But, if the one to whom you are speaking happens to be a submariner, the reaction is most likely to be an immediate and severe gastro-esophagal spasm!

To call the "Cat Futch Affair" a scandal is stretching it a bit. To compare it to the Tailhook disaster of sixteen years later is also a bit of overstatement. After all, the tailhook disaster involved the moral turpitude of dozens of naval officers. The "Cat Futch Affair" involved only one Naval officer; the commanding officer of the U.S.S. *Finback*, a nuclear-powered fast attack submarine bearing the hull number SSN-670. The commanding officer's failing was poor judgment.

Nevertheless, the "Cat Futch Affair" turned out to be an extremely painful experience for the submarine forces of the United States Navy. An official investigation was conducted into the event, and the commanding officer, whose name need not be mentioned, was summarily relieved of his command.

Finback, one of thirty-seven attack submarines of the *Sturgeon* class, was built by Newport News Shipbuilding and was commissioned 4 February 1970. She was finally taken out of service 28 August 1996. She was 279 feet long with a beam of 31 feet, a displacement of 4,780 tons fully loaded, and was manned by a crew of 107. She carried torpedoes and missiles and was one of the more active and highly decorated of the *Sturgeon* class vessels.

As is the case with embarrassing incidents such as the Cat Futch Affair, *Finback* will not be remembered for the numerous Cold War patrols she conducted, nor for the 750,000 miles she steamed. Nor will she be remembered for the seven deployments she made to the

U.S.S. Finback, Port Canveral, FL. February 13, 1994. (Official USN photograph)

U.S.S. Finback at sea, 1995. (Official USN photograph)

Mediterranean Sea, nor will she be remembered for being awarded the Navy Unit Commendation for her excellent work during Operation Sharp Guard in the Adriatic Sea in 1995. No, unfortunately, all of the "sweat equity" put into that submarine by hard-working bluejackets over her 26 years of "silent service" will have been for naught as far as the history books are concerned.

Finback will always be remembered for that fateful day at Port Canaveral, FL, when she pulled away from the dock with the music playing and Cat Futch, a local strip tease dancer, dancing bare breasted on her port fair water plane!

The Norfolk newspapers had a heyday with the news of this unusual event. The word "ecdysiast" became a household word. The Atlantic Fleet commander in chief was apoplectic.

And all of this in the name of morale. It was explained away as an effort to reward the troops for their efforts on a Caribbean Sea work-up cruise and to boost their morale preparatory to their Mediterranean Sea deployment.

While I am sure that the event did boost the morale of the crew momentarily, it proved to be disastrous in the long term. The Navy was on the threshold of a major sea change as it tried to incorporate women into its seagoing forces. Bare-breasted go-go dancers on fairwater planes was not the image the Navy recruiters were trying to project onto the television screens in living rooms across rural America.

We may have seen Cat Futches of an earlier generation performing for roistering submariners in movies like "Das Boot"…but not any more.

Chapter 11:
Heavy Seas

"To be at sea is to face the enemy"
- Victor Hugo "The Corvette Claymore"

HEAVY SEAS

I grew up going to the beaches along the south shore of Long Island, and was sometimes awed by the huge surf we would occasionally get there. But nothing prepared me for the typhoons, hurricanes, and just plain heavy seas which we weathered in my three years at sea. Whenever this topic has come up over the intervening years, people invariably ask, "Why didn't you just submerge when it got rough?" The answer has two parts.

For one thing, we could not stay down as long as most storms last. And for another, there was a danger in diving in heavy seas which we would not expose ourselves to unless it was necessary. This danger concerned what is called "righting arm." A characteristic peculiar to subs was that when we dove the boat, we changed its shape! This invariably comes as a shock to the person who asked the question. To the ocean we changed from the shape we all see in pictures of subs on the surface to the shape of the pressure hull alone. Our displacement got smaller. Also, our center of gravity shifted and, on top of that, our righting arm, the tendency of a ship or sailboat to remain erect, changed considerably.

There were a lot of changes happening very quickly during a dive, and if we were hit by a big wave at the wrong time, there was a chance to capsize. And if there is one thing you want to avoid on a sub it was that! Subs' ballast tanks are "free flooding." That means that there are big holes along the keel at the bottom of each ballast tank. If, for example, you turned a pail upside down and tried to sink it in your swimming pool, you would feel firm resistance, or buoyancy. But turn the pail upright and it goes to the bottom. So, we always rode out these storms on the surface, which was an extraordinary thing for me to see.

I continue to believe that we diesel sailors were a whole lot saltier—literally—than the nuclear-power folks. They simply sail out past the last buoy in the channel and "pull the cork," do their cruise, return, and surface in the same place. They too experience the isolation and the lack of privacy, but they don't experience the sea as we diesel folks and mariners have for a few thousand years.

Since we had torpedomen with little to do at sea, I, being junior, was put on lookout watches that mistakenly were considered, by some of the newer crew members, inferior to those watches below decks. Actually, the lookout watch was great—plenty of fresh air, I was always tan, and I got to see lots of things. As the cat bird's seat when we went through the Panama Canal and entered ports, I had the best seat in the house. Anyway, that was the good news. The not-so-good news was that with very few exceptions, we kept lookouts up even in huge storms.

When the seas were really big, we would stand lookout on the bridge next to the OOD instead of up in the shears. We'd keep the conning tower hatch closed and dogged, and we lashed ourselves with "21 thread" (half-inch line) to a pad eye on the splinter shield next to us, as soon as we got up there. We just stood there getting beaten around by the waves. It was actually fun and exciting for me, and any tendency toward seasickness was reduced considerably. I'd feel lousy below, but it was invigorating on the bridge in a big storm.

I recall vividly, in the Atlantic, waves resembling eight-story apartment buildings! I think I should point out that, unlike most ships, subs ride very low in the water. The deck of the bridge, where we stood, was no more than 10 feet off the surface of the water, so from our perspective those waves looked huge. We would head directly into the seas and we'd surf down the backs of the waves and plunge our thin bull nose bow deep into the oncoming wave. By the time the bow started to rise up on the next wave, it would already be covering the bridge, so we had to hold on to the splinter shield and actually be submerged in green, solid water! I would open my eyes and it was not foam, not spray, but GREEN. It was fun! We would whoop and holler and laugh and say,"Will you look at that son of a bitch!," or "Oh, oh, ...SSSHHHIIITTT!" I remember once losing my balance, and the wave washed me part of the way down the ladder to the main deck before I could hold on to something. Pretty exhilarating.

The whole issue of food in heavy weather was a problem for the cooks as well as the diners. We always heard profanity coming out of the galley when it was really rough. Cooking was just a nightmare. Yes, our pots and pans were trapped onto the burners by railings, but if they were too full, a good roll would spill a lot of the contents out on to the hot stove to create quite a mess. A yachtsman friend once used a phrase "a cocktail tack," meaning that he would steer a course which would result in smoothness so he could have a civilized drink. *Barbero* never had the luxury of a "cocktail tack"

What happened from time to time was that the cook became accustomed to the direction of the seas and could cope with them. All of a sudden, we would change course and stuff would begin flying all over the galley—some actually thrown by the outraged cook. We would hear all sorts of cursing and crashing. Sometimes the OOD was considerate enough to notify the cooks of a course change—often times not.

From the standpoint of eating during heavy weather, there were other problems to contend with. First, there were those whose appetites had vanished—they had other problems. In moderately heavy seas, we would spread out a rubber mesh tablecloth so the dishes would not slide into our laps as easily. But if the seas were really bad, we would simply get our food in a bowl, then find a place somewhere on the boat to wedge our bodies. Then, holding the bowl as if our hands were gimbaled, we'd attempt to eat. The other alternative for the cooks was to simply make sandwiches. The crew's mess in heavy weather always looked like a food fight had taken place.

Sleeping was the other aspect of living that was greatly affected by heavy weather. We quickly learned to sleep on our stomachs and hold on to the bunk's frame while we *were asleep!* I saw several guys actually tie themselves into their racks. It was really surprising that we could sleep at all. One of those sleep researchers would have had a field day on a diesel submarine!

The heavy weather, oddly, had less of an effect on the racks of those way down on the pecking order. There were, afterall, good racks and bad ones. The bad ones were so close together that when the man above was in his rack (someone was always there), it sagged so badly, leaving so little space that you had to decide whether you were going to sleep on your stomach or your back. You simply could not sleep on your side, nor could you turn over after you were there. After choosing, you'd slide in to the bunk to be trapped for the night. Even heavy weather could not dislodge those guys. I know. I had one of those racks when I first came aboard *Barbero*.

One night we were running parallel with the waves in reasonably heavy seas, running in "the trough," or parallel to the waves. The waves were coming from the port side, so the boat would roll to starboard with each one, never returning past the vertical. I was asleep and this motion was so regular that it did not disturb me.

Just aft of the tube doors were the choicest bunks in the room. There were two on each side mounted to the hull with more than the usual room between the upper and lower. My bunk was the lower one to starboard. The upper bunk to port was occupied, a dim light was on, and I was sound asleep. The boat, as it had been doing all night, rolled to starboard the usual amount, but this time it stayed there. I immediately woke up with this irregularity. Then the whole boat shuddered and the roll, which had halted very briefly, snapped farther to starboard. When it did not stop, I became alarmed. Just then the boat went so far over that the fellow in the upper bunk to port fell across the room and landed in my bunk! It was at this moment that I felt, for the only time in my life, that I was a dead man.

In an instant I knew that we were capsizing and I *knew* what that meant. The boat would spill the trapped air in the ballast tanks out of the holes along the keel, begin sinking immediatly, and implode shortly thereafter. I was absolutely terrified. The drip pans under the hydraulic gear in the overhead all spilled what to me in the dimness looked like blood. We had been hit by a rogue wave which had pushed us over *beyond* 60 degrees to starboard! We knew this because our big Sperry gyrocompass tumbled, and it would do that only beyond 60 degrees. I can still see this whole scene perfectly in my mind's eye, even after 37 years. There were lots of cuts and bruises among the crew. At sea, sometimes there is a very fine line between "cuts and bruises" and, "*Barbero* is overdue and presumed lost."

On several occasions the sea was so big that sea water came in the main induction valve up in the sail. This was a 36-inch opening inside the sail with a valve on it that was closed whenever we dove the boat. Its purpose was to supply air to the main engines while we were on the surface. Sometimes in calm seas we would close it so the engines would suck air through the conning tower hatch in order to clean out the stale air in the boat. But if the seas were high enough to force us to shut the main induction, they were also too big to allow us to keep open the conning tower hatch.

At any rate, water coming in the main induction is not good—it can swamp the engines and being without power in a big storm is deadly for any ship. So the decision was made to snorkel on the surface. The snorkel was raised, we buttoned up the boat as if we were submerged, which we effectively were, and we rode out the storm. We still needed a look-out since we were on the surface, so I would look through the periscope, which was nause-ating as hell and, of course, useless. It was like looking through a telescope while running down the street.

With respect to underwater noises, I know that each ship has its own sonar signature, like a fingerprint, and unique to the ship. It would not surprise me to discover that ships also had their own movements in response to heavy seas. I say this because Navy ships seem to be modified each time they go to the yards for overhauls. Adding sonar domes in the bows or installing new equipment all over the place has got to have an effect on how the ship responds to heavy seas. *Barbero*, for example, had a hangar aft of the sail and had her two main engines removed from the forward engine room. This surely accounted for the odd way she rode big seas.

All ships are like a see-saw, with the bow and stern rising and falling around a fulcrum somewhere in the center. The farther forward or aft you went, the greater the magnitude of the movement up and down. Both my rack and watch station were about as far forward as you could get, so I had to learn to live with my "living room" moving all over the place. We denizens of the forward room learned to hold on to things in the overhead as we stood around up there because the deck would sometimes simply drop out from under our feet, leaving us airborne.

The after room, for some strange reason, seemed to have a different motion than we did up forward. I know it defies physics, but it surely seemed different back there. In addition to the vertical movement, there was lateral movement also, which produced a distinct figure-eight motion. They also had to put up with the sounds made whenever the screws came out of the water.

Since everything on the boat was steel, either welded or bolted in place, we learned to always hold on to something, because being thrown into any part of the boat hurt like hell—nothing "gave." It was very common to see Band-Aids and old scars on foreheads.

There was a technique in going through those small watertight doors. It was sort of a hurdler movement with the head down and one foot out in front. The problem was that for a second or two you had to let go of everything. If the boat jerked suddenly in that second, you either got a kidney punch from the door frame or a TKO on the head! All that steel was unforgiving.

Big seas can do substantial damage to the superstructure, but so can ice. When we were off the Kamchatka we snorkeled for 42 days straight. This was in the winter, and there was ice all around. I don't recall hearing anything resembling ice striking us, but when we got back to Yokosuka we were put into the Navy yard for a few weeks in dry dock to fix a lot of damage to our sonar dome and superstructure. An extra few weeks in Yokosuka was welcomed by the crew.

There was another form of ice that built up from frozen spray. This applied to surface ships as well. If freezing spray was allowed to build up in significant amounts on a ship's superstructure, it could make the ship top heavy.

All but one of our cruises during the winter out of Norfolk put us in the warm Gulf Stream within a day. The one exception occurred when we sailed through cold coastal waters to Newport, RI, in order to fire some torpedoes at the range in Narraganset Bay. The weather was unusually cold, and we had a large build up of ice all over our sail and superstructure. The problem of the ice was easy for us to solve—we simply dove the boat for a few hours, which melted the ice, and then we steamed into port. I don't know what surface ships do about this problem, since diving is not an option.

—

Chapter 12:
U.S.S. Plunger (SSN-595)

"Like the destroyer, the submarine has created its own type of officer and man—with language and traditions apart from the rest of the Service, and yet at heart unchangingly of the Service."

- Rudyard Kipling: "The Fringes of the Fleet," 1915

I have been aboard many submarines in my naval career, but until Captain Dave Oliver, skipper of P*lunger*, invited me along on a short, one day trip, I had never gone to sea in one. It was an experience I will never forget. Of course, Dave was proud to show off his ship.

It was one of those perfect days as I pulled up in my staff car to the pier where *U.S.S. Plunger* (SSN-595) was moored. The third ship of the *Thresher/Permit* class of nuclear-powered attack submarines was a beautiful machine of war. She measured 278 feet in length at the waterline, drafted over 28 feet when fully loaded, had a beam of 31 feet, and displaced just over 4,300 tons (dived). Her four torpedo tubes were located halfway aft along her hull, two on either side, and angled slightly outboard. Her suite of passive, active, and countermeasures sonar was state of the art, and greatly enhanced her combat effectiveness in the primary mission of killing submarines.

Plunger's performance figures are still classified, but it is correct (and legal) to say that her top speed submerged was more than 30 knots and her operating depth was deeper than 1,300 feet. Her performance figures, though, were not that spectacular when compared to her Soviet counterparts. She had the one, single feature that made her a far more effective killing machine...she was quiet and deadly. That was always where the U.S. submarines had the edge over their competition.

I was scrupulous about being on time because, after all, it was a ship sailing, and good sailors don't show up late. Dave was waiting for me when I arrived. We went aboard and got underway almost immediately.

The deck at the very top of the sail was the surface conning station. That was where Dave stationed us to observe the experience of leaving port...and it is always an experience! The first thing that startled me was the need to don a harness not unlike the ones I wore whenever I went flying in a tactical airplane. The harness was intended to enable me to lock myself onto my perch and keep me from being washed overboard by an unexpected wave. Dave explained that a number of Naval officers had been lost at sea before they began wearing a safety harness.

The reason for this became evident to me almost immediately as we turned and headed south out the main channel past Point Loma. Although we were running at the prescribed speed (a leisurely 10 knots), there was a standing wave formed over the forward one third of the main deck. It was a solid layer perhaps six feet deep that extended almost all the way back to the forward part of the sail. The sea was relatively calm with no swell. It didn't take much of an imagination to picture how deep and rough that standing wave would be at a higher speed and under almost any kind of sea state. If it reached up to our perches even briefly without harnesses we would have gone overboard in the blink of an eye. It was a sobering thought.

Once clear of the channel we turned toward the submarine operating area and submerged. The remainder of my experience was spent in Main Con after a brief tour of the inside of *Plunger*. The purpose for the one day sail was to do a sort of sea trials following a period in port during which some repair work had been done on the ship pierside. As in all sea trials, the performance of the ship and its systems was examined sequentially. We dove first to one hundred feet and looked at ship systems for proper operation and, of course, leakage. I noticed that Dave carried a rag in his hand, and periodically he would disappear only to return after a few minutes, rag in hand and a thoughtful look on his face. The presence of water in the bilges of a surface ship is routine. On a submarine it is serious. All ships leak. That is why there are such things as bilge pumps. But, even tiny leaks on a submarine are treated with great concern.

Submarine operating depths have always been classified. But, in general, submarines in the World War II era operated routinely at about 400 feet. After the war, with newer designs, their operating depths increased to about 800 feet. When the first of *Plunger's* class, the *U.S.S. Thresher*, went down on 20 April 1963 off Nova Scotia, it represented a tremendous blow to the Navy's nuclear powered submarine building program. Her operating depth was estimated to be about 1,300 feet. She went down after an engineering failure in about 11,000 feet of ocean. It took the Navy five months before Lieutenant Commander Don Keach, operating a retrieval arm from the deep-diving submersible *Trieste*, was able to bring back a four-foot piece of *Thresher's* piping. I have always wondered why, in the early stages of design, development, and operational testing, submarines didn't do their work in relatively shallow water for ease of recovery. No one has ever explained that to me to my satisfaction.

On this beautiful day off Point Loma, *Plunger* went through a series of dives and level-offs, followed by a reverse series of ascents and level-offs. After each level-off, speed changes were made to assess other aspects of the ship's performance. Dave referred to this profile as "hogs and sags." One point of interest which has always stuck in my mind is the fact that speed restrictions at the various depths were imposed by concerns for ship survivability in the event that a catastrophic bow plane control failure occurred to the full-bow-down position.

Under such circumstances, emergency procedures would include blowing ballast, reversing engines, and regaining bow plane control. Of course, during all of these emergency procedures the ship would be descending, and the immediate concern would be to arrest the rate of descent before the ship reached "crush depth." The proper definition of crush depth is that depth below which the pressure hull will fail under ambient water pressure. Crush depth is always a design multiple of operating depth.

When a 4,000-ton submarine generates a substantial rate of descent, it takes an enormous corrective force to arrest it. Obviously, the deeper a submarine is operating, the closer it is to crush depth and therefore the slower it must go.

Ambient water pressure becomes enormous with increasing operating depths. Trieste, for example, experienced an ambient pressure of over eight tons per square inch when she made the record dive to the bottom of the Marianas Trench on 23 January 1960, piloted by Lieutenant Don Walsh and Jacques Piccard.

As we started on the reverse series of ascents and level-offs, Dave Oliver increased the up angle for each successive ascent. We ended up at a horrendous 30 degree angle of ascent at a speed of 10 knots. I remember hanging onto the periscope tunnel with my right arm crooked around it for support. Thirty degrees of angle seems much greater when experienced from the inside of a submarine than, for example, an airplane. Loose gear was falling off of working surfaces, and everyone else seemed to be merely hanging on.

Dave gave the order to level off at a depth of 100 feet and watched the man on the bow plane mistakenly pull back rather sharply on the control yoke rather than push it forward. Dave was quick to note the mistake and lunged over the man's shoulder to throw his weight against the yoke, pushing it forward. But the displacement, however brief, generated an enormous momentary rate of ascent which took several seconds to arrest. During those long seconds it seemed that everyone in Main Con was watching the digital depth read out located high on the bulkhead directly above the bow-plane position. The numbers, displayed like an automobile odometer, were whirling towards zero. The numbers reached zero and went back down to stabilize at about 75 feet.

We all waited and held our breaths…listening for any sound that might indicate that we had hit something on the surface. There was nothing but a blessed silence as Dave gave the order to slow and go to periscope depth. He raised the periscope and, hooking his arms over the handles, looked anxiously into the eyepieces as he whirled the scope through a full 360-degree arc, scanning the horizon for anything. There was nothing! Although the bow plane man's mistake was a tremendous breach of seamanship, I do not recall Dave reprimanding him. He must have done it later…leadership in action!

The return to the pier at Ballast Point was relatively uneventful. As I walked across the brow and saluted the quarterdeck, I felt that I had been privileged, on my first trip on a submarine at sea, to have seen a squared away crew, a shipshape combat vessel, and a real leader of men in action. It was a good feeling! Here was a ship prepared to go "in harm's way."

Chapter 13:
"The Loop's Too Big!"

"Twas Fultah Fisher's boarding-house,
Where sailor-men reside,
And there were men of all the ports,
From Mississip to Clyde,
And regally they spat and smoked,
And fearsomely they lied."
- Kipling THE BALLAD OF FISHER'S BOARDING-
HOUSE

Sailors have been wondering what to do with their off-watch time at sea ever since Noah. In the 50s on my boat, we had movies, cribbage, and cards—all done in the crew's mess. Because the crew was quite small, we all seemed to have several jobs—some *de jure* and some *de facto*. I had two *de facto* jobs. One cutting hair and the other showing movies.

The entire Navy apparently had one kind of movie projector, no doubt with a name like "Mk 1 Mod 3," and while it was not terribly complex, the Navy wanted you to go to a one day "school" to learn to splice film and operate the thing. I volunteered and went to the class. What was interesting was that my exalted new position of operator of the movie projector included selecting the movies as well as showing them. On a long trip I would pick out perhaps 40 movies and we would re-show the better ones.

I'd go over to the movie exchange in the duty truck a day or two prior to getting under-way. I would be besieged with requests from my shipmates for "shit kickers," John Wayne, etc. They had plastic-covered lists at the movie exchange, and I'd tell the sailor what to select from the back room. Forty movies was a lot to pick out, and one time I thought I'd vary things and get a few documentaries. So one night, far out to sea, I picked one about a M.A.S.H. unit in Korea, where the film maker followed the treatment of this poor guy who had stepped on a land mine.

The movie routine was to first get a cup of coffee, and then a good seat and settle in, while "The Greek" supplied grilled cheese sandwiches, popcorn, and other movie stuff. With everybody talking away, I rolled the documentery. The opening sequence was this poor guy being brought in on a stretcher and lifted onto the operating table. His face was charred black and the M.A.S.H. doctor opened the left eyelid and quickly went to the right, having decided, apparently, that the left eye was salvageable. He opened the right eyelid, quickly deciding that this eye was not salvageable, and took a sharp, pointed pair of tweezers, jammed them into this poor guy's eyeball, plucked it out and cut off the connections with a scissors! The scene took maybe four seconds and was utterly and totally shocking. The audience of 25 or so hardened submariners nearly killed themselves bailing out of the compartment. I was the only guy left in the forward battery after maybe eight seconds!

There exodus was accompanied by all sorts of "OH MY GODs," "JESUS CHRISTs," "SHITs," etc. The place was littered with half-eaten grilled cheese sandwiches, burning cigarettes, and cups of coffee—it was like somebody yelled, "FIRE IN THE HOLE." The crew never let me forget that night and possessed a certain caution for all further showings, always asking, "What's the movie tonight, Gillcrist?"

I was always uneasy when the captain joined us for a movie, because whoever was sitting near me in one of the better seats would get up and give the old man his seat. The crew, being pretty red-blooded Americans and generally from a different background than the captain, would often say pretty profane and vulgar things. The captain, I am sure, often regretted the visit. From the smoky dark would come, "Jesus, will you look at those tits!" My stomach would tighten a bit as I peripherally looked over to the captain. I'm sure he wished to show his humanity by visiting the Philistines in the forward battery, but there was a price to be paid.

There was a special language at the movies. Everyone, as soon as he was settled in their seat with their cigarettes and coffee, would shout "Roll 'em!" Whenever the machine was a tad out of adjustment, *everyone* would start yelling, "Frame it, God damn it!" But there was near mutiny if you let the projector start to chatter up and down. In that case, *everyone* would give the same advice, saying, "THE LOOP'S TOO BIG, THE LOOP'S TOO BIG!"

I really don't think anyone particularly cared about the movie. It was a social event, really, where we could sort of cut up and be ourselves, which under the best of circumstances was difficult on one of the old diesel subs.

Since we had very little room for anything, we economized by not having one of those real, no-nonsense, silvered movie screens, the kind that rolls up like a shade. When it was movie time someone would break out a bed sheet we reserved as our screen. They'd tie the sheet's two ends to some pipes and wiring in the overhead and, to keep the screen taut, attach two catsup bottles or salt shakers to the bottom corners by opening the bottle, laying the corner of the sheet over the mouth, and then screwing the top back on. The weight of the bottles pulled the wrinkles out of the sheet. The quality of the image was not as good as a real screen, but the compensation, very important in such a small space, was that we could watch the movie from both sides of the sheet. Of course, the guys on the other side of the screen had to put up with John Wayne shooting with his left hand and the sign behind him reading "NOOLAS."

Another form of entertainment on the boat was a time, maybe once a year, when the captain realized that we had not expended the current fiscal year's complement of small arms ammunition. I guess the presumption at the Pentagon was that we were practicing all the time to be good shots—nothing could be farther from the truth. They should have realized that the last thing you want to give a sub sailor is a loaded gun of any kind! I don't recall ever having any training in the Navy with real firearms—not once. The Marines spent lots of time firing weapons, understandably, but sailors knew nothing about small arms, except, of course, the gunner's mates.

So, one calm day we carried up all the guns and ammo onto the main deck and started hosing down the water with reckless abandon. There were Thompsons, M1s, .45s, and the piece de resistance—a .50 cal. machine gun in a mount on the cigarette deck aft of the bridge. Some of us had our own pistols; mine was a .44-cal magnum, and LT Murray had a .38-cal. I often have wondered what the rules were in the Navy about having firearms aboard ship. Surely pulling a .44 magnum out of your locker was *verbotin*, but on *Barbero* nobody seemed to care. There was this silly idea I had that if I ever had to be on a boarding party or abandon the boat, I was going to be prepared, so I had this giant pistol and a Randall knife in my locker. If this was supposed to be this fiscal year's small arms training for the crew, it was a joke. But the few of us who went up on deck made the most of it and had lots of fun—it was "John Wayne Day."

What represents fun and entertainment to one is not always the same for another, and nowhere was that more evident than between the officers and the enlisted men. In all the movies, when the director wanted to show the seamier side of town, he would throw a couple of sailors in the background. These "extras" invariably had a beer in their hands, hats on the backs of their heads, and were putting the moves on some female for the scene. The reality was that this image was to some extent true, but there were, particularly on subs, a significant number of fairly refined and quite intelligent sailors. I believe that this is even more true of the nuclear power sailors today.

One of the distinctions between officers and crew was background, and the other was age and maturity. Officers were generally older than a lot of the sailors, often married, and therefore acted in a more civilized way. Sailors are almost expected to raise hell, and officers are expected to set an example of behavior. Military literature is full of exceptions to these generalizations, of course, but I think these are fair representations to keep in mind.

After Carlos Dew left *Barbero*, LCDR Blount, a good and competent leader, arrived to take over as skipper. This was in the Pacific, where one of his favorite things was to be found floating all over the place—we called them "fishing balls."

The people along the Western Pacific rim were fisherman, and the device they commonly used to hold up their nets was a glass ball blown, it looked to me, from old melted down coke bottles. They were often a foot in diameter, and evidently people used them for decorations. The skipper developed a real appetite for these things, and the lookouts were instructed to keep a sharp eye out for the balls. When one was sighted, we would maneuver to snag it with a boat hook. I think this whole thing became a bit obsessive.

After a while one of my friends named Wolf volunteered to dive off the deck, managing not to bounce off the tank tops, to retrieve these stupid things. Wolf had attended swimmers school in Pearl, and I can only guess that that was the justification for letting a young sailor jump over the side in mid-ocean with no protection from sharks.

They collected quite a number of these things and kept them for themselves. For his efforts, Wolf was cut a share in the booty. It now occurs to me to wonder where the hell they kept all those balls in a sub with hardly enough room for stores. It also occurs to me to wonder how much time we spent, and lost, screwing around with them. Finally, in my cynical, advancing years, I don't think that I would have permitted, let alone encouraged, a 19-year-old to dive off the boat in mid-Pacific for some trendy decorations. Perhaps I am missing some hidden benefit to the Navy.

I mentioned that one of my de fac*to* jobs was cutting hair. If a sub did not have a doctor, nor even a laundry facility, it damn sure would not have a barber sitting around! So, one day after a long time at sea, I was feeling even more grubby than normal. I was not only dirty and wearing filthy dungarees, but my hair was over my ears. I just couldn't stand it any more.

In passing I mentioned it to a shipmate, and an idea suddenly came to me, "I'll cut your hair if you'll cut mine, is it a deal?" So we did it. The fact is that I was blessed with some sort of manual skills—I'm real good with my hands, consequently, my friend's hair looked really good. Ibarra, our yeoman, showed me a few tricks with the comb and scissors which really helped, and oddly I still remember them today. At any rate, it was obvious that the haircut I gave was a whole lot better than that given to me, because the whole crew began asking me for hair cuts and nobody asked the other guy. My hair sort of looked ok in the

Torpedoman Dan Gillcrist fires the 50 cal. machine gun on "John Wayne Day," U.S.S. Barbero, Western Pacific, 1959. (Dan Gillcrist Collection)

mirror, but it must have had lots of divots in the back which, of course, no self respecting sub sailor would mention to me, particularly one about to ask for a free hair cut himself.

Anyway, from then on I was the barber of *Barbero* and gave lots of hair cuts. After the Navy, my family and I lived several towns away from my parents and the house in which I grew up. I would, every weekend or so, drop by to see them and to do a little heavy lifting, things I did not want them attempting. My aging father would grab the sparse white hair over his ears as a signal to me to cut his hair. So I'd take him out on the back stoop, put a sheet around him with a big safety pin and, just as he did for me when I was growing up, cut his hair.

Chapter 14:
Nantucket Sleighride

"Allah is Allah—but I have two anchors astern."

- A Turkish Admiral writing to Lady Stanhope 1825

The remarkable painting by Winslow Homer of a group of swashbuckling New England whalers sitting in their longboat being towed along by a whale they have just harpooned always captures my imagination. The expressions of sheer exuberance on their faces says a great deal about early American seamen, the extreme hazards of their trade, and of the age of "wooden ships and iron sailors." Of course, there was a sailor positioned in the bow of the boat with a sharp ax in hand just in case the wounded whale decided to sound. If this happened, there were only a few seconds before the boat would be upended and drawn beneath the waves at an astonishing speed. The axman's job was to cut the harpoon towline with one swift stroke. The very lives of the boat crew depended upon this hardy sailor for his precision with the ax while standing in a boat that was being tossed about by the whale...a dicey assignment. The remarkable occurrence known as the "Nantucket Sleighride," however, is not without its modern-day counterpart.

The bane of my existence, when I was Assistant Chief of Staff (Operations) at CinCLantFleet, was trawlers. Usually, it was Soviet trawlers, but quite often it was otherwise innocent trawlers from the Scandinavian countries. By definition, trawlers fish from the bottom by dragging (trawling) conical-shaped traps along the ocean floor. By a broader definition trawlers also drag various net fishing devices through particular waters of the world to take advantage of the geographical breeding habits of all sorts of sea creatures. The specific venue for most of my aggravation was the Norwegian Sea. This was where our vast network of underwater listening devices produced its greatest yield in man-made undersea activity.

Of course these listening devices are connected by cable to our listening system...and most of the thousands of miles of cable is underwater...lying vulnerably on the ocean floor. Despite a modest effort to bury those cables, the very nature of the ocean floors with their shifting currents makes that task virtually impossible to accomplish completely. The cables, then, are vulnerable to almost anything being dragged across the ocean floor, be it innocent Norwegian trawling traps and nets or deliberate Soviet grappling hooks. Regardless of the device, once the cable is snagged, the trawling source continues to drag it along, picking up greater and greater weight until the tensile strength of the cable is reached and the cable parts.

I kept a cable repair ship fully employed almost year round repairing breaks. This is an incredibly complex task. First, the broken cable must be found, a monumental job in itself…finding one end, then the other, and buoying both off. They are found the same way the Russians found them…by grappling. Then they must be spliced and dropped back into the ocean only after a continuity test is passed. Then efforts to bury the cable are made. Along come the Russian trawlers with their hooks, and they break it again. It is a never-ending battle…an incredible technological war.

Naturally, as an anticipated adjunct of this war is for each side to watch the other doing its work. Therefore, covert movements, the cover of darkness, and bad weather are perfect for the conduct of both sides' operations. Appliqued over the top of all of these quasi-military efforts is the normal traffic of Scandinavian fishing operations of all sorts. The picture is further complicated by the operation of U.S. and Soviet submarines in the Norwegian Sea.

As mentioned in an earlier chapter, U.S. command authority is maintained with its submerged submarines by something called the "O Sub broadcast." The communications system utilizes extra long wave-length frequency (ELF) to "speak" to the submarines…a sort of one-way system. The submarines are able to listen to the broadcast by means of a trailing wire antenna. This antenna, ballasted for slightly positive buoyancy, is trailed behind the submarine, causing it to float above the submerged submarine, but just below the surface of the water. Submarines on patrol listen to this broadcast 24 hours a day. If the national command authority want a submarine to respond to a query, the ship must come to antenna depth, poke an antenna out of the water, and fire off a burst transmission. Then it dives to a safer depth and takes evasive action to prevent detection in case the source of the transmission might have been located.

As one might suspect, these trailing wire antennae sometimes get caught up in fishing nets and other devices. Naturally, the skipper of a 18,000 ton *Trident* submarine is not going to notice the slightly added drag of a fishing net and the boat to which it is attached. So, the stage was set in the Norwegian Sea for literally hundreds of what I laughingly referred to as "Nantucket Sleighrides!"

The events all seemed to follow a pattern. A Norwegian fisherman sits in his boat tending some fishing nets and smoking his pipe under the snow-covered panorama of some picturesque Norwegian fjord when he becomes aware of subtle motion. This occurs when the submarine trailing wire antenna first makes contact with the net. As the antenna takes up the strain and begins "gathering in the net" from below, the speed of the net, boat, and system gradually accelerates until the hapless fisherman realizes that he is rapidly proceeding outbound into the middle of the Norwegian Sea. His only recourse is to grab a sharp tool and cut himself free from the line that connects him to the net, not unlike the emergency action required of his counterpart off Nantucket a hundred years earlier.

What follows each occurrence is an official protest from the offended government with a demand for payment for damages inflicted. Naturally, the U.S. Navy's initial response is to "neither confirm nor deny" the existence of a U.S. submarine in the vicinity of the incident. After all, we would declaim, how do we know it wasn't a whale...or a Soviet submarine...or perhaps a Frenchman or even a Brit?

Initial attempts by me to see if the culprit was one of ours usually was met with silence. They didn't call the U.S. Navy submarine force the "silent service" for nothing! But, the fat would usually reach the fire when the culprit submarine's skipper gave the order to reel in the antenna at the end of the patrol. That's when the fishing net debris attached to the antenna became evident. Of course, such things only came to light in the end of patrol report...and that would be weeks afterward. If I had a dollar for every Nantucket Sleighride U.S. Atlantic Fleet submarines caused, I could retire...but then again, maybe it was a Frenchman!

Chapter 15:
Liberty

"There will be no liberty until morale improves"
- Anonymous

I reported aboard *Barbero* just after its return from a "Med Cruise," where its last port of call was Le Havre, France. The current in the harbor was perpendicular to the pier to which they were assigned to tie up, and it was swinging the stern out and away from the pier. Under the circumstances, the best solution was not to use the engines and drive up the pier, but to move the #1 line at the bow up the pier to the next bollard, so the boat could use

Torpedoman Dan Gillcrist relaxing topside, Roosevelt Rhodes, Puerto Rico, 1958. (Dan Gillcrist Collection)

the capstan and winch itself forward, out of the current. The captain had one of those cheer-leader-type megaphones, and he was shouting at the French yard workers on the pier, say-ing, "Move the line up the pier." There was no response. The French just looked at him. He repeated the request, adding a lot of pointing.

"Move the line up the pier." Still no response, as the stern moved farther away from the pier.

Now, with all sorts of body spin and pointing, he shouted, "Mov*e the line up the pier.*" Nothing. The "frogs" just stood there, looking at each other with shrugged shoulders. In utter frustration, the captain shouted down to the sailors on the maneuvering watch, forward of the bridge and asked,

"On deck there, can anyone speak French?" One of the sailors, probably well inten-tioned, said he did. The captain, speaking as though the poor sailor was also a Frenchmen, enunciating each word carefully, said to the sailor,

"T e l l t h e m t o m o v e t h e l i n e u p t h e p i e r." The sailor leaned out over the rail as far as he dared, cupped his hands to his mouth, and, shouting as hard as he could, told the Frenchmen,

"Move zee line up zee pier !"

I know God damn well that those Frenchmen knew exactly what was being asked of them, but, like all Frenchmen, they just wanted the Americans to pay for not knowing their language.

Nun in the Alley
Recently I read a funny definition of liberty; "Getting all dressed up in your best uniform, to go to the worst part of town."

My usual routine was to put on a set of "blues," catch a "crab," as we called them, and go to the hotsie baths of Yokosuka. While I was getting a long overdue bath, a kid would take the dress blues to get them pressed. Then, I'd walk to this very large enlisted men's club, which we called "the E M Crub," for an American dinner. Only then would I go to the bars which catered to submariners—they actually specialized. My favorite was "Bar Atomic."

One evening after a few beers, I was wandering about the area we called Black Market Alley, thinking that this was my first Christmas away from home and the folks. I was actu-ally feeling sort of lonely and sorry for myself when I turned a corner, only to find a nun sitting at the side of this little street, begging with a tambourine in her lap! An Anglo-Saxon nun, for God's sake—I was speechless, and immediately began feeling guilty. At the time I was a Catholic, and guilt was a basic tenet of the religion—we were good at it. At any rate, I only had enough money for a cab back to the boat, so I could not give her any of mine, but I remembered the money on the boat.

The torpedomen were the "inn keepers" in the forward room, which was a sleeping compartment for crew who worked aft somewhere, but it was our room, we were in charge, and we found money all the time whenever we cleaned up. We kept the money we found in a big jar, and the plan was to throw ourselves a party with it someday. Well, I decided, unilaterally, that that day had come, and there was not going to be a party.

Hailing a cab, I went back to the boat. I told the driver to wait and crossed the brow, dropped down the forward hatch, grabbed the jar with the money, returned to the waiting cab, and told the driver to take me back to the spot where he had picked me up. I was actually feeling pretty good about it, and my spirits were up. I walked up to the nun and plopped the jar into her tambourine. It must have weighed six pounds, and nearly tore the tambourine out of her hands. I don't recall saying anything at all, nor did she...her eyes said it all. I just walked away feeling good, although a bit embarrassed. When I informed the other torpedomen of my donation of our party money, it was fine with them—pretty good guys, I thought.

Volcano

This has to be unique in the Navy, but one time we went on liberty and took *Barbero* with us! While we were in Pearl, there was this new volcanic eruption on the Big Island (Hawaii). It just opened up in the middle of a cane field close to the sea, evidently spectacular enough to make world wide news. The volcano wasn't a week old when at quarters one morning while we were tied up to the wharf at the Sub Base, Captain Blount asked, "Who wanted to go over to the Big Island and look at the volcano?"

Well, the vote was along "party lines," i.e., the married guys wished to stay and the single guys wished to go. The captain granted liberty to the married guys on the spot, and we actually got underway soon thereafter!

Until then I'd never heard of such a thing, but it was feasible because, after all, we were not going to need fuel, supplies, movies, and all the rest. We would not be shooting torpedoes or missiles, so we really didn't need too many of the crew just to cruise over to the Big Island.

When we pulled into Hilo, the Army loaned us a couple of big trucks with which we drove out to the volcano. It was so new that there were neither police nor guards, nor any barriers whatsoever. In fact, there was no one even there at the time! We stopped pretty close to the volcano, parking on top of a gas station which had been covered in 15 feet of little BB sized cinders. The stuff was not ash, not at all like a powder. We were perhaps 200 yards from the edge of the hole where red globs of lava were shooting up high in the air. We felt fairly safe, since the lava was flowing out the crater's opposite side toward the sea. With every glob shot up into the air, there was a loud report, like cannon fire. It was spectacular! The irony was that just underneath the gas station's sign was a smaller one indicating, "No Smoking." Here we were, a bunch of young sailors witnessing a rarely seen natural event, the birth of a volcano. We walked around the base on still warm lava! This was my most unusual liberty, thanks to Uncle Sam and Captain Blount.

Hiding the Boat

The second time we pulled into Yokosuka was an awakening for me in a number of ways. Oddly, politics was one of the first things to strike me. We were assigned a pier in a remote part of the naval base, which made me think that they were trying to hide us from the Russians. On second thought, I figured that was ridiculous, since I was confident that our adversaries in the Evil Empire were a whole lot smarter than to be deceived in such a manner. It all became clear as I approached the main gate to go on liberty.

There was a large and very energetic demonstration just on the other side of the gate. What had happened, I believe, was the Japanese "left" found out that *Barbero* was there, and that she had nuclear missiles aboard. Remember, this was in the late 50s, and we were the first sub with "the bomb." It made the Japanese *very* uncomfortable, so much so that there were hundreds of bandannaed, banner-waving, shouting Japanese demonstrating at the main gate. I stood next to the marine guard, with USS *Barbero* sewn onto my shoulder, and hesitated for maybe a second or two before wading through the mob. Nobody was keeping me on base after 72 days at sea, 42 of which were submerged! I, by God, was going to get a "Hotsie Bath," get my blues cleaned and pressed during the bath, eat a big steak and a huge green salad, drink a good deal of Johnny Walker Black Label, and then play it by ear, and those crazy bastards were going to have to kill me first. Apparently, my feelings were displayed in both my face and demeanor, because they made a path for me through the mob.

Wahoo

Liberty is always associated with going ashore and getting away from your ship for a time. The crew of *Wahoo* had what I'd call a bit of liberty while underway! Subs in general, and particularly *Barbero*, seldom went to sea with other vessels. If you consider their missions, this makes sense. We only did it once, when we moved our home port from Norfolk to Pearl Harbor. We went around through the Panama Canal, accompanied the entire way by another diesel sub, USS *Wahoo*. *Wahoo* had the usual complement of four main engines, while we had only two, due to our conversion to a missile-launching sub. The obvious consequence of this was that *Wahoo* was a lot faster than we were. *Wahoo*, like all of us, hated to poop along at 12 knots when she could exceed 20 all day.

It turned out that the skipper of *Wahoo* was an avid fisherman like that guy on "M.A.S.H." He couldn't get enough of it, apparently, because they would run fast all night, get way ahead of us and then shut down their engines and drift all day fishing. Late in the day, we would come chugging over the horizon to catch up, then they would repeat the evolution. I must say that it was very comical each afternoon to see a United States man of war, a rakish looking, lethal submarine, with her rails lined with fishermen! It reminded me of those party boats I saw as a kid, fishing off the south shore of Long Island in the summers.

It must have been a lot of fun for them, because most of the watches were secured for that day's fishing. After all, who needed a helmsman and all the rest? I can just see the cook carrying up all those tuna sandwiches and lemonade for the fishermen on deck. Even as they would get underway as we approached, the captain would actually troll from the bridge!

We saw them once a day, each evening until we arrived off Papa Hotel—the first buoy entering the channel into Pearl. There the two subs fell into line for appearances. I really loved the informality and independence of the submarine service in those days.

St. Thomas

In the mid 50s my older brother Bob and I became very taken by the activities of Cousteau and particularly with his relatively new invention, then called the "aqua lung." The idea fascinated us. As a matter of fact, I even built one for my high school physics project from surplus airplane oxygen system parts based on a magazine article I had read. Bob, the real brains behind most of our enterprises, probably saved my life by somehow rounding up enough money to buy a real, store-bought, no-nonsense scuba outfit before I had a chance to kill myself with my physics project. In fact, had I tested it in a normal place instead of in six feet of dirty water in Baldwin Harbor, Long Island, I probably would have ended up contributing to a bumper crab harvest that year. We used the real one for only one summer before Bob went off to the Marines and I went into the Navy. After that, the scuba gear collected dust at our parents' home until I got an idea one day.

Barbero was scheduled to go to St. Thomas, among other places in the Caribbean, and it occurred to me to bring along the "lung," as we called it. No one objected when I lashed the scuba gear securely in the forward room as we got underway for the Caribbean.

The water in St. Thomas was unbelievably clear by comparison to the silty stuff we were accustomed to off Jones Beach, and I couldn't wait to get into it. I discretely went over the side of the boat, since I was unsure of any rules about diving around Navy ships. It was wonderful! I went all along the keel and even swam into a ballast tank. Then I went aft to sit on one of the screws (not such a good idea in retrospect). I never had to worry about compressed air to dive with since on a sub it is practically unlimited.

A British frigate was tied up across the pier from us that had some real divers aboard, not "shade tree" types like me. When they noticed me in the water, I was invited to come across and dive with them. Since I just couldn't go squishing my way across the brow of the august *Barbero*, I put on some dungarees over my swimsuit and carried my gear to the frigate, just in time, as it turned out, for their "tot."

For hundreds of years, British sailors have been given a ration of rum each day. It happens to be a really bad tradition that apparently they refuse to change. Nevertheless, as I was being introduced to the sailors on the fantail, each insisted I have a big gulp of his rum. Now there were quite a number of Brits on the fantail that day, all of whom insisted that this was a tradition of long standing, and furthermore, it would be a clear and present insult to refuse the rum. Another consideration was that I naturally felt an obligation to uphold the reputation of the United States Submarine Service and, of course, the Navy. I did not want them to think that this colonist couldn't hold his rum. After all this good fellowship, and in my case a bunch of rum, we went over the side to dive.

I went immediately to the bottom of the harbor and sat there, fascinated at being able to see the complete silhouettes of both hulls very clearly up on the surface. I could do this since the water was clear as a bell and a good 50 feet deep there. The rum by this time had begun working its dark purpose on my brain, when my air supply stopped abruptly and completely! Either those early models of scuba gear had no air supply warning system, or I missed the message in my intoxication. But, whatever it was, I was in big trouble.

I sprinted for the surface, which felt like a half mile away, and I honestly felt I would not make it. I didn't even have the benefit of a lung full of air since I had just exhaled when I found I was out of the stuff! What, no doubt, saved me was the very concept which I explained earlier in the piece "Free Ascent." While I thought I was completely out of air, as I raced toward the surface, that little "20 percent residual air" kept expanding as the surrounding water pressure decreased. I certainly did not feel like I was getting any air, but apparently I was. My Brit friends were none the wiser in spite of my gasps as I broke the surface like a Polaris missile, much more sober and a bit wiser.

Hong Kong

As I am typing this, Hong Kong is being turned over to the PRC. The TV news has been covered with stories from every conceivable point of view...what the crowds in Tienaman Square are saying...how they are responding in Shanghai...what the Brits at the club are saying over their gin and tonics...the view from some Chinese take out place, for God's sake...it's unbelievable! Last night while watching all this fuss on the TV, I turned to my wife Barbara and said, facetiously, "I've been there," which she of course knew. It made me think of liberty in Hong Kong as a 20-year-old sailor in 1960.

The thing about sea travel is that you get no forewarning, no milestones prepare you for the port you are sailing to—it's just day and night and ocean and time. You leave one culture and all of a sudden you are in a new one—sometimes radically different.

We pulled into the channel in Hong Kong early in the morning as the sun rose, and it was the most exotic thing I ever saw, before or since! This 20-year old sailor from Long Island was just not prepared for some place this exotic. Junks were busily crossing back and forth all over the place, hundreds of them. They all looked pretty ragged, but that is how they probably looked coming off the ways when they were launched. I had, prior to this, been accoustumed to only seeing Western sailing craft, and junks are their antithesis. They are no doubt great vessels, but completly different from ours in the West. The larger boats were for transporting goods, and the small ones were the water people's homes.

Like Japan, Hong Kong's economy has soared in the intervening years since *Barbero's* visit in 1960. There were a lot of poor people there in 1960, or at least they appeared poor to us at the time. Entire families lived on small boats no bigger than a medium sized dory. Hundreds of these boats were rafted with one another, with little channels left for their traffic. I suspect many of those people seldom got to the shore less than a hundred yards away.

I remember being almost stunned by a system in Hong Kong harbor. There was a lady called "Mari Su," who had a number of women working for her. She would make a deal with our ships wherein she would have her "girls" paint the ship in exchange for OUR

GARBAGE! We supplied the paint and equipment, and they would come along side in their little boats and get after it—scraping, priming and painting. Some would have their babies strapped on their backs while they did the painting. Now, I am not certain, but I suspect that Mari Su had a keen understanding of "American nature," because what she and the girls got was not exactly garbage. Sure, they took our cans and dumped them into their boats, and it was our garbage, but we went to great lengths to make it "real good garbage." Surely, Mari Su knew how we American sailors would fill our half of the bargin.

The crew's procedure, with respect to our garbage while in Hong Kong, was unspoken and spontaneous. We'd scrape our plates, being careful to separate edible food from simply trash. The leftover chicken went into one container, mashed potatoes in another, and so forth. We all felt guilty, as I'm sure Mari Su anticipated, and made sure that they got all the leftovers and a lot more from our galley.

Hong Kong had another "system" also new to me—it had more tailors per capita than any place on earth. Naval officers needed civilian cloths—suits, blazers, shirts, shoes, and the like. Sailors generally didn't. At home I had heard from my older officer brothers that if one ever got to Hong Kong, he should be sure to get some suits and shirts made. With that in mind, I got a cab and, instead of asking to be taken to some bar or Tiger Balm Gardens, like any normal sailor, I foolishly asked the cab driver to take me to a tailor shop. Now, there must have been thousands of tailor shops in that city, and I am certain that each had some kickback arrangement with the cabbies. Anyway, we pulled up in front of a shop and the driver took me inside to introduce me to the tailor, which would have normally been a dead giveaway. I just thought he was being polite! Then the tailor began plying me with liquor as I paged through the 1960 equivalent of *Gentlemen's Quarterly* to find a picture of the suit I wanted. By the time I got to the overcoat selection, I was pretty loaded. The tailor mailed all my bespoke clothes to my mother's house, and I did not see them until I left the Navy.

My brother Bob was, by this time, a poor starving student at the University of Alaska and in need of free clothing. It's not that I was all that discriminating at age 21, but after seeing myself in the overcoat, I determined that I was not about to be seen dead or otherwise in that thing. The tailor must have thought I lived in Murmansk. In fact, I did look quite a bit like Lavrenti Pavlovich Beriya in the coat. Anyway, when I offered it to Bob, he snatched it out of my hands like someone from the gulag. All he needed was a rope about his waist and a number on his hat.

Chapter 16:
Ditty Bag

"They bear, in place of classic names,
Letters and numbers on their skin,
They play their grisly blindfold games
In little boxes made of tin.
- Kipling - "THE TRADE"

I can still see the large room with numbered squares painted on the deck, each with a new cardboard box in the middle. The recruits were ordered to stand in a square, take off all their clothes, and put them all into the box, and write their mother's name and address on it. They next proceeded, naked as jay birds, to a line where they were examined by doctors and corpsmen. At the end of the line there were a number of tables where we were given all kinds of shots. The guy ahead of me on the line froze while the corpsman injected him again with the same stuff, thinking the naked male body at his little table was a new one! When the corpsman went to inject this same poor guy a third time, I spoke up. We were then directed to another line where our new, musty-smelling, ill-fitting uniforms were thrown at us as we made our way down the long counter. The supply sailors behind the counter read our sizes from a sheet each of us kept in front of us as we migrated along. Only then were we allowed to cover our nakedness with the uniforms we were just issued, looking like the boots we were. The entire experience was uncomfortable and humiliating. I imagine it was far worse for some of the recruits than others. The high school jocks were accustomed to being naked in the shower room, but for some it must have been a frightening experience. While the purpose of this whole evolution was a practical and necessary one, I think it served as a "pail of water in the face" wake up which said, "You're in the Navy now".

One of the items thrown at each of us was a silly sounding thing they called a"Ditty Bag." It contained a razor, blades, toothbrush, toothpaste, and several other things. None of us knew that the silly sounding name was as old as the British Navy, and not at all silly. For probably 600 years, sailors and officers alike needed a place for all their personal things aboard ships with virtually no room in them. This is a fact of life at sea as true and as applicable 600 years ago as it is for the brand new USS *Hopper* (DDG - 70) commissioned in San Francisco in September 1997.

* * * * * * * * *

The submarine service was advertised as voluntary, but to have a truly voluntary organization, you have to have a mechanism for the volunteer to also quit, to volunteer himself *out* of subs and with impunity. I suppose few "volunteer" military groups could meet this test. I'd like to be there when a Marine recruit at Parris Island tells his D.I., "All things considered, I'd rather be home." The U.S. Navy's submarine service has such a system— you can walk off the boat and no hard feelings.

Dupois was a mess cook on *Barbero*. It was a French Canadian name and pronounced "Dupueeee," but the crew called him "Dupuss." It was his first boat, and he reported aboard prior to our second WestPac cruise. Unbeknownst to us, the cruise had a little detour where we went to Japan via the coast of Siberia! The first leg was north from Pearl to Adak, Alaska, to top off fuel and then due west for what turned out to be a 72-day cruise with the middle 42 days spent snorkeling just off the coast of the Kamchatka Peninsula, all this in mid-winter.

Dupois was a completely agreeable fellow, seemingly suitable for sub duty, but he became increasingly apprehensive as the cruise progressed about the Russians finding us, and spent what seemed like all his off hours lurking around the sonar shack up in the forward torpedo room, asking whether there were any contacts. To add to his misery, he got pretty seasick when we were surfaced in rough weather and would tie a #10 can around his neck while he washed the dishes in his tiny scullery.

I clearly recall at the end of the cruise, as the brow went over to the pier in Yokosuka, Dupuee walking off the boat. He quit! Just like that. We never saw him again. He *unvolunteered* himself from subs, and I am certain that this was not held in any way against him. Who would want to be aboard a submarine, of all places, with a shipmate who did not want to be there for *any* reason? I had nothing but respect for the guy. This was just not for him, he no longer wanted to be aboard our sub, and the service allowed him to walk—a damn good policy.

* * * * * * * * *

There are a number of terms used by both the Navy and Marines which they assimilated during their lengthy duty in China in the early twentieth century. Both services spent quite a bit of time there. "Gung Ho," "chow," and "cumshaw," come to mind. Cumshaw was not simply a phrase, it was a system in the Navy.

Aboard the boat we were often confronted with new demands, largely due to additions of new equipment which did not exist when the boat was built back in 1943. Needed modifications were requested through BuShips (Bureau of Ships) in the form of a mountain of paper, drawings, cost figures, etc. But when the crew needed something welded, cut, or moved in order to make our jobs or living conditions a little bit easier, we seldom went the BuShips route.

One time we decided that it would make torpedo handling easier if we had two more padeyes welded to the inside of the hull in new positions. To avoid the onerous BuShips process and also to get the padeyes in as soon as possible, we used cumshaw. To begin with, we did not tell the gunnery officer. Instead, we went to the crew's mess and got an institutional size loaf of American cheese, some "horse cock" (bologna), several loaves of bread, and big jars of mayo and mustard. Then we "borrowed" the duty truck and drove to the welding shop, walked in to the supervisor, and told him what we wanted and handed over the goods. Our job immediately went to the top of the pile, and we had our padeyes welded to the overhead the next day.

We were utterly convinced that, while this was not regulation and in fact against the rules, it was efficient, fast, and cheap. The food could not have cost the Navy $20. We knew that this could get out of hand if done foolishly, but we knew what we were doing and so did the yardbird welder. We were not about to jeopardize the ship's safety. We did not need engineers and bureaucrats in the process. There is no telling how much money the Navy has been saved through cumshaw. If that infamous $2,500 toilet seat had been done our way, it would have been finished in a week and cost the equivalent of lunch for 20 yard birds.

* * * * * * * * * *

I'll bet that virtually every officer and sailor who has been in a shipyard has a few stories about yardbirds. These guys were the civilian shipyard workers who modified and repaired our ships. If the word were in the dictionary, it might look like this;

Civilian shipyard workers. Each assigned to a different "shop," which has a particular work specialty, a number and a color code. "72" shop, for instance, are the riggers, and they wear yellow hard hats. Yardbirds are ordinarily benign members of the worker class, unless one is unfortunate enough to be caught between them and the main gate when the quit whistle sounds at 4:45 p.m.

There were lots of stories of these guys stealing, stretching out their tasks, watching the clock and so forth, but there were plenty of stories which showed them in a positive light as well.

There was the one about the two guys who wanted to steal a long extension ladder from the ship yard. They tied the ladder underneath one of their cars. It naturally stuck out the rear of the car five feet or so, so the accomplice yard bird simply used his car to push the car with the ladder out the main gate, informing the Marine on duty that the front car would not start! Nobody said that these guys were stupid.

One story I recall showed yardbirds as being clever in solving problems. There was a heavy piece of gear which had to be dropped into a hole only slightly larger than itself, but since there was no purchase on top, the crane could only set the object down next to the hole using straps which were then removed. No one could figure out how to slide the thing into the hole and let it down gently to the bottom without having it get bound and stuck half way down. They were all savvy enough to know that if they let it bind crooked in the hole, there was no possible way to get it back out for a second attempt. Finally, a yardbird suggested that the hole for this very heavy thing be packed with shaved ice from the galley. When the ice was level with the deck, they slid the heavy piece of gear over the hole, aligning it precisely, and let Mother Nature do the rest! As the ice slowly melted, the equipment, guided by the yardbirds, gently sunk to the bottom of the hole without binding.

Our 40-foot periscope came back from the optical shop and was laying on blocks on the pier next to the boat. Naturally, the bottom was the business end with all the optics, range finder, and so on and was very, very delicate. I was convinced that there was no way to lift and reinstall the periscope without banging up this delicate end. I told this to the "72" shop guy, and he just laughed. They came the next morning with *two* cranes, one for each end of the periscope, lifted the thing 50 feet up while still in the horizontal position, and then slacked off the crane holding the bottom end until the thing was vertical! The periscope was greased up and slipped down into the boat. The yardbird looked at me like I was as green as a new banana, and he was right!

* * * * * * * * *

I'm not sure about the Marines or the Army, but in the U.S. Navy, the two best ships in the fleet are either the one a sailor just came from or the ship to which a sailor has just been ordered. Sitting around in the forward battery, a new crew member will regale his shipmates with how good the food was, or how good the skipper was back on the old USS *Has-been* BS-2. They'll go on and on about their old ship—the time we did this, the time we did that, it never fails. Conversely, the sailors who have orders to transfer as soon as they get back to Pearl, sound the same! "Man, I heard the *Grouper* is a great boat, it can really haul ass, blah, blah, blah." "The engineering officer is supposed to be one smart son of a bitch and not a prick like this guy." I hate to pose a problem and not have the answer, but this one is a mystery. If I'm not mistaken, this syndrome has always been a part of the Navy.

* * * * * * * * *

No story about life on an old diesel boat would be complete without describing how the hell we kept clean without showers and with almost no water devoted to personal hygiene. The answer is that none of us were very clean—we were all grubby to varying degrees. So, as an illustration, I will describe my weekly hygiene routine. Keep in mind that I was probably in the 80th percentile of cleanliness.

I forgot the day of the week, but once a week I went into the little washroom in the forward part of the crew's mess where there was a shower stall filled with stores and two small stainless steel sinks. I'd fill the sink with water, no more than six quarts, and wash my hair. Then I stripped and washed my entire body with soap and a wash cloth (in the same water). Next, I shaved off the week's growth (in the same water). By this time, the specific gravity of my six quarts of H_2O was changed considerably. I'd then drain and refill the sink with the last six quarts of water which I allotted myself and rinsed my hair, face, and body and put on a new set of clothing. It was the second best feeling a sailor can have, and was certainly the best feeling one ever got on a submarine! This conservation of precious water on diesel boats was self-imposed. We were the crew of *Barbero*, we were literally "all in the same boat," and there was no way any of us would jeopardize the safety and well being of the rest by wasting water.

* * * * * * * * * *

Everyone in the Navy knew that subs had especially good food. When you thought of carriers or other ships, you did not think of food. There were other associations, of course, but food was not among them. The reason for this, I believe, was an effort to make what were uncomfortable conditions a little more bearable. I am sure that there were destroyer sailors who were uncomfortable too, but the policy of the Navy was to give us both extra money, known as "sub pay," and also to allow more funds for food. Units in the Navy were alloted so much per man/meal, and submarines were given extra funds. So, when The Greek ordered stores for *Barbero*, he always got special stuff, like frog's legs and the best steaks. We would have cookouts on the pier where he grilled our steaks to order over charcoal on half of a 55 gallon drum. When we had our ship's picnics ashore, the food was always terrific.

Perhaps The Greek (Chief Reader, our head commissaryman) was unusual, but he always seemed to go the extra mile for the crew. On Christmas in Pearl, he would leave his family to come down to the boat to make sure the guys with the duty and us unmarried youngsters were taken care of. He did this even though he did not have the duty himself. I even saw him empty a bottle of his own bourbon into the eggnog! Something tells me that, while he was special, he probably was not all that unusual among submarine cooks. Subs were known for good food because we had more money to spend, but also because we had people like Chief Reader.

There was a policy on all the old boats of an open galley. I am not aware of any other ships doing this. In fact I don't know how big ships would ever police such a thing, but it was true on the old diesel boats. Open galley meant that if we were hungry, we could break out some food or make ourselves a sandwich! It was like home in a way. The only condition was that we clean up after ourselves. It was great and special treatment for us, and we knew it and appreciated it. I don't know what the retention rates were for sub sailors, but I'll bet they were high.

The odd thing was that we seldom took advantage of the open galley policy, because we were fed so well. The food at meals was family style, very good and virtually unlimited.

In addition, the cooks seemed to be very aware and ahead of the curve. When we'd show movies in port on weekends, popcorn and grilled cheese sandwiches would appear. We would not have to ask—we would decide among ourselves to watch a few movies and we'd all of a sudden start smelling food!

Submarine service was considered "arduous sea duty." Given the living conditions that I have already described, there was very little the Navy could do to make the boats in any way homey or comfortable—they were what they were. They simply could not make a sow's ear into a silk purse, no matter what they did to the boat. However, they could and did make up for it with the chow situation. For nearly all of us, the food was far better than mom's. After three years aboard *Barbero*, I went home and had to adjust a lot to "home cooking." That was when I first began to cook for myself—*Barbero* had spoiled me.

* * * * * * * * *

This story is for the engineering types. One of my shipmates who came aboard shortly after me was a very bright engineman (if I am once again excused for another oxymoron). His prior assignment was as the engineman on a very small, experimental sub with a crew of perhaps six or eight. When he described the little boat I was at first fascinated, and as the story progressed, I became appalled! His boat was propelled by reciprocating engines—I think they were gasoline. So far, so good. But they were designed to run while submerged with the oxygen source being hydrogen peroxide broken into its two components, hydrogen and oxygen! Very dicy stuff indeed. The best way to elaborate on the idea is to describe a type of torpedo we had at the time, the Mk 15, which ran on similar principles.

All torpedoes run submerged. The non-electric ones, which ran on burning fuel, needed an oxygen source. The conventional torpedoes of the time were the Mk 14s, which carried a large compressed air flask to provide the oxygen, and were powered by a little turbine engine fueled with alcohol. These were very stable and safe little vehicles to get 800 pounds of HBX explosive reliably to a target. The range and speed of the Mk 14s were largely limited by how much air, alcohol, and water (for cooling the combustion and providing steam for the turbine) it could hold. These range and speed limitations spawned the Mk 15.

The Mk 15 looked the same as the Mk 14, except it had a much smaller air flask and a larger fuel flask and an additional flask full of hydrogen peroxide, H_2O_2. I'm not talking about the stuff we get at the pharmacy that is in the 3 percent solution; I mean a highly concentrated and very unstable version. Here is how the torpedo worked.

The H_2O_2 was pushed through a heavy walled chamber inside the torpedo stuffed full of round metal screens coated with cobalt, which acted as a catalyst. The concentrated H2-O2 broke down into its components of two very dangerous elements, oxygen and hydrogen, plus the byproduct of such a breakdown, heat. The stuff coming out of the back of this chamber was sent to a combustion chamber, where alcohol was introduced in a spray and the brew was ignited. Water was sprayed into the after part of this chamber, and the hot, high-pressure slurry was then run through the turbine. The result was a very high speed, very long range and very, very dangerous vehicle which had to be constantly monitored whether it was aboard a sub or in the base torpedo shop.

Back to my shipmate's little boat, they broke down the hydrogen peroxide and ran the hot gases essentially into its engine's "carburetor." The energy the engine produced went to turning the screw and running a compressor that compressed the exhaust from the engine so it could be vented into the sea.

The whole idea of being at 200 feet in a little room with the processes I've just described going on a couple feet away from me sends chills down my spine. Needless to say, the Navy scratched the program after awhile...thank God! I've always had a lot of respect for that engineman.

* * * * * * * * *

I think the naming of Navy ships, particularly men-of-war, is very important. For the most part, the Navy has done a good job. Most sailors must be proud to have their ship's name sewn on their shoulder. Battles like Antietam Creek, Chosin Reservoir, Bunker Hill, Anzio, Belleau Wood, Lexington, Guadalcanal, San Jacinto and the like are perfect for a man-of-war; battles are great names for ships. Lord knows we have no shortage of great fighting American warriors from all the services to name ships after—O'Bannon, John Paul Jones, Nimitz, Eisenhower, York, Murphy. There must be hundreds of candidates with the Medal of Honor or a couple of Silver Stars to name ships after, and of course the Navy has. I am particularly fond of the names of old Navy fighting ships like *Wasp, Bonhomme Richard, Hornet*, and *Enterprise*. One great fighting ship's name—*Shangri La*—came out of thin air. The press asked FDR where in the world Doolittle's bombers, which had just bombed Tokyo, had come from. He replied, surely with his famous grin, "Shangri La."

But I have a problem with using the names of politicians, bureaucrats, and places you would never, ever voluntarily, travel to like, Wichita, Albany, Lubbock, Kalamazoo, and Duluth.. Who the hell wants to go into harm's way on the USS *Kalamazoo*? The crew would all be hoping that the enemy wouldn't find out the name of their ship!

I guess state names are ok, but they are marginal for me, personally. However, cities are absolutely out, as far as I'm concerned. It is here that I draw the line in the sand! Hell, we have an entire class of fast attack submarines named after Los Angeles, for God's sake! Some of the "boomers" (fleet ballistic missile subs) are named after famous Americans. What branch of the service was Francis Scott Key in anyway? Or Sam Rayburn, or George Washington Carver? Name the building the band practices in after Key if you want, but not a submarine. At least Ulysses S. Grant was a warrior. Hey, call me old fashioned, but what ever happened to naming submarines after fish? Submarines have a colorful history when it comes to names. Fish are perfect for submarines, and there was a time when subs *all* had fish names. Here is a sampling;

Albacore	Amberjack	Angler
Archerfish	Barb	Batfish
Billfish	Blackfin	Bluefish
Bluegill	Bowfin	Dolphin
Drum	Flasher	Skate
Carp	Gar	Grouper
Growler	Kingfish	Lionfish
Mackerel	Pompano	Plunger
Perch	Redfin	Puffer
Marlin	Flying Fish	Trigger
Tarpon	Pickerel	Snapper
Sea Leopard	Remora	Bonefish
Tusk	Sea Devil	Pampanito
Carbonero	Hammerhead	Sea Poacher
Bullhead	Sea Owl	Tang
Puffer	Queenfish	Scorpion
Seawolf	Shark	Swordfish
Thresher	Tunny	Wahoo

* * * * * * * * *

Whenever I run into someone who either considers his military experience as negative or is completely indifferent about it, I almost feel sorry for him. Perhaps I am one of those people who have selective memories, expunging the bad experiences. This must be true to some extent, since I must have had a bad time now and then. I simply have no recollection of them. All the Navy experiences housed in my memory are pretty good and sort of wholesome, actually.

On a day-to-day basis, I did not think about defending western civilization and its right to produce roll-on deodorants. Rather, it was a way of life that I lived for a few years. I was pretty happy with it as a young fellow in my formative years. It was for me a period, from 18 to 22 years old, when I had a chance to catch my breath and consider things such as what I wanted to do in life, whether to go to college, marry, have children, and those sorts of things.

Joining the Navy out of high school and going to college after the Navy was, for me, productive; good timing. If my guess is correct, it would have been a better course for a lot of my contemporaries than to have entered college straight out of high school, not having any idea about their direction in life. However, there was a perceived risk that my family had—I'd never go back to school afterwards. Rather, I'd get married, or there would be some obstacle to further schooling. After all, that happened to many soldiers and sailors.

I have no regrets about when and how I served my country. I had a good, wholesome experience in the Navy, and it came at the right time in my life. The experience and the maturing prepared me to be a far better student when I did get to college, to be a better employee, a better neighbor, and a better citizen.

Chapter 17:
The Bubbleheads

"All the regulations and gold braid in the Pacific Fleet cannot
enforce a sailor's devotion. This, each officer in command
must earn on his own."
- LCDR. Arnold S. Lott: "Brave Ships, Brave Men"

One of the nicer epithets which aviators give to submariners (the accent is on the third syllable), is "bubblehead." There are worse nicknames, but those are reserved for particularly obnoxious members of the community. This particular one was only moderately disagreeable. But he made up for this with hubris...enormous hubris. Which is worse? Who knows? The problem was that at the time he was also the Chief of Naval Operations (CNO), while I was Assistant Deputy CNO (Air Warfare) and, for a few months, Acting Deputy.

My eternal recollection of him, rightly or wrongly, is that he never, ever, invited me to sit down in his presence. When summoned in for something, I would walk into his office, notice that he was not looking up...but concentrating rather on some piece of paper on his desk. I would end up standing at his desk for some ill-defined period of time while he finished up what he was reading. Invariably he would sign the document, toss it into his out basket, then look up at me. That was my cue to open the conversation, and that was when he would look at me for the first time.

I suppose I was expected to stand at some form of military position, like attention or parade rest, which I never did. I couldn't force myself to do that...even though I was a mere rear admiral, and he was a four-star admiral. At the time I had just recovered from my second hip replacement and would dearly have loved to be invited to sit down. But that never happened.

I would observe, parenthetically, that in all of my dealings with other people, regardless of how our ranks may have differed, I have never been so rude as to treat any guest that way.

Notwithstanding all of the aforementioned, there is a philosophy of life which I adopted a long time ago that has sustained me through the worst possible examples of leadership. It is a simple way of thinking…one which has left me totally free from that form of stress normally associated with people who have a hard time dealing with a difficult boss!

I ask myself the following question…the answer to which is always the same and always a source of solace. "I have been shot at by some of the best anti-aircraft gunners in the world. I have had surface-to-air missiles chase me around the sky. I have survived 167 missions over Vietnam. I have ejected twice from stricken aircraft and survived. I have made more than 900 carrier landings. Having survived all of the above, am I now going to let some pompous pissant give me an ulcer?"

Always, the answer is a resounding no!

On the positive side, he was a genuinely honest person who tried hard to be nice. Unfortunately, he was never able to pull it off. I felt sorry for him. He clearly had hit the stops of leadership ability and the "Peter Principle" had kicked in. As CNO he was in way over his head.

In the late summer of 1984, when the Deputy CNO (Air) was out of the office, the hotline rang on his desk. That meant that the CNO was on the line and wanted to talk personally with his deputy. Normally, I didn't answer it, but something told me to walk in and pick up the receiver. "Paul Gillcrist here, Admiral. The boss is out of the office. Is there anything I can do for you?"

"I hope so," he answered. I could tell from the sound of his voice that he was in a good humor. "I'm working on the speech I'm going to give to the Tailhook Convention, and I need a few facts. I'm not sure you can come up with them." I knew about the speech. It was the first time a non-aviator CNO had ever been invited to be the banquet speaker at the convention. This was before the ill-fated 1991 convention at which bad things occurred. I sensed that since his brother, a retired captain and aviator, had talked him into accepting the speaking invitation, he wanted to do it well.

The CNO went on to explain that he had been the commanding officer of the cruiser USS *Oklahoma City* in the Tonkin Gulf and had managed to shoot down a North Vietnamese MiG with a surface-to-air missile. The shootdown had been in conjunction with an aerial engagement in which there had also been an air-to-air shoot down of a North Vietnamese MiG by a U.S. Navy F-8. The CNO had very cleverly formulated a speech plan which was certain to enamor him with his audience. He would show how he too had shot down a MiG. Such an announcement to a group of spirited Naval aviators was certain to elicit an enthusiastic audience response. The CNO was sitting at his desk playing the tape of the two shoot downs…the tape that his tactical officer had made of the UHF radio frequency channel being used by the F-8 pilot and the *Oklahoma City* radar controller. "I'm trying to find out who the pilot was who shot down the other MiG. His call sign was *Nickel Four Two Three*. Can you find this out?"

"Certainly," I answered. "That's easy." He was genuinely surprised at my response. After all this time (almost 20 years), he apparently thought the information might be irretreivable. In actual fact, I had worked in the office that compiled those statistics when this particular aerial engagement occurred. I knew exactly where the answer was and in which file cabinet. Within minutes, I returned the call and told him the pilot's name. He happened to be an acquaintance. Then came the question which I was anticipating…and I was already relishing my response, which I knew would blow his socks off.

"Do you think," he asked, "that this pilot would be in the audience?"

"No, sir," I responded, my heart jumping with glee at the inevitable outcome of this conversation. "I am absolutely certain that he will not be there." There was a pause before the next question came.

"How can you be so sure?" the CNO asked, his voice filled with curiosity.

"Because he is in jail!", I responded. It took every bit of restraint I had to keep from laughing out loud.

"What?" was the shocked response. I explained that the pilot in question had long since resigned from the Navy and gone into business on his own. During the course of that business he had managed to get on the wrong side of the law and was serving a stint in the slammer as a result. I made it sound so matter-of-fact in my explanation that one could infer that I didn't think it was any big deal! His response was predictable.

"Typical fighter pilot!" was all he said before hanging up, knowing full well that that was my own aeronautical background.

The speech went well, I was told. But the piece de resis*tance* (and the point of this story) occurred at a reception on the floor of the hall in the hotel where all of the contractor booths and displays were located.

The spirit of camaraderie was everywhere. The sense of being a part of a wonderful fraternity was evident in the exuberance of everyone present. People were enjoying their cocktails and mixing with one another, swapping sea stories and, in general, having a wonderful time. The idea that those young fleet pilots were able to mix and exchange experiences with their counterparts from another era of Naval aviation…genuine war heroes…was simply heart-warming.

One of those youngsters, a lieutenant (junior grade) who had enjoyed perhaps one stinger too many approached the CNO on unsteady legs and greeted him with an ingratiating smile. Realizing that this wonderful exchange of ideas and camaraderie did not exist in the other Naval communities (surface warfare and submarine), the young man volunteered the most insouciant observation that the CNO had probably ever heard. The young man announced, in a loud voice,

"You Bubbleheads don't have anything like this, do you?" The admiral "was not amused."

PART II:
Skimmers

"I wish to have no connection with any ship that does not sail fast, for I intend to go in harm's way."

- John Paul Jones

I remember well sometime in about 1972 when the U.S. Navy's surface warfare insignia first appeared in the Pentagon. Up until then one could spot a surface warfare officer a hundred feet away by the fact that he wore no identifying insignia on his left breast above the ribbons. Submariners wore dolphins (gold for officers, silver for enlisted personnel), and the aviators wore gold wings. The surface warfare officers wore no identifying insignia. I suppose that the insignia for the submariners and aviators meant that they had undergone a rigorous (and dangerous) training regimen, and for qualifying, had earned the right to wear a special insignia. There was no training regimen for surface warfare officers. Ergo there was no identifying insignia. In 1972 that was forever changed. Surface Warfare Officers School (SWOS) was created, and its graduates were declared eligible to wear a special insignia which, at a distance, looks strangely like a pair of wings.

There was a sense of distaste among the submariners and aviators, I knew, about the surface warfare insignia. Submariners underwent a very stressful training program capped by a very dangerous unassisted escape from the bottom of a 100-foot water tower. Tough stuff! The aviators, on the other hand, had to learn to fly, and graduation exercise consisted of landing aboard an aircraft carrier. Also tough stuff! By comparison, the SWOS training program was a "walk in the park!" So, the aviators and submariners disdainfully took to calling them "Skimmers!" The epithet stuck.

I have a theory about the differences between ship and airplane drivers...and why those distinctions exist. The theory goes something like this...and it goes to the heart of the way the two career patterns differ. In the case of the surface warfare officer, he goes through a carefully designed training regimen to learn to operate a naval ship...how to get under way, how to maneuver, how to refuel at sea, how to fight the ship and, finally, how to get her back to port and moored. All of these evolutions require the very finest of teamwork among the half dozen people on the bridge team, those on the fo'csle who handle the mooring lines, those in the main propulsion spaces who generate the power used by the ship to maneuver, those on the signal bridge who handle visual communications with other ships, and those in the combat information center who are the keys to fighting the ship as a weapons system. Of course, there are others whose jobs are equally important…like weapons, supply, personnel, etc.

When a surface warfare officer, acting as officer of the deck, wants to maneuver the ship, he checks with the navigator hovering nearby to be sure that gentleman concurs with the intended course change. If the maneuver is complicated, he also checks with combat to be sure his planned course and speed changes are correct. Then, and only then, does he issue the order. "Right standard rudder," he calls out in a loud voice to the helmsman. "Steady up on new course of two eight zero." The captain is usually there watching all of this, along with the navigator. The young officer can also issue orders to the helmsman like, "All engines ahead full." If at any time he has second thoughts about his orders, he can always modify them and reconsider the consequences of adherence to them by his bridge team. All he has to say is, "Rudder amidships" or "All engines stop." The ship can slowly come to a halt in mid-ocean while he confers with combat, the navigator, or the captain. In response to all of these orders, the petty officers manning the engine order telegraph and the helm must repeat them as the bosun's mate writes them down in the ship's log. A slow, careful, methodical, and stodgy business…but a system which has been proven effective over several hundred years. On a typical four hour watch, steaming independently, the OOD might change course or speed once or twice, or perhaps not at all.

By comparison, the pilot of a tactical Navy airplane (like a *Hornet*) might have occasion to change course 50 times on a typical single plane two hour navigational flight. He might change throttle settings several hundred times. He never asks anyone's permission. There is no one to ask. There is no navigator to check it out with in advance…and no combat information center to be sure his planned changes are correct. If there is any doubt about the correctness of his decisions, coming to "all engines stop" and going dead in the water while he holds a conference is definitely not an option. His airplane is in motion and must stay in motion, or it will fall out of the sky and kill him. The decisions he makes about power and speed can kill him if they are bad ones. Other maneuvering decisions can kill him just as easily. The standard aviation career pattern regimen develops a young officer who learns to make decisions quickly but wisely…and to be accountable for them.

On the other hand, the career surface warfare officer learns to get consensus from other professionals before making decisions. He also knows that those same consensus people will probably share a portion of the blame if things should go badly. Is it any wonder that after a dozen years "before the mast," the career surface warfare officer is quite a different type of decision-maker than his counterpart in Naval aviation?

My thesis draws no other conclusions than the fact that senior surface warfare officers are characteristically quite different than their aviator counterparts at the point where the two career paths come together…in the command of major combatant vessels!

Chapter 18:
Marcus Aurelius Arnheiter

"You can make a mastiff hear reason, astound a bull, fascinate a boa, frighten a tiger, soften a lion; but there is no resource with that monster—a cannon let loose."

- Victor Hugo: "The Corvette, Claymore"

Anyone who knew him simply had to put him at the very top of his or her list of "most unforgettable characters." I first met him in the spring of 1948, the year I entered the Naval Academy. After several attempts to write this chapter, I finally had to settle on the adjective "intense" to describe Midshipman Arnheiter. Although we were thrown together by circumstances that warm summer in 1948, I cannot count him as a friend. But I did like him.

Marc stood about 5 feet 10 inches tall, had a pair of piercing black eyes that always seemed to hold a fierce, evangelistic glint, and always wore his jet-black hair in a short military cut. His skin was swarthy, and he spoke in a loud, oratorical tone of voice. He had a great sense of humor, and could display the most impeccable manners when he wanted to do so. He was well above average in the intelligence department, and seemed to have no difficulty with Naval Academy course work when he felt the inclination.

The first vestige of military structure to which midshipmen were subject in those days was what was called the "cutter crew." The derivation of the name was simple. It was the number of persons it took to fully man an 18 foot cutter...12. The cutter was a small boat powered by five banks of oars, the kind one often used to see at the beach for use by lifeguards in rescue operations. The five banks of oars plus a coxswain and a safety observer/signalman made up a cutter crew. We stayed in our cutter crews for the first several months of plebe summer indoctrination. One of the men in my cutter crew was Tom Winkler, who hailed from New Orleans.

Tom's close associate was Marc Arnheiter, who was a member of an adjacent cutter crew. The reason they were associates was their mutual (and unusual) backgrounds. They both had washed out of West Point in their first year and had come directly to the Naval Academy to start all over again. Furthermore, Marc Arnheiter had spent the year prior to his

West Point stint at the Citadel. So, Marcus Aurelius Arnheiter had already seen two solid years of first-year indoctrination (spell that hazing) before he ever showed up at Annapolis. It was like having survived two boot camps in succession and then starting a third. To me, at the time, it seemed like a form of masochism!

Marc and Tom brought much of the lore of previous disciplinary regimens with them. They were quick to share most of it with us. After all, it made the pair seem like two wise old owls imparting their hard-earned wisdom with the rest of us. Aping a West Point upper-classman, Marc or Tom would snarl, "Sweat your imprint on that wall, Mister," then show us how a West Pointer would slam his back up against the nearest wall in full attention (chin tucked in, stomach sucked in, and eyes riveted straight ahead) when so directed. They also shared tricks on how to get the best spit shine on a pair of shoes in the shortest time. They were a wealth of information when they got together to relate experiences. Our cutter crew listened to them as though they were oracles!

When the summer indoctrination ended, Marc and Tom ended up assigned to companies in other battalions, and we lost contact. Occasionally, I would see Tom, but hardly ever did I see Marc. After graduation we three lost track completely. Marc went into the surface Navy and pursued a career in destroyers. Eventually, his intensity caught up with him off the coast of North Vietnam on 31 March 1966. In attempting to engage the enemy as commanding officer of the destroyer escort, USS *Vance* (DER-387), Marc was court-martialed and subsequently relieved of his command. The events surrounding his career's demise were described by a journalist named Sheehan in a book entitled *The Arnheiter Affair.*

It was openly known that the Navy's execution of the Vietnam War was heavily weighted in favor of the aviators as far as combat action was concerned. It was an air war. Occasionally, a U.S. Navy combatant vessel would come into direct shooting contact with North Vietnamese forces, but it was rare. Even when "Linebacker" operations were kicked off in the summer of 1968, actual exchanges of shots between U.S. vessels and North Vietnamese shore batteries were infrequent.

There was a simple reason for this…it was stupid for a Navy ship to engage a shore battery in a duel. In fact, the rules of engagement for surface units were very explicit…do not steam within range of an enemy shore battery. Certainly, Linebacker operations involved U.S. Navy surface ships bombarding lucrative targets along the coast…but not when those targets were "covered" by shore batteries. Generally, there was no weight and size limitation to North Vietnamese shore battery guns, nor their defensive fortifications. Therefore, by definition, the shore battery could shoot larger shells farther than say, a Navy destroyer. It was not until the Navy pulled a couple of World War II battleships out of mothballs that this immutable equation changed.

There were a few Navy destroyers who were severely criticized for being overly aggressive in "trolling" for enemy shore fire. Marc Arnheiter's peccadillo fell into that category. I recall trying to read *The Arnheiter Affair*, but finally gave it up. It was not good reading. The author clearly did not understand his subject matter deeply enough to do the job of recording what was really a benchmark in Naval history.

Marc even garnered the support of one of our classmates, Eddie Shiver, an aviator who had earlier resigned his commission to pursue the practice of corporate law. Eddie defended him during his court-martial. The story of the court-martial is one which I will leave to Eddie to tell if the spirit ever moves him.

So, all connection with Marc Arnheiter ended until eight years after graduation, when our paths crossed one summer night at the U.S. Naval Medical Center in Bethesda, Maryland. It was vintage Arnheiter! I had been hospitalized at Bethesda for 16 months as a result of a serious airplane accident in 1959. I was near the end of my incarceration, and was allowed to leave the hospital for an hour or so in the evening to go to supper with a friend. I walked with the aid of a hinged brace on my right leg. It was about 10:00 in the evening when I walked up the steps to enter the main entrance to the hospital rotunda. As I neared the top of the steps I saw the unmistakeable silhouette of Marc Arnheiter, dressed in civilian clothes and pacing back and forth with a worried expression on his face. The rotunda was only a few short steps from the emergency operating room. I immediately felt compassion for him. It was obvious that a loved one was ill and he was waiting for the outcome of a difficult emergency procedure. I conjured up all sorts of dire events as I approached him, that would have put him here at this hour. He seemed terribly preoccupied. I greeted him, and we chatted a bit before I offered to take him down to the hospital cafeteria for a cup of coffee. He declined.

USS *Vance* underway in the Pacific Ocean. (Official U.S. Navy Photo)

I decided that he needed someone to talk to…someone who would listen to his sad tale. So I asked him what had happened…what sad set of circumstances had occurred to bring him to Bethesda at this late hour; and what, if anything, could I do to help in this time of need.

He turned to me with a sad expression and said, with a straight face, "My dog was run over by a truck!"

"What?" I almost shouted in disbelief. "Your dog was run over?" I was incredulous. He nodded somberly. "And you brought him here? To Bethesda?" I asked. He nodded again. I couldn't help but ask. "And they took him?" He nodded again, adding an explanatory note.

"They wouldn't take him in the emergency room. So I raised so much hell that the doctor finally agreed to see him. They are looking at him now!"

"Where?" I asked, still incredulous.

"In my car," came the deadpan answer.

It was truly vintage Arnheiter. That was 36 years ago. There was a note in a 1971 edition of the academy alumni association magazine that Marc Arnheiter had been injured in a fall while leading a group of Boy Scouts on a mountain climbing expedition. The fall was serious enough that Marc was retired 1 February 1971 with a 60% disability. I have not seen nor heard from him since! Marc Arnheiter was the Naval Academy class of 1952's answer to the legendary Philo McGiffin!

Author's Note: Commander Philo McGiffin, a graduate of the Naval Academy class of 1912, served on the China Station before World War I. He ingratiated himself so successfully to the Chinese leaders who were then intent upon beginning a navy, that they offered him a commission in their navy and an immediate promotion to admiral. Much to the consternation of the U.S. Navy, he accepted! The rest is history.

Chapter 19:
Dreadnaught

"...terrible as a dragon and huge as a mountain; destroyer even of the strongholds of heaven, and a weapon like a fire-raining monster."

- Inscription etched on Zam Zammah, the first cannon cast in India.

I have always been convinced that one can never fully appreciate the awesome power of a battleship until he goes to sea in one. For example, a 90,000 ton nuclear-powered *Nimitz* class aircraft carrier is truly incredible in its size, speed, and in the destructive power that can be delivered by its embarked air wing. However, there is something about the *Iowa* class battleship that is even more overwhelming. The battlewagon, by comparison, is smaller, displaces less, rides lower in the water, and seems, at least pierside, to be a less imposing combatant vessel. But once at sea the true value of the weapons system becomes evident.

My introduction to the battleship occurred in the summer of 1950 during my second-class summer cruise as a Naval Academy midshipman. *USS Wisconsin* (BB-64) anchored in Annapolis Roads that May, and we loaded aboard her for a summer cruise, first in the Caribbean, then on to northern Europe. It was to be a cruise which took us to places like Portugal, Scotland, and, of course, the Caribbean Sea.

By some stroke of good fortune I was assigned for the early part of the cruise as turret captain in the No. 3 turret (the aft 16-inch gun mount). There were three turrets on that class of battleship, two forward and one aft. Each turret contained three 16-inch guns. The turret sat atop what is called a barbette (the tube which extends below decks). Within the barbette were sleeping quarters (the best enlisted quarters on the ship, because they were air-conditioned), as well as the necessary equipment to continue feeding the huge 2,000-pound shells into the magazines of the three guns as fast as they could fire them. The barbette was air conditioned because the powder bags for ready service were stored there. The rounds were brought from the ship's magazine to the barbette, and thence by ammunition hoist up to the gun deck, where they were fed into the breach and rammed home by a powerful hydraulic ram. Once the round had been rammed home, a series of powder bags was placed in the breach and also rammed home behind the round. The powder bags, made of silk, were 16

U.S.S. Wisconsin (BB-64), Hampton Roads, VA, October 1, 1996. (Official USN photograph)

inches in diameter (just like the round) and about 14 inches deep. Different loadings called for a different number of powder bags. Five was the maximum number used with an "equivalent service round" to get the maximum range of 54,000 yards (27 nautical miles)!

When I say I was turret captain, I meant "midshipman turret captain." This means that someone was always looking over my shoulder. But, when *Wisconsin* sailed from Annapolis Roads that spring, she headed for the island of Vieques off the coast of Puerto Rico, where we were to shoot the guns before heading for Northern Europe. On the main gun deck inside the turret, the crews for the three guns competed for honors as the best and the fastest on the ship. They competed first with each other, then with the other two turrets. Somehow, I recall that I managed to instill in the three crews enough competitive spirit that it almost cost me a trip to the bridge and a thorough dressing down by the captain.

We were cruising off the coast of Vieques, readying ourselves for a Naval gunfiring exercise. Once preparations were completed we began firing, first turret No.1, then 2, and finally it was our turn. Our first several rounds went off smoothly. First No.1 gun, then two, and finally three. Their re-loading times were fairly competitive, and I confess to egging them to greater speed in my enthusiasm to beat the other two turrets.

Sitting in the turret captain's seat, I was able to watch the flight of each round after it left the barrel. The one ton rounds were huge, and nutated (like a poorly thrown football) in flight. The optics of my periscope were fabulous, and visually following the flight of each round was not difficult at all. Also, sitting there behind 14 inches of case-hardened armored steel gave me an incredible sense of security. The slanted face of the turret was specifically designed to take the full shock of an incoming 16-inch round and cause it to bounce off! I could only imagine the noise level inside the turret if that ever happened. We would all be deafened for life, no doubt...but alive!

The protective belt of armor at and below the waterline was equally impressive. The battlewagon was an almost unsinkable man o' war. It was interesting to note that when *Wisconsin's* sister ship, *New Jersey,* was brought into action in the Persian Gulf War, its crew felt comfortable that anything the Iraqis chose to shoot at them would simply bounce off.

The time came for my number three gun to fire again. I watched as they loaded the round, dropped five bags of powder onto the loading ramp and rammed them home. The firing signal came to me from CIC over my sound-powered telephone headset, and I squeezed the trigger. The roar was deafening, and I watched the nutating round arc inland toward the target, which was a concrete bunker 25-feet thick. The round punched through the reinforced concrete as if it was cheese, and the entire bunker erupted in smoke and debris...a direct hit!! I was delirious with joy and pride until I noticed hurried activity inside the turret. I looked in to see my No. 3 gun crew ramming another round into the breach without clearance. Before I could stop them, they ran the hydraulic ram into the bore and the deed was done! It was in there for good, and the only way to clear the bore was to fire the gun! It made me uncomfortable that they had acted without approval in doing so, and I made a mental note to take them to task after the exercise was terminated. No big deal, I thought! But, it turned out to be a big deal, after all!

"Terminate the exercise," came the call over the sound-powered phone. I was stunned, but only long enough to absorb the implications of my status. I had a round chambered without permission. The next call on the phone sealed my fate. "Report all chambers clear!" In sequence turrets one and two reported all chambers clear. Then came my report, and my throat was suddenly very dry as I reported.

"Turret three reporting guns one and two clear. There is a round in gun three!" There was a two second silence before my earphones exploded.

"What? Turret three, understand you have a live round in gun number three?"

"Yes, Sir", I replied meekly. There followed a series of obscenities from the weapons officer the like of which I have not since heard in my 33 years of duty in the Navy.

"Who was the @#$%^&*+ idiot who authorized that?" the strangling voice asked.

"I did, Sir!", I responded weakly. There was no way I could blame it on an over eager gun crew.

"Wait one," the voice said.

It was about now that I noticed that Wisconsin was turning and accelerating away from the gun line. I can only imagine the scene between the weapons officer and the captain. The ship began a 360-degree turn to get her back onto the gun line for another run to clear the No.3 barrel in turret three. We fired it and the rest was history. I suspect my movement to the navigation training program on the bridge was directly connected to the incident, but no one ever actually told me so.

The transit across the North Atlantic Ocean to Europe was one of sleepless nights as I learned the intricacies of celestial navigation. Teams made up of two midshipmen each were put under the tutelage of a Chief Boatswain's Mate. Each team was required to keep track of *Wisconsin*'s progress across the North Atlantic. We did this purely through celestial navigation by which, four or five times a day, we shot fixes on the stars, moon, and the sun. Evan Parker was my navigation teammate, and our first star fix as we passed 200 miles east of New York harbor was inauspicious, to say the least. It took us at least three hours to resolve our five star fix, and when we had plotted it, we found U.S.S. *Wisconsin* to be somewhere just south of Albany, New York. We improved considerably over the next ten days. But, since the sun set, that time of year at high latitudes, as late as 11:00, we were forced to stay up late. By the same token, sunrise occurred at about 4:00 in the morning. It was a long transit.

Each morning there was a ritual which sticks in my mind to this day. It was called "holystoning" the deck. There was only one small part of the deck, forward of the number one turret, where there was wood to holystone. I believe it was an area reserved for ceremonial purposes. It was the only way I can explain an expanse of main deck of a ship made of 46,000 tons of armored steel that was inlaid with fine Philippine mahogany. It was probably 30 feet wide and 75 feet long. Each morning after breakfast the Chief Bo'sun would line up six of us in our bare feet with our trousers rolled up. Each of us was given what looked like a four foot length of broom handle and a pumice-like stone the size and shape of a brick. In the top of the brick was a depression worn (obviously) by the constant abrasion of a broom handle. This was where we thrust the bottom end of the broom handle.

The bo'sun lined us up side by side, standing athwartship and facing forward, and we bent over the brick holding the broom handle high and low with both hands. The end of the stick was held tightly in the groove in the brick. A sailor with a hose sprayed sea water onto the deck ahead of us, and the bo'sun exhorted us to move the bricks back and forth in unison. Moving ahead at a very slow pace, we sanded the mahogany surface with those holystone bricks vigorously. Normally, sailors used to holystone the wooden decks of their ships to the tune of a sea chanty, not only to break the monotony, but also to give rhythm and efficiency to the process. So, we sang.

If we didn't sing loud enough, the bo'sun reminded us that we "could stay here all god damn day." He started out with an old tune. Once we caught on, we found that we could make it fun. In a loud baritone the bo'sun kicked it off, and we swung our holystones to the beat of the tune.

"Away, away with sword and drum,

Here we come, full of rum.

Looking for someone to put on the run,

The armored cruiser squadron."

The tempo was increased ever so slightly with each stanza After about 20 stanzas we were going so fast the rhythm broke down and, laughing aloud, we would regroup and start all over again. I never knew how many stanzas there were to that sea chanty...but the Chief Bo'sun knew them all. It was a daily ritual imposed, I assume, by someone who wanted to instill in us a sense of what it had been like in the old days when the Navy was comprised of wooden ships and iron men. Maybe it was the bo'sun's idea. Maybe it came from higher up. The only classmates whose names I can recall who holystoned Wisconsin's foredeck with me were Walt Gragg, Evan Parker, and a guy named Roesch. The rest have faded from my memory!

About this time, as we were getting into the higher latitudes west of the British Isles, a monster storm bore down on us like the Grim Reaper. As I was later to learn, this turned out to be the "mother of all storms." Meteorologists will tell you that since there is friction between the air and the surface of the water over which it passes, there is a direct relationship between certain of the parameters which are obtained on the open ocean. One of these important parameters is surface wind velocity, and the other is "fetch." Fetch is the distance of open water over which a surface wind has the ability to interact uninterrupted. The stronger the wind and the greater the fetch, the greater will be the size of the swells (or seas). The swells of the storm through which *Wisconsin* plunged that spring were more than 75 feet from the troughs to the crests...the height of a six-story building. The wind velocity was measured at over 100 knots! As our bo'sun mate put it, we were in an "ass-kicking storm."

As a good seaman should, the captain turned the ship into the wind and maintained engine rpms for about 12 knots. The battleship climbed up over each monstrous sea swell, then dove down, digging her bow into the next swell. Enormous walls of sea water raced down her weather decks all the way up to the 04 level. Ladders and catwalks were carried away, and a nest of large acetylene tanks was torn loose on the 03 level. All access to the weather decks was restricted. Because of our heading into the seas, we only experienced the roller coaster ride of pitching up and down, and there was little rolling. Finally, for reasons not explained to us, the ship turned to the northeast and we began quartering into the swells. The combination of rolling and pitching had its effect, and two thirds of the crew began to experience violent sea-sickness. It was one of my greatest fears. I could get car sick or airsick at the drop of a hat as a child.

The Chief Bo'sun told us that "a full stomach doesn't get sea sick." Walt Gragg and I decided to test the thesis and ate like we were ravenous...which we were not! In fact, the atmosphere on *Wisconsin* was conducive to sea sickness. Everywhere was the smell of vomit and stomach bile. People were "heaving their guts out" everywhere we looked. Not having the option to go out for a breath of fresh air only aggravated conditions. It was awful.

One day during the noon meal, Walt and I were seated side by side at a long mess table oriented athwartships. There were perhaps a dozen midshipmen at the table, most of them queasy at best. We stared listlessly at the food which the messmen had slopped on our aluminum trays.

It was far from a tantalizing culinary display. But, true to our pact, Walt and I ate like reluctant trenchermen. Since the table was sitting crossways, the effect of the rolls was substantial. In fact, the trays slid back and forth with each roll. On one particularly heavy roll, Walt's tray slid over in front of me momentarily before returning to its position in front of him. During its brief visit to my position, I stabbed my fork into a piece of the entree and ate it. He did the same to the tray belonging to the man on his right. Then the ship rolled back, and I was now looking at the tray of the man on my left. I performed the same bit of larceny on that tray too. Walt, watching me, did the same.

We began laughing...at first quietly. Then it became uproarious. With each subsequent roll we laughed harder. The tears were running down our cheeks and the others at the table were becoming increasingly annoyed at us. It somehow wasn't very funny to them. Finally, during one monstrous roll, the folding bench on which we were seated collapsed. There was food everywhere, and Walt and I only laughed harder. By now our messmates were furious at us. After extricating ourselves from the mess of spilled food, we decided to get a breath of fresh air despite the prohibition to all hands from venturing onto the weather decks.

To be safe from prying eyes, we climbed as far as we could go inside the superstructure of the ship... all the way to the 0-11 level. This was 11 levels above the main deck, and six levels above the bridge. The last three levels were, in fact, up vertical runged ladders hand over hand. At the top of the last ladder was a small hatch. We undogged the hatch and crawled out onto a very narrow catwalk…into the teeth of 100 mile-per-hour winds. As we crouched there on our hands and knees, we held tightly on to the hand rail. We knew instinctively that if we tried to stand up we would be blown over the rail and never be found again. Our position so high above the ship's metacenter caused us to move fore and aft and sideways through huge arcs of space. During the height of a roll we could look vertically down into the sea.

I recall the peculiar phenomenon of extremely high winds. It was hard to breathe, droplets of sea water stung like bbs, and the wind force tore open the buttons on my chambray work shirt. Speaking was out of the question…the shriek of the wind was unbelievable!

But the real drama was unfolding beyond the ship. Everywhere we looked was horizontally driven water…sheets of it…torn from the tops of swells and hitting with the force of a fire hose. The sky was not visible…just driven water. The monstrous seas were scary in their sheer enormity. When the ship settled into the trough, the wave crests towered over us. The bow would dig into the oncoming swell, and the forward part of the ship would literally disappear underwater. Then the bow would surge upward and reappear, and a huge wall of sea water 20 feet high would race aft, tearing ladders loose and finally cascading over the rising stern like a waterfall. It was nature's power in its ultimate form. No one who saw it could ever forget! Walt's words, shouted into my ear, adequately described my own feelings at the spectacle

"Holy s—t!"

We finally made it back down to the main deck without being caught and decided to descend to the mess deck directly below and go to our bunks. No useful training could be done under such conditions, so the midshipmen had been allowed to got to their bunks to try to get some rest. As we approached the ladder leading down, the ship lurched, and I fell against the stanchion holding the hatch open. My body weight knocked the stanchion loose, and the enormous hatch began to fall onto its coaming as I fell through the hatch opening. The fall to the mess deck was probably about eight or nine feet, so my right hand instinctively grabbed the edge of the coaming. I swung by one hand and looked up to see the hatch about to fall onto my hand. In a fraction of a second I realized that the hatch (weighing several hundred pounds) was about to amputate all of my fingers on the cutting edge of the coaming! My mind told my hand to let go…but it was too late. There was a resounding clang and I felt considerable pain in my right hand as I hung there.

Someone lifted the hatch up and off my hand as I swung my feet over and dropped onto the ladder. To my utter astonishment my fingers were all intact. One of them hurt like crazy…my ring finger. My brand new class ring had been flattened like a doughnut. It had absorbed all of the force of the descending hatch, saving my fingers from the guillotine. It took a trip to the sickbay to finally get the ring removed from my mangled finger…with no permanent damage! Later that fall I took the ring to a jeweler and learned that the charge to repair the ring exceeded its original cost. My next stop was a pawn shop (my first visit ever to one of those establishments), where the proprietor gave me 20 dollars for it. A few years later during a return visit to Annapolis, I stopped at the pawn shop to reclaim the ring. Of course, it was long gone. So much for rings. As far as I am concerned the ring was a bargain...regardless of the price. It saved all of the fingers on my right hand...and my Naval career!

Somehow, I knew that the captain, sitting in his chair on the bridge...watching the same spectacle through the windows, was reveling in the feeling of hurling himself against the most powerful forces of nature in the one vehicle most prepared to overcome them...a 50 thousand ton Dreadnaught!

Chapter 20:
HMS Leopard

*"It is upon the Navy, under the good Providence of God, that the
wealth, safety and strength of the kingdom do chiefly depend."*
- Preamble to the Articles of War, Charles II

The moment Stu Harrison and I saw her, I knew exactly what we were going to do. The most recent in a long line of her majesty's ships bearing the name, HMS *Leopard* lay at anchor ("swinging on the hook," as we used to say) inside the Grand Harbor of the port of Valetta on the island of Malta, looking every inch the British man-of-war that she was. Valetta is the capital and principal port of Malta, an island situated between Sicily and Africa, the scene of many historic battles in World War II. It is famous in naval aviation as the site where the great British naval fighter, the Glouster "Gladiator"—a 1934-vintage biplane—made its last heroic stand (against modern German fighters!).

The two of us, Lieutenant Commander Stuart Harrison and I, represented that dangerous combination, a couple of bored sailors on liberty with absolutely nothing to do. We had seen all that there was to see in Valetta. The afternoon was warm. It was a quiet Sunday in April 1962. Our own ship, USS *Shangri-La*, an old *Essex*-class aircraft canter, lay at anchor a little farther out in the harbor.

We'd had perhaps two gin and tonics each at the club on the naval base, and then decided to do a bit of sightseeing. There really are not too many sights to see in Valetta...and we had seen them all. Therefore, it shouldn't have surprised us that we each thought, standing on the quay at Valetta, at the same moment, of visiting a British man-of-war.

At a distance of about a quarter mile the ship had the menacing look of a vessel built to punish the enemy. Designed as an antiaircraft frigate of the 2,500-ton displacement class, she sported four 4.5-inch guns in two twin turrets, two twin 40 millimeter Bofors gun turrets and, for an anti-submarine weapon, a Squid triple-depth-charge mortar. I knew from the air intelligence officer's briefing of several days ago that *Leopard* could make over twenty-five knots at flank speed, had a complement of 195-205 officers and "ratings" (as enlisted

HMS Leopard F14/37 SFPU, Caribbean Sea, 1963. (Official Royal Navy photograph)

men are called in the Royal Navy). The ship measured 330 feet in length at the waterline, had a beam of 40 feet and a draft of twelve feet at combat load.

Tied up at the quay wall was *Leopard*'s liberty launch. The Brits called it the liberty boat, and it was manned by a senior boatswain's (bo'sun's) mate and a non-rated engine man. The boat had just arrived from a trip to *Leopard*, and Stu and I had assessed the professional way in which the bo'sun had brought her in to the quay wall. He had a little ship's bell on the launch, which he rang very ceremoniously whenever he wanted to call for a power change. One bell obviously meant "all engines stopped" (the launch only had one engine). Two bells meant "all ahead one third," three bells meant two thirds power, four bells called for flank speed (probably fifteen knots), and five bells meant "all engines astern full" (there was only one backing speed). Both boat crewmen were dressed in immaculate whites and were obviously very proud of their ship, whose name was emblazoned on a sign attached to the launch's handrail as well as painted on her transom. The rating had the ship's name woven into the band of his cap.

The bo'sun had just ordered the engine to be shut down, verified the security of the two lines attaching her to bollards on the quay wall, and stepped ashore to enjoy a smoke. Stu and I studied the picture of an old British salt, puffing on a cigarette on a quay wall with his launch in the foreground and the parent ship, a Royal Navy frigate, in the background. It was the kind of tableau one could expect to find in a painting on the wall of a maritime museum, for example, at Greenwich.

We approached the bo'sun and identified ourselves as naval officers from USS *Shangri-La*. Then we asked him if ship's visiting hours were still on. The time was about three p.m. He flipped the cigarette onto the macadam quay, ground it out carefully with his shoe, and came about three-quarters of the way to attention. I sensed in him the willingness to recognize our status as naval officers, but in a grudging sort of way, since we represented that "upstart navy from the colonies." He was, in a word, deigning to speak with us.

"Well, Sir," he said to me, "we really don't 'ave visiting hours as such. But, I'm sure our captain would be 'appy to 'ave you aboard for a look around."

I told him we would be delighted to come aboard for a visit and thanked him very much. I am not sure whether I expected him to jump into the launch and take us right out ... but he didn't do that. Instead, he lit another cigarette and reverted to his ruminations, which he had been enjoying before we came along and interrupted them. He was obviously on some kind of schedule, perhaps every thirty minutes, and did not intend to interrupt it for two U.S. Navy lieutenant commanders who obviously had absolutely nothing to do at the moment. Stu and I waited, talking to one another in low tones for about ten more minutes. Suddenly the bo'sun finished his cigarette and addressed us as though we had just this moment arrived. "Well, Sirs, if you would come aboard now, we will go out to 'the ship.'" Sailors the world over always refer to their ship as "the ship," as though she were the only one in the harbor. To them she is!

As the launch neared *Leopard*'s port side, or unofficial, accommodation ladder, I watched for the subtle signal which I knew must pass between the bo'sun and *Leopard*'s officer of the day, telling him that he carried two unannounced visitors requiring some modicum of professional courtesy. Had we been in uniform, he would no doubt have brought us to the starboard, or formal, ladder. I never saw the signal. We came to a stop alongside the accommodation ladder with a gentle rubbing of fenders, and the crisp, professional ringing of the engine-order telegraph signals. I found myself wondering idly how many times the bo'sun and his engineman had performed that little bit of nautical showmanship.

As we stepped off the launch and onto the bottom step of the accommodation ladder, I noticed that the OOD, telescope tucked under his left elbow, had moved to the top step of the ladder in anticipation of our arrival. Doubtless, he had looked us over with his telescope while we were en route. The telescope had been decorated with the same white line and marlinspike seamanship that U.S. Navy bo'suns use to decorate their OODs badge of authority.

Stu stepped onto the quarterdeck, came to attention, then turned toward the ship's White Ensign fluttering on the stern, rendering it the standard tribute paid by a naval officer in civilian clothes. "Request permission to come aboard, Sir," Stu asked in a loud voice.

"Granted," came the reply in the clipped, crisp British accent, "Welcome to her majesty's ship *Leopard*." I followed suit. A sallow-faced leftenant gave us the standard escorted tour of *Leopard*, which took about thirty minutes, then delivered us to the wardroom for refreshments. This was, I thought, why Stu and I had really ventured aboard. We wanted to see how they served liquor aboard a Royal Navy vessel since it is not customary—or legal—for liquor to be carried in U.S. naval vessels except for medicinal purposes. We soon found out.

Our escort had already informed us that they were expecting the ship's commanding officer to return at any moment with almost all the rest of the officers. It seemed that they were defending the ship's honor at a football (soccer) match over at the naval base. The escort was obviously going to baby-sit us until we either left or the Captain returned, whichever occurred first. He led us down to the wardroom, located aft on the deck directly below the quarterdeck.

A steward's mate appeared as if by magic and began setting up the bar. I assumed that it was in preparation for the returning soccer team, and not for us. Nonetheless, when he was set up, he offered us a drink. We accepted, and Stu and I slowly began sipping what must have been our third gin and tonic of the day. I did note that the Bombay gin was poured sparingly into the glass. For that I was silently grateful. The time was about four p.m....sixteen hundred hours.

We stood at the bar chatting. It was a pleasant atmosphere. The wardroom was commodiously appointed, the afternoon was warm and balmy...and the gin and tonic was pleasantly refreshing...not heavy. On one bulkhead was one large mahogany plaque decorated with a coat of arms and *Leopard's* name. Further along on the bulkhead was a magnificent, framed photograph of Her Royal Highness, Queen Elizabeth the Second.

Suddenly, there was a commotion on the quarterdeck. Stu and I could tell from the sounds of ribaldry that the soccer team was returning victorious. Moments later the officers among them piled into the wardroom and headed straight for the bar. Our escort made introductions all around, and the Skipper most graciously insisted on refreshing our drinks. There seemed to be a sense of anticipation in the group which I couldn't quite fathom until the commanding officer, with an extremely straight face, explained that they had received two new officers this very day and that they were all looking forward to their proper initiation, which was about to begin. We were very fortunate, he pointed out, that Stu and I had happened aboard at the perfect time to witness their time-honored initiation ceremony.

The two newly arrived "subleftenants" were summoned to the wardroom to meet all the officers, as well as "our two Yankee friends from *Shangri-La*." The two young men, Arbuthnot and Strothers, were young indeed. I estimated their ages to be no more than early twenties. Beer seemed to be the refreshment of choice for the victorious soccer team from HMS *Leopard* as the afternoon wore on. The combined effect of several beers each, the exhaustion of having played a vigorous game of soccer in the blazing Mediterranean sun, and the pleasant relaxation in the wardroom had its effect. Most of the gentlemen in the wardroom were in high spirits, and nearly everything anybody said seemed to be hilariously funny.

At some juncture, someone asked the Skipper when they could start the initiations. "Right away," he announced to a chorus of hoorays. "Lieutenant Atherton, front and center," the Skipper roared. A lean whippet of a young man stepped forward, and with a great effort appeared to be keeping a straight face.

"Yes, Sir," he said.

"Atherton," the Skipper announced, "You are currently the wardroom record-holder in our event. Would you be so good as to demonstrate to our two new officers, as well as to the two Americans, how to do the drill?" As an afterthought, the Skipper added, "Oh yes, Atherton, feel free to go for a personal best if you wish."

"Aye, aye, Skipper," Atherton said enthusiastically, "I'd like very much to give it a bloody go for an all time wardroom record." There was a roar of approval from everyone in the room.

"Hear, hear," someone shouted. "An all time record. Hear, hear!" Someone else chimed in, and there was a toast to Atherton with many "hear, hears" echoing from the crowd.

Some chairs were cleared away from the wardroom between two scuttles (portholes), one on either side. The bar had been set up next to the forward scuttle on the starboard side of the wardroom. In response to a nod from the Skipper, the bartender poured a full beer into a fresh glass and placed it on the bar in front of Lieutenant Atherton. The Skipper consulted his wrist watch and the wardroom grew silent as he watched the sweep second hand march around toward the twelve o'clock position. When the hand passed the 50 mark, the Skipper intoned, "Ten seconds." At exactly the twelve o'clock position he shouted, "Go!" and punched the stopwatch's "start" button.

Atherton, who had been standing at full attention in front of the bar, shouted, "What Ho!" and downed the glass of beer as fast as he could gulp it. Slamming the empty glass onto the bar top, Atherton sprinted across the wardroom and literally dove through the scuttle, apparently reaching up to grasp an unknown stanchion outside and a little bit above the aperture. Swinging his body, legs and feet completely outside the scuffle, Atherton athletically pulled himself upward and out of sight. We could hear him scrambling across the deck above us at a full sprint, port to starboard.

At this point, I noticed the bartender refilling the glass of beer Atherton had just emptied. There was a scrambling and huffing as Atherton's feet, then legs, and then body appeared through the starboard scuttle. As soon as his feet touched the deck he rushed to the bar, scooped up the glass of beer and gulped down its contents. As he slammed the empty glass down on the bar the Skipper punched the stop button on his wristwatch and shouted, "Mark!" He studied the watch for a moment to a hushed room, and then announced calmly," Twenty-two point four seconds, a new wardroom record by one-tenth of a second!"

The ovation was deafening! There were shouts of "A new record," and "Hooray," and "Would you believe it?" Several officers came up to Atherton, who was puffing heavily, and pounded him on the back. "Bloody good show, old man," several of them said. It was a rare moment of camaraderie in HMS *Leopard*. There, in the middle of the Grand Harbor in

Valetta, Malta—a sovereign slice of the British Empire—a noteworthy athletic achievement by one of its warships was being celebrated.

I took the opportunity to observe the expressions on the faces of the two young "subleftenants." They were a study in adulation...for the event itself, for the record holder, but most importantly for the histrionics. This was camaraderie...esprit de *corps*...morale-building...male bonding...the stuff that had made the Royal Navy the most feared in the world for centuries. To say that Strothers and Arbuthnot were entranced would be understatement.

When the commotion died down the Skipper took the floor again. "Gentlemen," he announced, "may I have your attention. We will begin the real part of the initiation in a few minutes. Please take this opportunity to charge your glasses." The bartender busied himself filling glasses and took advantage of the quiet moment to announce to the Skipper in a voice that was perhaps too loud, "Skipper, we seem to be running out of bitters." The Skipper nodded and made no other reply.

"Which of you young gentlemen would like to try his hand at a go-around?" the Skipper asked. He was staring directly at Strothers and Arbuthnot. Both volunteered simultaneously. The Skipper picked Arbuthnot, the taller and rangier of the two new officers. "Very well, Arbuthnot. Have a go at it. But, remember, although we will be timing you, it will be unofficial since it will have been your first time." I noted that the bartender had already filled a new glass for the potential new pretender to the throne.

The young "sub-leftenant" drew himself erect and took several deep breaths while the Skipper consulted his watch. "Ten seconds," he intoned. Time seemed to stand still as the breathless wardroom watched with great interest. "Go," shouted the commanding officer of HMS *Leopard*, punching his stopwatch.

"What Ho!" shouted Arbuthnot as he seized the glass. The young officer was not as deft as his predecessor and spilled beer down his shirt front in the process of gulping it down. Slam, went the beer glass on the bar top. The gangling figure of "sub-leftenant" Arbuthnot arced across the small room and went partly through the narrow scuttle, then stopped for a moment while he clawed at the invisible stanchion on the deck above him. It was clear to Stu and me that this attempt was not going to threaten the record set by Atherton a few moments earlier.

We all listened to Arbuthnot's footsteps pattering across the overhead and watched with great interest as he re-entered the starboard scuttle, fell to the deck, raced to the bar and downed the second beer. You could have heard a pin drop as the Skipper, with much drama, studied the dial of his watch. "Twenty-seven seconds," he announced very solemnly. Not bad, Arbuthnot," he observed. "Not at all bad for a first try." He turned to Strothers and asked, "What about you, Strothers. Are you ready for a go?"

"Yes, Sir," the young man responded. The near maniacal glint in his eye told me that no isk was too great to ensure that he beat Arbuthnot's time. Strothers was shorter and more olidly put together. I judged that he might very well beat his peer.

I was also acquiring the impression that I was witnessing a carefully scripted performance that had probably been replicated elsewhere on other Royal Navy ships for decades...perhaps even centuries. Strothers did better, I thought, until he landed on the deck inside the starboard scuttle and his feet went out from under him. Down he went with a crash. The delay in scrambling back to his feet cost him a few precious seconds. He was clearly crestfallen when the Skipper announced his time as twenty-nine point seven seconds. For the second time, while refreshing everyone's drinks, the steward at the bar announced to the Skipper in a voice that was again a bit too loud, "Skipper, we are just about out of bitters." Again the Skipper acknowledged the remark with nothing more than a nod.

My instincts told me it was time for Act II. The Skipper began the action by addressing himself to Strothers. "Strothers," he opened with a frown. "You need more traction if you ever hope to set any kind of record aboard *Leopard*. Why don't you go down to your cabin and put on a pair of gym shoes. Then we'll give you another try at it. This time, however, I warn you that it will go into your all time average record book, which I keep." A chastened Strothers disappeared on his mission. The drama unfolded as I watched the Skipper turn to Arbuthnot.

"Arbuthnot, be a good fellow and go below to the spirits locker. Bring us two bottles of bitters. Here, take the keys...and be quick about it." As soon as Arbuthnot disappeared, the wardroom, as if on cue, sprang into action. Every piece of furniture was quickly moved. It reminded me of a stage crew moving sets between acts. Each person seemed to have his assignment clearly delineated...and he did it with speed and precision. The bar, which was on wheels, was rolled aft to the other scuttle. The chairs and tables were all moved to new positions such that to a new, inattentive, or perhaps alcohol-impaired observer, it might appear that nothing had been changed. The framed photograph of Her Royal Highness, the Queen, had even been moved to a new spot behind the new position of the bar. The large, mahogany *Leopard* plaque remained where it was because it apparently was too large to move and was attached to the bulkhead securely.

During this activity there was a great deal of low volume snickering. The sense of anticipation was overwhelming. Timing seemed critical. Whatever was going to occur had to happen after Strothers returned to the wardroom, but before Arbuthnot got back. It was obvious to Stu and me that such opportunities came only rarely. The gentlemen of *Leopard's* wardroom were clearly intent upon getting the most out of this one. Within a minute Strothers reappeared wearing sneakers and a brighter gleam in his eye. As he approached the bar the Skipper addressed him with a neutral expression that must have taken every ounce of composure he possessed: "Well, Strothers, are you ready for another go at it?"

"Yes, Sir," the young man said. "Very good," the Skipper responded, and consulted his wristwatch. The bartender poured the glass of beer, and the entire wardroom held its breath "Ten seconds," intoned the Skipper. My grin was so broad that it took a very stern sideways glare from him to warn me to wipe it off my face. I glanced over at Stu. He was managing to look more serious, somehow. It must have taken superhuman effort!

"Go," shouted the Skipper.

"What Ho!" cried Strothers as he downed his beer and darted across the wardroom toward the new scuttle. I had already divined what the surprise was going to be. Armed with a little more experience, and determined to do better this time, Strothers made a much less tentative dive though the scuttle, half twisting in mid air to grasp at the stanchion, which everyone but Strothers knew was not there. Strothers' head and shoulders disappeared through the scuttle with the legs and feet quickly following. Then we heard the yelp of fright, followed by a long, drawn out wail. There was the sound of a splash and a great deal of laughter as Stu and I ran to the port side scuttle. There was about a twenty foot drop from the scuttle to the water, and Strothers' entry point was about ten feet aft of the port accommodation ladder. We saw the boatswain's mate of the watch standing at the bottom of the ladder, boat hook in hand, pulling a chastened (but smiling) "sub-leftenant" Strothers toward him.

From the look on the sailor's face I could tell that he had done this countless times before. Of course, Strothers was sent below to change into dry clothing before Arbuthnot returned with the two bottles of bitters. Arbuthnot, when he returned, was subjected to the same indignity as Strothers, and managed it with as much aplomb, and with no hint of a clue from the man Strothers, a hapless victim only a few minutes earlier (his straight face was a flawless production). All in all, it was a wonderful day for the wardroom of HMS *Leopard*.

Later, as Stu and I rode the liberty boat back to the Valetta quay, we ruminated over the notion that ships of Her Royal Highness' Navy had similar rites of passage for their young officers and enlisted men, probably dating back centuries. From Khartoum to Mandalay, from Cairo to Capetown, from the West Indies to Australia, wherever the men and ships went, British sailors and soldiers have maintained their esprit de corps with similar capers, aimed at easing the pain of family separation and cementing the bonds of mutual understanding only acquired through shared adversity. Kipling called them the "Sons of the Widow:"

"Hands off o' the Sons of the Widow,
Hands off o' the goods in her shop,
For the Kings must come down and
the Emperors frown,
When the Widow at Windsor says, 'Stop"

Chapter 21:
"Sixth Fleet, Arriving"

*"Traditions of the Royal Navy? I'll give you traditions of the
Navy—rum, buggery, and the lash."*

- Winston Churchill: To the Board of Admiralty 1939

Whenever a senior U.S. Naval officer arrives aboard a Navy ship, regardless of the mode of transportation or the location of the ship, the officer of the day ensures that his arrival is properly announced. The ship's loudspeaker system, the "1MC," sounds with the distinctive bells and the Chief Boatswain's Mate's call: "Ding, ding. Ding, ding, W*isconsin* arriving." This, of course, would mean that the commanding officer of the USS *Wisconsin* had just arrived. When he leaves, a similar announcement is made, indicating that he is departing.

However, when the aircraft carrier, *Saratoga*, reported in for duty with the 6th Fleet in the Mediterranean in 1971, there was the foreboding sense that the new fleet commander might pay us a visit on a less formal basis. As the CAG on *Saratoga*, I was only mildly interested in such matters, since I normally had little to do with visit protocol. But, like Air Force General Curtis LeMay, the new fleet commander had a reputation for unexpected visits. Sometimes they were traumatic. The legend that was being bandied about at the time was of a visit the gentleman made to one of his ships as it lay tied up to the fleet pier in Naples, Italy. The commanding officer of this particular vessel had enjoyed a late night of liberty on the town after an extensive period at sea. He felt that he deserved the right to let his hair down this first night in port.

At exactly 0730 on a Saturday morning, the three-star Admiral (commander of the 6th Fleet) arrived pierside, and his presence was not noticed by a rather lax quarterdeck watch until it was too late. He was halfway across the ship's brow when the bo'sun's mate of the watch recognized him and seized the telephone to call the skipper's stateroom. The fleet commander held up a warning hand and the bo'sun, understanding the signal, placed the telephone back in its cradle...filled with foreboding. He also knew instinctively not to ring the ship's bell and announce the arrival of the surprise visitor over the 1MC.

The admiral knew this class of destroyer like the back of his hand and proceeded down the passageway, followed by a nearly distraught officer of the day, and headed for the stateroom of the sleeping skipper. Without knocking, the huge man walked into the stateroom. Picking up the poor commanding officer's uniform trousers, which had been thrown over a chair, he shook him gently. The skipper rolled over in bed and opened his eyes, grumpy at being awakened this way. There, standing in his crisp khaki uniform bedecked with the insignia of a three-star admiral, was his boss, twice removed! It was an apocryphal story. But, I have no doubt that its original version was true.

So, there was a certain amount of anticipation as *Saratoga* "in-chopped" into the Mediterranean Sea that our ship might get such a surprise visit. This was especially appropriate since recent message traffic from that gentleman to his ships had urged utmost security precautions, particularly for those ships which carried nuclear weapons. The terrorist threat in the 1970s was a "hot button" topic for all the armed services.

A few months later we were operating in the Tyrrhenian Sea west of the Italian Peninsula. It was mid-morning, and we were just about to begin re-spotting aircraft for a day's flight operations. At the time we were working a noon to midnight flying schedule. I happened to be up in the air boss's roost (primary flight control), and someone called out a visual sighting on a U.S. Navy *Sea King* helicopter approaching at low altitude. The air boss's voice boomed into the radio frequency reserved for flight operations (land/launch frequency): "Navy helicopter approaching *Saratoga* from the east, identify yourself." There was no answer. The alert air boss then pushed a button on his communications panel and notified first the bridge, then the Marine Air Detachment. That took all of three seconds. Next he picked up the bullhorn and ordered the "Tillie," an enormous crash and rescue crane, to drive out into the middle of the only available landing area, blocking it off. Now the helicopter couldn't land, even if it wanted to do so, without permission. By now the air boss's assistant had arrived and continued to attempt to establish radio contact with the helicopter.

Finally, an extremely nervous voice came up on the radio and identified himself as the helicopter pilot, saying that he was en route on a ship-to-ship mission and was developing engine difficulties. He asked permission to land. The air boss told him to "wait one!"

By this time the Marine Detachment, fully dressed in helmets, flak vests, and armed with M-14 rifles, had deployed themselves out of sight in the catwalks on either side of the number one and two elevators.

Now we were ready! The air boss directed the Tillie to clear the landing area and gave the helicopter clearance to land. The helo touched down, its passenger door opened, and three men dressed in camouflaged uniforms darted out, carrying hand weapons. One of the three stopped when he saw the platoon of Marines appear out of the catwalks on either side, weapons pointed at him. The other two dashed for the catwalk and were wrestled down to the flight deck and hand-cuffed by several very eager Marines. I thought the hand-cuffing was rather roughly done and clapped my hands in approval. We all knew the drill. The invaders were supposed to dart to the catwalk and disappear into the bowels of the ship, hiding out until the operation was over. They were supposed to be terrorists carrying explosives powerful enough to severely disable the ship if properly placed. I was proud that *Saratoga* had passed her first test.

At this point, the commander of the 6th Fleet walked sedately down the steps and was met cordially by the ship's executive officer…who couldn't hide his smile. I met with the admiral during the course of his three hour visit and tried to answer his questions regarding the maintenance support of my air wing's aircraft in a dispersed mode of operations which he was considering. I was definitely not in favor of the whole idea, and I think that fact came across loud and clear during the course of my answers. That afternoon he departed to the ringing of the bo'sun's pipe and bell and the announcement: "Ding, Ding. Ding, Ding, 6th Fleet departing."

Several months later *Saratoga* received a message from 6th Fleet asking for a firepower demonstration and air show for the flagship's dependents' day cruise. Each year ships are allowed to take their crew's dependents out for a day's cruise to include demonstrations of the ship's activities. The 6th Fleet flagship was *Springfield*, a cruiser homeported in Gaeta, Italy, a few miles south of Naples. The request would, of course, be honored. I set my own staff to the task of writing an operations order for the best firepower demonstration the fleet commander had ever seen. Then, in the few days preceding the dependent's day cruise, we practiced several times to get our timing perfect.

The demonstration would open with a simultaneous supersonic low pass by a pair of F-4 Phantoms coming from opposite sides of the ship. Then an RA-5C *Vigilante* would pass over the ship, dumping fuel from its empennage vent mast. When the plane was directly over the ship the pilot would engage the afterburner that would torch off the dumped fuel in a long stream of fire behind it that was quite spectacular.

There would also be strafing attacks by a section of two A-7 *Corsair* IIs on a smoke light in the water alongside the ship. That would be followed by a low altitude bombing pass by a pair of A-6 *Intruders*, which would each drop 22 five hundred pound bombs in the retarded mode. This would be done on another smoke light in the water alongside the ship. Next, two F-4 *Phantoms* would drop a parachute flare ahead of the ship, then come around and shoot a live Sidewinder air-to-air missile at it. As soon as that was over an SH-3 *Sea King* helicopter would come close alongside the ship, firing their M-61 machine guns at another smoke light. Then they would dip their sonar dome in the water and hover for a few seconds before scooting away.

In order to ensure that there would be no glitches, I decided to ride the helicopter in the left seat with the squadron commanding officer, Commander Pete Braun, in the right seat. We would direct the show from a position close on the port quarter of the ship. Furthermore, our own air wing air show announcer, Lieutenant Commander "Pear" Favre, would be lowered from our helicopter via a hoist to the deck of Springfield, where he would announce the show over the cruiser's loud speaker system. Pear received his nickname from the general shape of his body, and was one of Fighter Squadron 31's premier radar intercept officers. After the show we would retrieve Pear via helicopter hoist and fly the return flight to *Saratoga,* which was in the area. The last thing that happened was a slight "curtsy," which Pete Braun executed with his helicopter just before we departed the area.

The air show went well, with only one glitch which I suspect nobody noticed, even though it almost gave me a heart attack! A smoke light had been put in the water ahead of the ship, intended to pass down the starboard side. We in the helo were on the opposite side of the ship directing traffic. Just before the first A-7 commenced his strafing run the OOD on *Springfield* decided to turn right to take the smoke light on his port side. This was in violation of the Op Order which I had provided to *Springfield,* and effectively placed our helo directly in the path of the ricocheting bullet stream from the A-7. The *Corsair* had already rolled into his strafing run when I saw what was developing. He never saw us! I yelled over the radio: "A-7 in strafing run, abort your run. Abort your run. ABORT YOUR RUN!" He aborted and let us move to the starboard side of the cruiser.

After we retrieved Pear Favre, after Pete had done his curtsy, and after the air wing participants had departed, I heard the 6th Fleet commander's voice come up on the radio giving us all a "well done!"

It was about a month later that *Saratoga* had a catastrophic sea water intake gasket failure that flooded a main machinery room. It took a month to effect the repairs in the harbor in Athens. The day we steamed out into the Aegean Sea to recommence our deployment, *Saratoga* experienced an identical failure on the gasket in the other main machinery room. This time the crew took appropriate action and shut off the main intake stop valve in time to prevent any damage. Nevertheless, *Saratoga* went dead in the water, and the ship sounded general quarters. Of course, the carrier notified the 6th Fleet by immediate message, and *Springfield* just happened to be in the area.

It was as beautiful a day as one can find in the Aegean Sea in the summer…blue skies and an azure ocean. But *Saratoga* looked obscene! She sat there "as idle as a painted ship upon a painted ocean," surrounded by garbage! The failure had occurred just after the bo'sun's mate had announced the dumping of trash and garbage from the fantail over the 1MC.

In the pandemonium that followed sounding of general quarters the Bo'sun's Mate of the Watch failed to announce the termination of the dumping. Normally, it doesn't look bad, because the trash and garbage disappears in the wake of the ship as it passes on. But *Saratoga* was dead in the water, and there was an ever-widening circle of jetsam surrounding the ship. It looked absolutely awful. I was feeling personally embarrassed at the sight when someone shouted, "Here comes *Springfield!*" Lo and behold, I looked to the east and there, hull down on the horizon, was a pillar of black smoke. *Springfield,* the 6th Fleet flagship, was coming straight at us at flank speed. How horrible! That was my second encounter with *Springfield.* The third encounter proved to be much more memorable!

The time came late in Saratoga's Mediterranean deployment, for a change of command for the 6th Fleet. The new commander had been ordered in, and certain people from *Saratoga* (including the CAG) had been invited to the ceremony. *Springfield,* looking every bit the neat, clean, and trim flagship she was, sat there pierside in downtown Naples where the ceremony was held…and what a ceremony it was!

Springfield was sitting virtually in downtown Naples. I went aboard and was escorted to a seat bearing my name in about the third row center. There were a number of local dignitaries present; perhaps moreso than one might find at the average 6th Fleet change of command ceremony. That was because the departing commander was being elevated to a four-star assignment as commander of the Material Command...the chief logistician for the Navy. His relief, a friend of mine and also an aviator, had a great future. So, it was a pleasant ceremony for me to attend. The usual ritual was followed until time came for the honors to be rendered to the senior officer present, who was a participant, the commander-in-chief of the NATO Southern Command, CinCSouth. We all stood stiffly at attention while a 20-gun salute was fired by *Springfield*'s saluting battery. At the report of the first gun, I was startled by the loud echo which bounced off the tall glass skyscrapers surrounding the pier. I let my eyes wander and saw thousands of faces in the windows watching this spectacle of NATO unity being performed under their very eyes. The windows all shook with each succeeding gun report.

My gaze returned to the three principles on the speakers' platform and found their expressions to be a study in scarcely contained delight. They were obviously taking pleasure in the fact that thousands of Neopolitan businessmen, normally a sophisticated class of Italians, were being forcibly reminded of their reliance upon the United States Navy. I wish I had a photograph of the three men; a brand-new, three-star admiral taking over, the outgoing three star-admiral about to put on his fourth star, and their boss, another four-star admiral. It was no coincidence that the ceremony was held in mid-morning on a working day and right in downtown Naples!

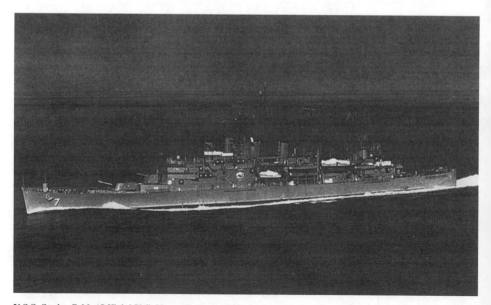

U.S.S. Springfield. (Official U.S. Navy photograph)

Five years later I found myself working for the very same gentleman who gave up command of the 6th Fleet that day. By now, he had been elevated to command of the Atlantic Fleet (CinCLantFleet), the unified Atlantic Command (CinCLant), and the NATO command, Supreme Allied Command Atlantic (SacLant), all at the same time. He was about to retire and was sending me to make what turned out to be my last visit to *Springfield*. The man scheduled to relieve him at CinCLant happened to be the 6th Fleet commander. By way of bringing his relief up to speed on numerous issues associated with the three-hatted job, he sent me over to do the briefing. I carried two filing boxes containing important files about the hottest issues. One box, which was unsealed, contained issues regarding the CinCLant Fleet and CinCLant assignments. The other box was sealed with a NATO security emblem.

I was not supposed to know what was in the sealed box. For me it was a dilemma. I was not so foolish as to suppose the incoming commander would refrain from questioning me about the contents of both boxes. I would look and sound foolish if I tried to answer the NATO questions without bringing myself up to speed at least on the general subjects…and I would certainly be expected to know the answers. What to do? The admiral's executive assistant, a very wise captain, understood my problem when I explained it to him. Without a word he reached inside his safe and handed me a new NATO seal. He just looked at me, never saying a word. Our gazes met, and we understood one another perfectly.

The flight in CinCLantFleet's specially equipped P-3 Orion took 11 hours from Norfolk to Naples. The entire flight was spent boning up on the issue papers in both boxes. Just before we landed in Naples, I scraped off the broken NATO seal, licked the new emblem, and sealed the box again. I remember walking up to *Springfield* tied up at the pier in Gaeta. As I stepped onto the brow and prepared to come aboard, carrying my two filing boxes, I heard the familiar sound of the bo'sun's pipe and bell on the 1MC, "Ding, ding. Ding, ding. Captain, United States Navy, arriving!." It was a good sound!

Chapter 22:
"You May Fire When Ready, Gridley"

"Leave the artillerymen alone. They are an obstinate lot."

- Napoleon I, 1769-1821

Every plebe at the U.S. Naval Academy is required to memorize certain items of naval historical trivia. One of those are the immortal words by Admiral Dewey to the captain of the armored cruiser *Olympia* at the Battle of Manila Bay in 1898, "You may fire when ready, Gridley." Captain Charles Vernon Gridley followed instructions, and the rest is history.

Twenty-seven years after graduation from the Naval Academy, thirty-one years after I was required to memorize that deathless phrase, the words came back to haunt me when USS *Gridley* nearly caused an international incident. The setting for this rather dramatic incident occurred in about June 1978 in the Caribbean Sea, a few miles southeast of the southeastern tip of Cuba. That particular stretch of ocean was set aside for live gun firing exercises by Navy vessels operating out of the Naval base at Guantanamo.

At the time of the incident *Gridley* was a guided missile destroyer (DLG-21) from the Atlantic Fleet, and was in the Caribbean to conduct some training exercises, including the firing of her two twin 5 inch 38 cal. gun mounts. Since this was to be a competitive exercise to qualify *Gridley* for the award of the Atlantic Fleet Battle Efficiency E, a judge was on hand to ensure that the rules contained in the fleet training manual were followed.

Accordingly, 24 hours prior to the exercise, an international notice to mariners (NOTM) was issued and broadcast to ensure no ships accidentally wandered into the area. It was both a political as well as a safety measure. The rules governing such competitive gunnery exercises (GunExs) were fairly complicated to ensure both a fair evaluation of the combat readiness of the participant, but also the safety of all ships involved. The target was a sled containing a vertical wooden surface about the size of a billboard. The sled was towed behind an ocean-going tug or other utility vessel at a prescribed speed and over a carefully defined geographical course. Of course, the tow cable was long enough to ensure that the towing

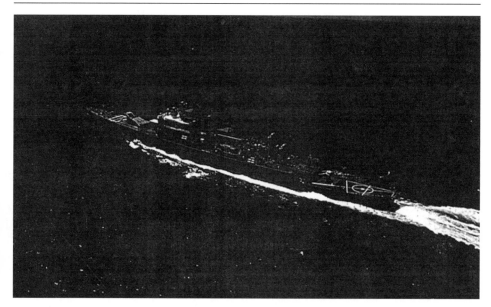

USS *Gridley* underway in the Indian Ocean. (Official U.S. Navy Photograph)

vessel was not put in any great jeopardy, and the firing range was set at 75 percent of the maximum range of the gun being evaluated. For the 5-inch 38 cal. gun that range was 10,000 yards (roughly five nautical miles).

The stage was set for the drama when *Gridley* set sail on the morning tide from the base at Guantanamo. By 10:30 a.m. she was in position at the prescribed northern edge of the exercise area, awaiting the arrival of the target. The skipper of the ship was on the bridge, and his ship had already been called to general quarters. The gun crews had been drilling for months, and everyone was anxiously awaiting the opportunity to compete with all other 5-inch 38 shooters in the Atlantic Fleet for the prize. The skipper was dressed in battle garb, his khaki shirt buttoned all the way to the neck, the cuffs of his wash-khaki trousers stuffed into his socks, his battle helmet snugged down tight and his Mae West life vest firmly secured around his chest. He fingered the binoculars slung around his neck nervously as the judge, standing next to him, announced in a pompous tone, "Captain, you are cleared to commence the exercise as soon as the target appears."

At that moment I was sitting at my desk at CinCLant headquarters, unaware of who or where *Gridley* was. The squawk box broke my concentration with an ominous announcement. I recognized the voice of the CinCLantFleet duty officer next door in the command center.

"Sir, the CinC is in the command center. You had better get in here!" Sensing the urgency in his voice, I dropped what I was doing and moved swiftly through the 3 cipher-locked doors that constituted my own secret access to the command center. When in a hurry, I used this special access route. No one else knew all of the cipher codes. No one else used this access. Within ten seconds I was standing at the rear of the CinCLant duty officer's desk in the middle of the amphitheater, asking him in a whisper what was going on. The reason for the whisper was that there was an interesting tableau of flag officers all standing there watching their four-star boss, who was also standing on the duty officer's dais holding the telephone to his ear and listening carefully. Standing at a respectful distance watching the CinC was his three-star deputy, and next to him was the Marine Corps major general from the staff. My own boss, the chief of staff for operations, was absent. For this reason I felt emboldened to do what I ultimately did. It was so quiet in the huge room that I thought I could hear my own heart beat. The duty officer filled me in on the circumstances in a whisper.

It seemed that *Gridley* had just fired upon a Soviet Navy combatant vessel! The announcement nearly caused me to have a heart attack…and fully explained the solemn expressions on the faces of the three flag officers present…as well as their presence. The expression on my own face, deciding what I should do, compelled the duty officer to add some important details. Remember, readers, we were in the middle of the Cold War.

The details included the fact that a Soviet AGI was towing a *Foxtrot* diesel-powered attack submarine right through the middle of the firing exercise area, international notifications to the contrary, notwithstanding. *Gridley's* skipper spotted the pair of Soviet vessels on the horizon approaching from the southeast with his binoculars, and mistook them for the tow ship and target! Since this was precisely the moment and place at which he expected the tow ship to appear, the mistake was somewhat understandable. Furthermore, the submarine under tow on the surface looked remarkably like a target sled, since the submarine's hull was still below the horizon (hull down), and only the submarine's sail was visible. Unfortunately, the tow vessel didn't look anything like a U.S. Navy tow ship. Nonetheless, it was a remarkable coincidence!

It is quite unusual in the U.S. Navy to see one ship towing another, except in a dire emergency. In the Soviet Navy, however, it is a routine procedure. Soviet naval combatants routinely tow other combatant vessels all over the oceans of the world, especially for long transits (like this one from the North Cape to Cienfuegos, Cuba). I am convinced it was done to conserve fuel. The duty officer mentioned one other fact with which, he properly guessed, I would not be familiar. In accordance with the fleet training manual, the first round of a firing exercise, the "calibration round," was always aimed 25 miles aft of the target. This was done as a safety measure. I thanked the Lord for this important tidbit of information, because it helped me to make what I believed to be the right decision.

Back on board *Gridley*, the skipper asked for target range from combat information center (CIC) and told the weapons officer to stand by to open fire when the range decreased reached 10,000 yards. The judge nodded his approval, and the Skipper gave the order, moments later, to "fire, when ready!" A few seconds elapsed while the after gun mount made a few minor adjustments to the elevation and azimuth of the gun barrel…then there was a thunderous explosion as flame belched from the barrel, and the 75 pound general-service round was on its way. Wanting to observe the impact of the "calibration round," the Skipper adjusted the knurled focus knob on the binoculars and nearly had a heart attack. He immediately recognized the distinctive silhouette of a *Foxtrot* submarine. Pandemonium broke loose on *Gridley's* bridge!

Her skipper did a few other things in his panic. Of course, no one on the bridge had observed the impact of the calibration round, and therefore had no idea where it had gone and whether the Soviets might have seen it…or, perish the thought, even been hit by it.

To his credit, the skipper acknowledged the political implications of what he had just done and initiated an immediate flash precedence voice satellite message to CinCLant headquarters. Unfortunately, someone in the Oval Office at the White House intercepted the message, and an Army lieutenant general immediately got on the line asking for details a mile-a-minute. The poor skipper was now paying the penalty for using a flash message precedence to inform the fleet headquarters. As I walked into the command center, the CinC was listening to the conversation between the Skipper and the Army general in the Oval Office.

The Skipper had also initiated communications with the Russian tow vessel by flaghoist, flashing light, and several radio channels. Furthermore, he had dispatched his helicopter to the tow ship to attempt to see what, if any, damage had been done and to establish communications.

I waited for a pregnant several minutes and reflected upon my future. I was fairly in the dark as to what was being said over the telephone, and was reluctant to walk over to the communications cubicle and eavesdrop. But I reflected on what the CinC had told me when he interviewed me for the job. "I expect you to run things. If you need help, ask. But, I expect you to run things!" His message had been clear then, and I remembered it clearly now. I knew I must not wait another second for some stupid Army lieutenant general in Washington to f—k things up and create an international incident! I took a deep breath and held out my hand to the CinC. "Sir, may I have the telephone, please?"

There was an audible gasp from the two flag officers standing behind the CinC. The CinC looked at me, and for a terrible two or three seconds I found myself contemplating retirement. Then, without a word he handed the telephone to me. As he did so I glanced at his three-star deputy and saw that his face was ashen. It was now too late to turn back, so I decided to be bold…to do what the CinC had hired me to do…to run things!

I dialed the two number code which was the CinC's own personal override code. It was designed to intrude on any channel, override it, and take over the line. Of course, no one but the CinC was supposed to use it. But, he himself had directed that I be given the code. I assumed that he did that in case I ever saw fit to use it! Immediately, I found myself in voice communications via satellite with the skipper standing on *Gridley's* bridge. The lieutenant general in the Oval Office was now in a "listen only" mode…for better or worse. I heard another audible gasp in the room. I had just cut out the Oval Office! Then I spoke in what I hoped was an authoritative voice.

"*Gridley*, this is CinCLant with instructions to follow. How do you read? Over." The skipper's voice came back immediately.

"CinCLant, this is *Gridley*. I read you loud and clear. Ready to copy. Over" I chimed right in before someone tried to override me.

"*Gridley*, your instructions follow. Cease all firing. Cease all communications with the tow vessel. Recall your helicopter. Stand clear of both the tow vessel and the ship under tow, but maintain visual contact. Report to this command at 15 minute intervals until further notice. Please acknowledge. Over." The skipper's voice came back sounding enormously relieved.

"CinCLant, this is *Gridley*. Wilco. Out." I handed the telephone back to the CinC and, turning on my heel, walked out of the command center and back to my office. It wasn't until I sat down at my desk that I realized I had been holding my breath. I just sat there waiting for the inevitable telephone call from the CinC, firing me! The squawk box told me a few minutes later that "all flags had left the command center." A minute later the red telephone rang. It was the direct line to the CinC's office. I picked it up and again held my breath. The CinC's gruff voice uttered only two words.

"Not bad!"

I explained about the calibration round and guessed that no one on the tow vessel or the submarine had heard the gun report, nor seen its impact since it was a practice round and therefore contained no explosives. Further, I suggested that the Soviet officers were probably all in their wardroom enjoying a mid-morning vodka and hadn't the foggiest idea they had even been shot at.

Why should we needlessly create an international incident until we're sure they know what happened? He agreed, and hung up with a final directive. "Okay. Keep me informed."

The lessons which came out of this incident were three:

1. Do your best to know all there is to now about what's going on.
2. Do what you think is the right thing
3. Be prepared to accept the consequences for your actions.

Author's Note: The Russians never mentioned the incident at the time. It was 5 years later, when I was in Washington, D.C., on my last tour of duty, that I saw the first official acknowledgement of the incident. It appeared in a small article in the back pages of the *Washington Post*, announcing the fact that the U.S. government had officially apologized for the accidental firing of a Naval gun in the direction of a Soviet vessel off Guantanamo.

Chapter 23:
Burial at Sea

"Where principle is involved, be deaf to expediency"

- Mathew Fontaine Maury, 1806-1873

One of the things I was required to memorize in grammar school was the corporal works of mercy, the last of which was to "bury the dead." Since, at the time I'd never been to a funeral, much less an interment, it seemed foreign to me. So, I never gave it a thought. But, to the commanding officer of the USS *Bigelow*, the last corporal work of mercy was the thing which ruined his whole Naval career!

During my stint at CinCLant headquarters from 1977-1979 I had occasion to order the burial at sea of literally hundreds of former seamen. It was an honor reserved to sailors of all ranks, and it was performed on a routine basis. All a person had to do was make an official request to be buried at sea, and if he were a former Navy man, the Navy would do it. My incoming mail always seemed to have at least one request on Monday morning for a burial at sea. One of my staff men would pick a likely ship scheduled for some sort of training in one of our operating areas. I would sign the message designating the ship and the date. The remains, be it a coffin or a cremation urn, would be delivered to the ship in question just before the ship sailed.

It was left to the ship's commanding officer to pick the time and place for the funeral. The only stipulations to which he was required to adhere were the format of the events. At the determined time and location (more than 50 miles away from the coast) the ship would slow to "one bell," and the funeral detail would be called away. An honor guard would be formed up, the chaplain would read an appropriate excerpt from the Scripture, the honor guard would fire the three volleys, the flag which had been draped over the casket would be folded, and the pallet which held the casket tipped up, allowing the remains to slide overboard into the sea. All hands, at parade, would salute as Taps was played by the bugler. It was a fitting end for a sailor who had spent a portion of his life at sea.

Of course, there were some details which needed strict adherence...such as knocking out the special plugs in the bottom of the casket so that it would fill with sea water and sink. Also, there would be arrangements for delivery of the flag to the designated next of kin, and so forth. In my two years at CinCLant I do not remember any glitches...except for *Bigelow*, of course!

Sometime in the summer of 1978, I believe, a burial at sea detail was assigned by me to *Bigelow*, a destroyer based out of Norfolk. The casket was delivered to the ship just prior to her sailing for a shake-down cruise to the Caribbean Sea. The captain, a dedicated Naval officer, determined that he had time to do the burial honors in the Virginia Capes Naval operating area before heading south. So, *Bigelow* set the honor detail for mid-day, and slowed to render proper honors to the departed seaman. The ceremony was conducted with scrupulous attention to all of the details referred to above...including knocking out the flooding plugs in the bottom of the casket.

The ceremony was carried out well, the scripture was well-chosen, the honor guard fired the salute, and the casket was slid over the side with proper honors. Taps was played, and orders were given for the ship to hold her course and speed until the casket sank beneath the waves. But, it didn't sink!

The skipper, eager to get on his way to his commitment in the Caribbean Sea, initiated a 360-degree turn to come back alongside the still-floating casket to see what had gone awry. Nothing was apparently wrong, so *Bigelow* initiated another turn and came alongside for a second look. The casket was floating like a cork in a storm!

What to do? The skipper had a scheduled exercise to conduct in the Caribbean Sea and needed to get on his way. On the third pass by the buoyant flotsam the skipper decided on a radical procedure.

He knew that the water-logged casket would be a chore to snag and haul back aboard. It also now presented a hazard in that its water-soaked remains would have to be returned to Norfolk, since there would be no assurance that another burial attempt would not be equally unsuccessful. It was time for decisive action. He ordered his weapons officer to equip three of his best marksmen with M-14 rifles and to shoot a few holes in the casket in order to encourage it to sink.

The firing began, and after considerable "holing" of the wayward casket the skipper saw it begin to settle a little lower in the water. He felt much happier, and initiated yet another turn on "the firing line" to see the end of this wretched business. Unfortunately, the casket still floated, although a little lower in the water. There were two more firing passes, and the casket began to have the appearance of having been through a major battle! It was so full of holes that it was difficult to conceive of its continuing to float. But, continue it did!

By now the skipper was in a frenzy of frustration and foolishly ordered that one of the ship's 20 millimeter automatic cannons be loaded. On the next pass the explosions of the cannon rocked the ship as geysers of water erupted around the errant casket. The holes made by the cannon were enormous by comparison to those made by the rifles...and still the casket floated. It was bizarre!

As I re-read this description the notion that the poor departed seaman was somehow wreaking his revenge upon the skipper of *Bigelow* for some past offense endured, keeps coming back to me. The poor seaman simply refused to leave this world and enter the watery grave his family had selected. Against all known laws of hydrodynamics, that wretched casket continued to float!

As luck would have it, someone in the crew had a grudge to pick with the skipper. Perhaps he had felt the skipper's wrath at Captain's Mast! Anyway, this individual got his hands on a movie camera and proceeded to record the mayhem being inflicted upon the departed seaman's remains by rifle and cannon fire...for posterity. The casket finally sank after being torn virtually to shreds by 20 millimeter shell fire. *Bigelow* headed south, and the incident was set aside by the skipper as yet another anomaly of life at sea.

The movie ultimately found its way to a television studio and then was flashed into the living rooms of people all over America...much to their outrage, indignation, and horror. How could any self-respecting Naval officer do such a thing? Of course, the J-3's office at CINCLANT (my office) caught the brunt of the inquisition, which ensued...both from on high and from the media. After all, was it not I who had sent the burial tasking message to *Bigelow*?

The President was aghast! The Congress was horrified! The Defense Department was furious! The press was indignant! The CinC, my boss, was disgusted! My state of mind could only be described as venemous!

How, we all asked, could anyone be so stupid and uncaring? After all, a minor exercise in the Caribbean Sea couldn't be so important as to cause a ship's commanding officer to lose all sense of perspective and propriety! But, it apparently did just that.

It took several days for the initial firestorm of bad press to subside somewhat. A formal investigation was initiated by the immediate superior in command of *Bigelow*, the two-star Cruiser-Destroyer Group Commander. The recommendation that the skipper be relieved of his command immediately was carried out with dispatch.

Needless to say, there was an immediate message from the Commander-in-Chief of the Atlantic Fleet to all concerned describing the procedures (in nauseating detail) to be followed in conducting burials at sea. Subsequently, I examined every tasking message which I signed detailing burial at sea with far greater scrutiny than heretofore. As I signed the first few, I recall asking my staff assistant whether the commanding officer in question could "handle the detail?" Ruefully, I reflected on the changing circumstances. Heretofore the question of a combatant vessel's ability to punish the enemy had been the paramount consideration. Now, the question seemed to be how well it could bury the dead!

PART III:
Brown Shoes

"You may talk of gin and beer,
When you're quartered safe out here,
And you're sent to penny fights and Aldershot it.
But when it comes to slaughter,
You'll do your work on water,
And lick the bloomin' boots of 'im that's got it."

- Rudyard Kipling: "Gunga Din"

As long as I can remember, aviators have worn nice-looking cordovan shoes with their summer khaki uniforms. As previously mentioned, the surface warfare officers wore black shoes with their summer khaki uniforms...thus, the distinction of "black shoes and brown shoes"...and never the twain shall meet, I often thought.

Sometime in the 1970s, I think, that quintessential mechanism of bureaucracy, the Uniform Board, decided that brown shoes had to go. The thinking was that distinctions and divisiveness between the two communities, the surface warfare community and the aviators, would blur and ultimately disappear...how silly!

So, we aviators all stopped wearing brown shoes with our uniforms and relegated them to the civilian part of our wardrobes.

Then, during the reign of "the enfant terrible," Secretary of the Navy, John Lehman, when aircrew retention rates had plummeted to an all-time low, he re-instated brown shoes. His calculation that the shade of our shoes would turn the tide of years of bad leadership is vintage Lehman.

Now, my son informs me, the Navy, in its infinite wisdom, has found the Solomon's Solution. Everyone can now wear brown shoes with the khaki uniform. The Navy's leadership is truly gifted!

Chapter 24:
A New Mistress

"Nothing is more binding than the friendship of Companions-in Arms"
- Hilliard

"The Green Machine" was what Marines called it in later years. In my time, (1956) we called it "The Crotch." All the name-calling disguised an unreasonable and deep seated affection for the Corps. We hated to admit to this affinity. An oft times expressed saying, "Eat the apple, f—k the Corps," further hid our feelings.

Young men will always be lured into the Marine Corps. The Corps is like Circe, calling out to passing sailors, luring them onto the rocky shoals of life. Many a mariner has answered the Corps' siren call and been transformed into a swine like Odysseus' men.

It isn't the posters or the John Wayne movies. It's probably a defect in the psyche. We were all carrying some excess baggage when we volunteered. Perhaps young men need to prove something to themselves, and like a middle-aged man in need of validation, acquire a new mistress...The Corps.

The Corps has crept into my ruminations often through the years. We were lovers back then, sharing many a moment of heightened awareness. One of those moments, a vivid memory of the Corps, is of a rainy day at Parris Island.

It was a light rain—a mist, really. Enough so that the green fatigues became black with mixed sweat and rain. The darkness caused by the storm clouds scudding in off the Atlantic belied the mid-day hour.

My mind's picture is of one of the recruit platoons. They were a compact, relaxed unit, jogging along the road at a rhythmic, mile-eating pace. The DI, keeping pace to the left, had become bored with counting cadence. The guidon bearer was giving voice to a favorite marching tune about a girl named Sue. Ninety male voices were singing the chorus with gusto, leather boots drumming.

Robert Gillcrist (center) gets his stripe on board U.S.S. *Wasp*, 7 June 1948.

The greens and browns of the land mixed with the skin tones of the jogging marines. Black, white, brown, yellow, and red; just as surely the bounty of America as are wheat and corn.

They were moving along a country road which was curving, rising before them like destiny. The Corps. Going in harm's way. On that rainy day, I had been sent to the Post administration building on some errand. That was how I happened upon the chanting platoon. I was returning to the company area; running along that same country road, jogging to their cadence, keeping pace with them, a hundred feet back.

The platoon had just left the post exchange. They had been given a rare opportunity to go in to the exchange to buy a toothbrush, or towel. As was understandable, the boots hit the candy counter hard. The DI running alongside the platoon was warning all, stridently, "be advised, when we reach the company area, every piss ant will be search for '*pogie Bait.*'"

Then, as in a dream, as the pounding boots evoked thunder, the platoon rained pogie bait. And the road ahead of me was suddenly littered with Hershey bars; at first, a trickle, then a deluge: hundreds of them. These I picked up as fast as I could, stuffing them into my blouse, until my fatigues were stretched to the limit. Then, because I looked like a clown, I left the road and raced through the woods to Platoon 356's quonset huts.

A quick look for the DIs, and into the hut I went. Without a word, I dumped my loot on the concrete floor.

And, as with a mistress, despite the infatuation, there were annoying things about the Corps. The constant hunger was one of them. It seemed like we were always hungry. There was a time on the Aircraft Carrier Wasp when on the "Dog" watch we were so hungry that we stole and ate some lemons. To be fair, it would be impossible to create an accommodation that would allow Marines free access to food. Simply wouldn't be possibly.

At Parris Island, the hunger was acute, because one of our DIs had a habit of marching us to the mess hall and then, before releasing us for chow, warning the Platoon to be in formation by the exit of the mess hall before he arrived there.

As soon as we fell out, we would all run through the mess hall without stopping to eat in order to be in formation when the DI came around the corner of the mess hall at a brisk pace. The DI would find us in formation and continue with our afternoon training. He was probably on a diet, and this ploy suited his plans nicely. We probably represented a kind of surrogate support group.

In the beginning, at Parris Island, we were restricted to those spartan steel quonset huts at night: huts shaped like a tin can cut in half lengthwise. There were even guards. The guards were offically called Fire Watch. No one was permitted to leave the huts at night, not for the head, not even for a drink of water. The Corps knew from past experience that some of us would bolt if given the slightest opportunity.

And so it was one night that I lay so thirsty that I couldn't sleep, listening to the night sounds of 30 exhausted recruits. As I lay marking time in my bunk, it occurred to me that there were fire extinguishers at all four corners of the hut—*water* filled extinguishers.

Hopping out of my bunk in my skivvies, I padded barefoot to the nearest fire extinguisher and squatted next to it in the dark. With some trepidation I unclipped the rubber hose and sucked tentatively. In a moment my throat was enjoying a cool draft of alkaline water. Between the gulping and the satisfied rumbling of my stomach, another boot heard me. A voice from an adjacent bunk asked, "What the hell are you doing?"

It was a fair question, considering the circumstance. "Shove off" was my reply. But by then he was out of his bunk, sensing something good, like maybe an attempt to escape. In no time, the entire quonset hut was awake, busily draining all the fire extinguishers.

And, as we all know, mothers will always send cookies to their sons in the service. The mothers of the recruits at Parris Island were no exception. The DIs hated to see us enjoying ourselves, so we rarely got to eat those cookies from home. What would happen was that the victim would be made to read the saccharin letter from his mom or girlfriend in a loud voice while the rest of us stood at attention as sand fleas roamed, feeding at the corners of our eyes. Afterwards, the DIs would take the treat and "keep it for us."

And that was what led to an inspiration on another sleepless night as I lay in my bunk, suffering hunger pangs. I got to thinking about this *keeping*. My imagination kept rerunning a film clip of the DIs eating all those cookies. Then I realized that they were lean, hard Marines. No way did the drill instructors eat cookies.

What a revelation! I sat up abruptly, wide awake. The DIs must wait till dark and then haul those packages over to the big green metal dumpster behind their quonset hut. Suddenly, I was out of my bunk, as furtive as Papillon the night of his escape. The fire watch was pacing between several huts; no problem if I timed it right.

Flitting through the night like a ghost, moving from shadow to shadow in my skivvies and barefoot, I reached the dumpster. A breeze was coming in off the ocean, soft and damp. The Camp was as quiet as it would be all night. By feel, I located the access door on the side of the steel container. Very slowly, in case of squeaky hinges, I eased the metal door open. All was quiet, so I hitched up my skivvies and hopped in.

With the container door shut it was as black as death. The bulk of the debris in the dumpster was paper and cardboard, so I sat quite comfortably. Look for an unopened cardboard box, I reasoned. Sure enough, by feel and in no time I came up with a potential box. Opening the box was as exciting as Christmas, despite the atmosphere of the dark smelly dumpster. I was proud of myself, because on first try I had come up with a whole box of cookies.

Sitting in the dumpster, feeding in the dark, I mimicked a monkey. First, I'd feel around, then pick up an object, smell it just in case, and then gobble it down. What a sight it must have been. Nirvana was suddenly interrupted by a rustling noise just outside the dumpster. For a second I thought a DI was about to throw in some trash. But the noise was so controlled, the movement so furtive, that I realized that it was probably another enterprising recruit. As my competitor slowly eased the door open, the devil made me roar at the top of my lungs, What's your name, Boot?

I suspect, from the scent lingering in the air and the damp earth, that he wet his skivvies as he frantically bolted into the night. Long afterwards I still laughed about that recruit's absolute conviction that a DI sat in the dumpster each night waiting for any opportuning souls. My infatuation with the Corps ended when I finally realized that there were many other exciting, tantalizing mistresses out there in the world. The Corps was much too jealous a mistress to allow me to make even a passing acquaintance with another, and so I bid adieu.

Many a contemplative moment since Viet Nam, I've harkened back to the day my close pals and I had all been given an opportunity to train as helicopter pilots. My pals sat in the quonset, grouped around me, trying to change my mind about flying and the additional time I would have to sign up for.

Remembering the humiliating failure of my eyes to pass the Navy flight physical some time earlier, I declined. My guardian angel must have been whispering in my ear. Had I gone along with those bright, fun-loving young men, my bones would probably be hidden in some jungle thicket until eternity.

Chapter 25:
The Making of a Marine

"We few, we happy few, we band of brothers:..."
- Henry V Act IV

His first recollection of Him was of one fall day in 1945. There was a knock at the door, and Peter opened the door to find a big, lean, tan, stranger standing there; unsmiling, wearing a Naval officer's uniform.

When the 6 year-old asked what the stranger wanted, the man pushed past him and walked in as though he owned the house, which he did. Pete's mom was equally unsmiling. It had been three years, sufficient time to wound the marriage, just as surely as enemy fire damages and destroys.

Peter didn't know what to do about this stranger. Peter felt an instinctive need to protect his Mom. He just didn't know what to do. The stranger walked about the house like a time bomb ready to go off, a bomb that Peter wanted to go off somewhere else.

They were difficult times for the whole family. Peter took the brunt of the discipline. His younger brother was too young to feel the impatience, the anger; to suffer the injustice. Peter sat in his room licking his wounds often. His mom was no longer that haven in times of stress. She had her own to deal with. And after three savage years in the South Pacific, the stranger had rendered gentlemanly manners.

One day, sitting in the 5-inch gun tub aboard the carrier Wasp, Don Colyer told me of the manic life style of the stranger, the war veteran. Each morning, Peter had to fall out for inspection at six a.m., his child's body rebelling. Peter would be ordered to stand at attention next to his bunk, tummy sucked in, chin tucked.

Every morning, the stranger, the *officer*, would inspect Peter's clothes and shoes. Then he would actually flip a quarter on Peter's bunk to check for tightness. They were long and difficult days for Peter. The officer didn't have a job to go to yet. Instead, he spent his time roaming the house like a tiger—pacing: always unsmiling. Peter lived in fear of the officer, the alpha male. His fear fostered a deep need to seek the officer's approval. Peter tried his best to gain that approval, but it was elusive and rare.

With the passage of time, the slow turning of the clock that children suffer, the mother and father reached some sort of accommodation. The thawing was slow, but eventually there was reproachment. The father, who was called Don by his fellow veterans, eventually began to talk to the 6 year old in common, everyday conversations.

And from time to time the veterans would gather to sit and tell sea stories in low voices, as if validating their recollections. The story telling was generally stimulated by a few drinks. There was one sea story that the six year old never forgot. That sea story took place on a little known atoll. The Officer's ship was attacked by Japanese planes and sunk. The surviving crew managed to float towards the atoll, grouped together for protection.

As the group neared shore, one man jerked and groaned, then slipped under in a swirl of blood-stained sea water. The group then heard a distant shot, and then another crew member was killed, and another. There was a hulk of a destroyed landing craft laying in the surf nearby, and the remaining crew struggled through the sea, frantically seeking shelter in the twisted, burned steel of the hulk. The crew clung to the hulk all afternoon, floating in a suddenly cold sea as the Japanese sniper moved invisibly to new positions, seeking out exposed crew and killing them. And behind the survivors, the frenzied thrashing of the feeding sharks would be embedded in their memories for eternity.

The officer hung on doggedly as his crew slowly were executed around him, wondering when night would come to hide them from their executioner; wondering if the survivors should try to go ashore in the night, and which direction along the beach would lead to freedom and which would lead to death. Sitting there in the gun tub, Don Colyer's voice was barely a whisper as he told the story. I imagined 6 year old Peter, sitting cross-legged at his father's feet, mouth open, eyes wide with fright. The officer continued his story, speaking in awe of looking down the beach in a state of abysmal despair, having lost his command and crew, and seeing three raggedy-assed Marines jogging along the beach toward the survivors.

The Marine's canvas leggings were missing, their sandy fatigues slapping their legs, their distinctive cloth-covered helmets were jouncing about. The three Marines came with their M-1s at port arms as if out for an evening run. There was no fear in those Marines— none. The Marines, who were only in their teens, had seen far too much death. Unlike the cowering survivors, they came on like Judgement Day, jogging along three abreast, all business. Only in their business, they dealt in lead.

There was a presence about the Marines that said there would be no quarter. The Marines would take no prisoners. The trio jogged along the beach, willing the sniper to take a shot—just one. And he did. Perhaps the sniper felt the presence of death himself, because he missed. It was to be his last shot. The three Marines rushed like grim reapers into the jungle where the thick green growth masked the dull thuds as the three M-1s sought him out. For some time Peter had felt an overwhelming need to gain his father's respect. In that moment of the telling of the sea story, it was apparent to the boy that though his father respected little, he respected the Marines.

And so it was, that the vulnerable little boy sitting at his father's feet made a vow. When he grew up, he'd change his name to Don, and that one day he'd be a Marine.

Chapter 26:
The Detachment
(A Rogues' Gallery)

"Yes, barrin' an inch in the chest an' the arm, they was doubles o' me and you;
For they weren't no special chrysanthemums—soldier an' sailor too!"
- Kipling

There were about 60 Marines in the detachment onboard *Wasp*. When my brother asked me to describe them in a chapter of "Spindrift," my mind went blank. After some thought and discussion with my shipmate Colyer, and the aid of a photograph of the starboard watch of the detachment, I was able to piece together the names of a meager few of those lively characters with whom I lived, cheek to jowl, for so long. What follows, in order of rank, is a brief, fleeting recollection of some of the Marines. As you will surmise, some I liked, and some I was uncomfortable with.

Captain Weita was a mustang: a Marine who came up through the ranks. During the assault on Iwo Jima, he was a private. He survived the landing and those endless days of fighting, and decided to make the Corps his life. Captain Weita was a stocky guy with a steely jaw and piercing blue eyes. The detachment didn't know what to think of him until he sneaked a woman aboard one time and we found out.

What happened was that *Wasp* had visiting hours on Sunday in New York and Captain Weita sneaked some shapely visitor down to his cabin. Things apparently went so well that *Wasp* was one hundred miles at sea, noon Monday, before the acrobatic team realized it. After that episode, he was our kind of guy, and we'd do anything for him. He definitely had style! Captain Weita was the antithesis of another CO whose yoke we languished under, who handed the entire detachment a personally autographed, framed portrait of himself. We all threw them in the dumpster. It wasn't the sort of thing that a marine did!

Lt. Francis X. Kelly, "Francis," was the executive officer of the detachment. He was a New Yorker who had hung out in Gilhooley's, next to the old Madison Square Garden, on 49th Street, in another life, drinking beer. This made me comfortable with him. Kelly was also a Manhattan College grad, another point in his favor. For some reason, the detachment considered him a wimp. As a result, they were disrespectful in sly ways. Because Kelly had ultimate faith that I would not fail any inspection, he never checked closely. As a result, I'd make bets with the detachment as to whether I could go through a close inspection while wearing argyle socks, or no dress shirt under my jacket. It drove them crazy, because I never got caught. The disregard that Kelly sensed added to his command problems, and eventually caused psychosomatic back problems. We might have been crazy, but we weren't stupid!

First Sgt Potter was an anachronism, struggling with the changes in The Corps. We all called him "The First Lady," for no good reason.

Staff Sgt Perez was another veteran of the War in the South Pacific. When we watched the Marine combat film footage of the assaults on Iwo Jima and the other big battles, he'd laugh uproariously as the Japanese stumbled out of caves and were burned alive with flame throwers. He called them "smoked scirrokies."

Gunny Wirth was as close to a saint as a Marine could get. Now that statement is something of a quantum leap for anyone's imagination, but it was true. Gunny put up with more crap from Colyer and me than was necessary, and frequently swept things under the carpet on our behalf. We certainly didn't deserve his good will. Thanks, Gunny, wherever you are.

Sgt. Jones was a big black guy with an even temper and a good sense of humor. Sgt. Jones took great pleasure in describing obscure sex acts to the author. He liked to bring up the subject on a late night watch in front of an audience. He'd laugh uproariously at the reaction that he'd get each time. The author was something of an *innocent* back in those days.

Corporal Bancroft was a quiet man who gave the false impression that he was meek. In fact, Bancroft was a tough marine who was a good squad leader. He was in the heavy

"The Detachment," U.S.S. *Wasp*, **June 1958. Robert Gillcrist is pictured at left end rear row. (Official USMC photograph)**

weapons section with Colyer. He and I were interested in the same gal for awhile. I think they got married after he was discharged. I liked him anyway.

Corporal McLean was a wee little man. He would attach himself to Colyer and me when we went ashore, and with regularity, would start a fight with some smaller group of paratroopers, say. It irritated us that he was so calculating in picking a group that would not be able to defend itself against the three of us. Within the detachment, we felt that a fight should be kind of like a summer rain squall. Something that came up unexpectedly, was a bit noisy, and passed quickly, leaving everyone a little damp and uncomfortable, but strangely refreshed.

Brogan was a product of the slums on the lower east side. He was a brawler extraordinaire. He was a petty thief, and lazy, as well. Brogan bunked in the machine gun section, along with Colyer. One day I had to explain to Brogan that there was not going to be any more nonsense on my watch. Although I was only a private at the time, I was corporal of the guard and responsible for the running of my watch. Much to my surprise, Brogan realized that I meant it and would take whatever steps were necessary. After that we got along.

One night as we were ready to begin our watch, Brogan came to me and asked to be placed in the guard shack because he was very tired. I said, "Tough," and put him in with the nuclear weapons. Later that night as I was making my rounds to check on the watch, I found Brogan asleep. As I lifted his weapon prior to awaking him, the nuclear weapons officer walked in and discovered the problem. Brogan was in deep trouble. On many occasions since, I've wondered if a better manager would have been perceptive enough to see the problem and make the necessary changes before the problem arose.

Radivitch had been a lineman for "ole Mississip." Now, it's not that anyone ever did it, but hitting Radovitch would have been like Sunday-punching a spreading chestnut tree. Tough wasn't the word for him. Radovitch did have a soft spot, though, and I did occasionally see him cry. It was usually when we were in some dingy camp town bar and he had consumed a case of beer. Someone would inevitably drop a nickel in the juke box and hit "Jambolia." As the tune played, Radovitch would start to cry. It seemed that playing football and all the perks that went with it at Ol' Mississip had been like a "comped" weekend in Heaven for Radovitch, and the reminder of "Jambolia" set him off. I think a football injury ended his college years. How a Mack truck ever got out on the field, though, I can't imagine.

Radovitch was from Steel Town, and had never been over on the right side of the tracks until his junior year when the Wildcats kicked ass and made state champs. After that Radovitch's eyes were opened, and the scholarship came in the mail, along with the women who came in all manners of size, shape, color, and octave.

In boot camp, the DI could not seem to make either an impression—or, incidentally, a dent—in Radovitch. The DI tried his best, taking Radovitch into the showers every night and attempting to beat the shit out of him while Radovitch stood at attention. Radovitch rarely spoke of the ordeal. I envision the two of them meeting some day; a chance passing of two ships, only there will be no need for an ambulance if no one is around to witness the event.

Trout always made me uncomfortable. He was like a steel trap that was hidden somewhere nearby. You were always on the edge of anxiety. Trout was so mean that he probably has gone through life peeing on every toilet seat that he used, just to spoil everyone's day. He was predictable to the extent that he would screw you if given an opening. And therein lay the problem. You had to cover all bets when dealing with him. Trout came from the deep South, and was probably inducted into the Clan at birth. I can see him today, rocking back and forth on the porch, chuckling over bygone "Coon Hunts."

Sly was an apple-pie American boy. This innocent appearance hid a mean streak and a vicious nature. Most times this worked in Sly's favor when he had one of his many confrontations. Sly would identify the situation immediately and, while his opponent was still repeating the required hyperbole, saying things like "there's no anchor tied to your ass," Sly would haul off and floor his opponent with a lightning-fast blow to the jaw. Sly was true to his name.

"Wetback" Salcido. Where to begin? I doubt that Lloyds of London would insure Salcido, no matter what the premium. He was the most accident-prone guy I ever met. Colyer recently reminded me of the time Salcido ran through a glass door. I guess he was in a hurry. Salcido was a Latino who we all called "Wetback." He insisted that he was from LA and had been born in this country, but we got such a rise out of him that we continued to call him Wetback.

Salcido was an excitable guy. A good example of his minimal grip on himself occurred on a lively night in Boston. We were taking a cab from one watering hole to another, and were slightly bombed, all of us. An argument began about which hot spot to go to. Salcido lost his temper and told us all to go to Hell, and then he resolutely stepped out of the cab. The only problem was that the cab was roaring through the streets of Boston, doing 40 miles an hour at that precise moment.

One day Salcido discovered a trick. It was after lights out one quiet night, and we were all sitting in the head, preparing for the midnight watch, polishing shoes or cleaning wet gear. Salcido walked into the head and said, "Hey look guys." He then took a swig of lighter fluid and a lighted match and blew a fine spray of the fluid over the match. The effect was a dramatic plume of flame that practically reached across the entire head. We were all suitably impressed, until Salcido hiccupped and inhaled the rest of the fluid. In an instant his head and oily black hair turned into a torch.

As chance would have it, one of the Marines had been given the duty of mopping the head floor as punishment for some minor infraction. In that moment, as we all froze and stared at the staggering, moaning torch that was Salcido, the mop handler reacted. He stepped into a swing that would have sent a hardball over the fence and nailed Salcido full in the face with the long-handled wet mop. The impact was so powerful that Salcido flew back to the bulkhead with enough force to be knocked out. Fortunately, the flames were put out along with Salcido. We carried the smoking Salcido to sick bay as fast as we could. The duty corpsman wanted to know what happened, but we staunchly denied any knowledge of the accident. Later, when Salcido recovered, they asked him what happened. Wetback hadn't a clue!

Apparently, a wet mop moving at one hundred miles an hour wipes out all memory. Perhaps I should contact the New England Journal of Medicine. This new method could replace shock therapy. What you'd do is to instruct the mental patient who was due for therapy to go through a particular door, and behind the door you would place a 300 lb. orderly with a name like Bruno, armed with a filthy wet mop; poised, a wet grin on his vacant face.

"Tackhammer" Schohammer. Back when Shohammer had joined the detachment we discovered while in the showers that God had shortchanged Shohammer in the male anatomy department, so he was immediately christened "Tackhammer," meaning a small, delicate hammer used to drive upholstery tacks, as opposed to say a framing hammer used to drive 20 penny nails.

Now, in any normal, responsible societal group the citizenry would have thrown a net over the likes of Tackhammer. But as was evident, we were not in the mainstream on *Wasp*. Tackhammer was just another of many slightly dysfunctional characters in the Detachment, along with Salcido, Sly, Faucet, Brogan, and on and on. One of Tackhammer's idiosyncrasies was to demonstrate a few steps of the chain-gang shuffle, or the Rogue's March, whenever the detachment was in formation, something he learned on the job, so to speak.

An example of Tackhammer's state of mind took place during a riot in one of the ship's crew compartments. These group fights happened every so often out of frustration, or maybe due to the incipient race problem. On this occasion the Marines were called out to quell the riot. It was part of our job description. Since the early days of the Navy the officers' quarters were always aft of the mast. The knaves pressed into service by the press gangs were quartered before the mast, and the marines were quartered amidships as a buffer, to keep the officers safe from the crew.

As I've said before, times had not changed too much. On this night, Lt. Kelly, the detachment executive officer, gathered the pumped up Marines together for a pep talk before the big game. He didn't have the sense to recognize that we were already primed to go. And so, with Lt. Kelly in the lead, we moved through the ship to the trouble spot. When we reached the compartment where the riot was in progress, the watertight hatches were all dogged tight. Tackhammer stepped past Lt. Kelly and took the steel pipe off the rack to force the dogging latches open for the Lieutenant. We always became suspicious when Tackhammer was pleasant to anyone. He swung the hatch open, revealing a pitch dark compartment. Evidently all the lights had been broken in the fight. We could hear cries, whimpers, and sounds of combat coming out of the pitchy-dark. Now, Tackhammer, "of grace a gallant henchman," said to a very hesitant Lt. Kelly, "Let me go first, sir."

Without waiting for permission, Tackhammer dove through the black hatch and disappeared. Kelly hesitated for a second more, than took a deep breath and started through the hatch. There was a thud, and Kelly went down, his boots sticking up over the hatch combing, immobile. The detachment was both surprised and puzzled. Then out popped Tackhammer's face with a big grin. He saluted all present with the dogging pipe and waved us into the melee. Now we could go to work unsupervised.

Fawcett was a pretty squared-away guy. He just didn't fit in with the certifiable collection of nuts in the detachment. As a result, he'd end up with a problem. One problem that I should have taken care of but did not properly handle had to do with one midnight watch in some port. Fawcett had watch on the forward line, the bow line. We had a Hawaiian sergeant whose name escapes me. The Hawaiian was a thug who probably runs a prostitution ring today.

Anyway, the Hawaiian had been ashore and had gotten into a fight, injuring his opponent badly. In an effort to sneak aboard unseen, he climbed up the bow line, over the rat shield, and was almost home free when Fawcett saw him. Fawcett asked the sergeant what he was up to and got floored for his question.

Fawcett complained to me when I made my rounds as corporal of the guard. He felt that I should put the attack on report. This was one of life's moral decisions that I probably should have handled better. I found the Hawaiian Sergeant and confronted him. Remember, I was only a private, a rank of another magnitude entirely, especially on sea duty. After considering all the angles, like a Marine being jailed and the detachment and loyalty and Fawcett's hurt chin and pride, I told Fawcett to stop bellyaching and did nothing. Probably not one of my better decisions. Incidentally, Fawcett became the detachment haircutter when I refused to do it any longer.

"Hat" Holder most probably had a first name, but I never heard it. We all called him Hat Holder because of his penchant for offering to hold our hats when there was a fight in the offing. You see, we all spent a considerable amount of time polishing our barracks caps, and while a fight was one thing, a ruined barracks cap was quite another. "Hat" would offer to hold the hats rather than risk getting his ass kicked.

Another one of his quirks was to steal small things. Probably kleptomania. It was as if he didn't know he was doing it. There was a time when Hat and I shared adjoining racks. One night I started having nightmares, and thought I was being force fed some kind of sewage. I awoke to find that Hat and I were sleeping with our mouths about an inch apart. Our breathing rate was exactly the same except that as Hat exhaled, I'd inhale. We lay there exchanging the same lung full of stale air for God knows how long before I went into a nightmare. It was the moment I decided to get out as soon as possible.

"Indian" Mowatt's complexion was swarthy. His face was rounded and as smooth as a baby's. Mowatt's temperament was as smooth as his face. We called him Indian because he was a Navaho. Only one time did I see him lose his temper, and then he was twice as fast as I was. For some reason, although I liked Indian, I never went on liberty with him.

"Apache" was the only Apache Indian in the detachment. He was short, bow-legged, flat faced, and taciturn, with thick straight dull black hair. He had a habit of going off on liberty by himself. Once he came back, thoroughly beat up and in a rage. We all kidded him about being ambushed and of the dangers of drinking Firewater.

Sullivan was a slightly built guy who went to Providence College. For whatever reason, he quit college and joined up.

Don Colyer was my shipmate for the entire hitch in the Marines. Colyer appears as either the hero or foil in the majority of these sea stories, as well as in another manuscript entitled "Black Sheep."

Pignano was called "Killer" because of his success with women. One of the following stories is about him.

Goldberg was a little Jewish guy who took far too much needling from the rednecks. I use to stand up for him regularly, but the abuse he took didn't seem to bother him.

Patten was a good-looking young man who took the Corps seriously. When he was transferred off *Wasp*, Colyer and I never expected to see him again. Then one day at the Brooklyn Navy Yard, he walked into the mess hall. Patten was wearing a business suit and carrying a .38 caliber pistol. We chatted over lunch and Patten told us about being a courier and traveling all over the place. Colyer and I were about to be discharged, and this meeting almost tempted us to sign up for another tour of duty. I am sure Patten stayed in the Corps. Next time I'm in Washington I must check the Wall.

Steve Carter was by far the smoothest and handsomest Marine in the detachment. Carter could get a laugh out of any situation. I used to marvel at his self-confidence with the women. He once told me his secret. He was a great dancer, so he'd ask some woman to dance. Once they were in sync, he'd move in and hold his partner close. The trick as Carter told it was to watch the woman's ears. After her ears had slowly turned cherry red, Carter would simply disappear with another conquest. The women were crazy about Steve. Carter had apparently attended one of the Ivy League schools. After the school asked him to leave because of some misunderstanding over the Dean's wife, Carter lived an idyllic life in Spain with the daughter of the commandant of the Garde Civil, gamboling on Majorca until his father finally cut him off. Coincidentally, his lover cut him off shortly thereafter, and Carter decided to join the Marines.

"Lieutenant" Gillcrist is the author, and unfortunately it would take another volume for the writer to describe this fine fellow in sufficient detail to be appreciated by the reader.

Chapter 27:
Surprise!

"Even knaves may be made good for something"
- Rousseau

An aircraft carrier is a humming, throbbing, steaming, gurgling being. On my first approach to *Wasp*, reporting for duty after infantry training, it was apparent to me that *Wasp* was alive, but sleeping. Closer inspection over the next several months made me liken the carrier to a city-state. *Wasp* was a steel Sparta. A state whose God was war, a paladin whose territory was the seven seas. Awesome power lay within *Wasp's* steel chrysalis.

Wasp was an aged ship, a veteran of the Second World War. It was an Essex-class carrier built in the frenzy of desperate construction that was what the Japanese alluded to when they spoke of "arousing the sleeping giant." And, like many a veteran, *Wasp* had its *souvenir de guerre*, that made it limp when in a hurry, the result of a Japanese torpedo. One visible example of the expedient methods used to build the ship was the head in the Marine quarters.

The toilet was a long stainless steel trough; a steady rush of salt water through the trough kept it clear. On a rack behind the trough were a stack of wood slats. To use the facility, the user reached up and grabbed two slats and arranged them across the trough. Then you sat on the slats and took care of business. It was a social event, since there was no partitioning. On occasion, a trouble-maker would bunch up toilet paper, set it afire using lighter fluid, and drop the conflagration into the water at the upstream end of the trough. The users would all jump up in succession as the flaming raft passed under their respective bottoms.

Life aboard *Wasp* was grossly lacking in privacy. It was demeaning and claustrophobic, as well, even for someone from a large depression-era family. Despite all the ills righted and the changes in what we called "Rocks and Shoals" (Naval Regulations), the quality of shipboard life was not too distant from the environment that Lord Nelson sought to correct.

Shackling, and bread and water, were still practiced during my tenure as a brig guard. In fairness, I ran my watch in the brig like boot camp. All in all, it was an active, strenuous, regulated existence. It was penance, as in penitentiary.

One of the lasting memories of my stay at Parris Island was my first sighting of "brig rats." They were shuffling along, "lockstepping," with several guards herding them. The guards were all carrying shotguns in a business like manner. The message was clear. If you tried to run for it, they'd shoot you dead. During my time in the Corps, I came very close to joining those ranks on several occasions. My bad temper was always waiting patiently in the wings; eager for a grand entrance. And that is just what happened one Thanksgiving night in Boston. It so happened that my bunkmate Colyer and I were confined to ship for several months for one of our escapades. The sense of confinement that Colyer and I endured was honed to a fine edge during the holidays.

And so it was, that on Thanksgiving Day evening, in honor of the occasion, I was released from confinement and given a few brief hours ashore. The three dollars in my uniform pocket suggested an evening with little promise.

A long walk from the dock at the South Boston Naval Shipyard to the center of Boston cleared the cobwebs. It was a quiet night, as is always the case after families gather to rejoice in thanksgiving. The world was sleepy, sated, and secure in snug harbors. After a brief, disappointing stop in Scully Square for a beer at one of my favorite haunts, I headed back to the ship, resigned to a thankless Thanksgiving.

On the return walk to the ship, a sense of grievance burgeoned. Enough was enough! There was still sufficient money in my pocket for a pitcher of beer at the Enlisted Men's Club outside the shipyard gate. It wasn't much to be thankful for, but it would have to do as a Thanksgiving feast. Night had fallen by the time I reached the Enlisted Mens Club. My thirst was legendary. Anticipation was riotous. Looking up at the windows of the club, I saw darkness. The bloody place was closed for Thanksgiving.

In an instant, all the accumulated wrongs, ills, and grievances converged, and in the collision of emotions, I lost my temper. The club's entrance door was in front of me, so I took a firm grip on the handle, intent on breaking the lock, and lunged with all the pent up anger I could no longer contain. The next thing I knew, I was lying on my back looking at the night sky. The door wasn't locked. I had practically pulled the door off its hinges. In a nanosecond I was on my feet, strolling into the darkened club, humming, "I'm in the money."

The club was the motherlode of cheap, weak tap beer. This was like winning Lotto. There was no hesitation; no decision to make. This was my Karma. The club was familiar ground, so I headed unerringly for the lounge bar in total darkness. I reasoned that if I left the lights off, I could spin out the evening and never be discovered. And if I was found out, who cared? As I entered the lounge, humming a tune, a sultry feminine voice softly called, "Is that you honey?" I was speechless; probably just as well, since my voice would give me away. A grunted affirmative seemed to satisfy her.

Moses couldn't have been any more astounded than I was, when God gave him the Tablets. The analogy ends there, though, because the ten commandments were the farthest thing from my mind at that moment. Whatever light was available was behind me, so I couldn't see anything. She rushed into my arms; all silk, softness, and perfume, and gave me a torrid, lingering kiss. Murmured endearments, the burrowing into my arms, the human warmth all worked its wonder on the Convict. My cup runneth over. Valhalla!

Suddenly, the lounge was bathed in light, and our embrace was the center of attraction of a sea of astonished faces. The entire lounge was filled with surly scurvy chief petty officers. Some of the swabbies in the back couldn't see the events unfolding and began to sing a wavering, drunken version of "Happy Birthday."

Their senior members in the front rank, collectively faced with the outrage at having a hated Marine private, a keeper of the keys to the brig, no less, caught *indelicato* with the wife of the chief whose birthday they were about to celebrate, were in shock. The transition from Valentino to Jesse Owens was a difficult, but necessary, one for me. With a Homeric effort I released my grip on her ample butt and sprinted for the nearest exit with the grace of a Rhino, strewing cafe tables behind. Urged on by the banshee screams of the woman and the epithets of a hundred drunken chiefs, I flew. The thunder of 200 government-issue black oxfords pounding across the dance floor spurred me on as the drunken mob took up the chase, stumbling over the tables and chairs strewn in my wake, cursing.

Fleetness of foot, fear of dismemberment, darkness, and a fervent prayer combined to win the day. I made my escape. Strangely, for the first time that day, I felt a sense of genuine thanksgiving. But then, as I climbed the after brow of *Wasp*, my spirit grieved. Pondering this sensation, I realized that in my haste, I never even saw her face! Those poignant words "To have loved and lost is better than to have never loved at all," seemed to take on new meaning.

Chapter 28:
The Pimpernel

"They seek him here, they seek him there, those noncoms seek him everywhere..."
- Anonymous

Anyone who has ever been in the service knows how important it is to become invisible from time to time. And so it was that when my class at Sea School had all been assigned to a ship and I was intentionally left to rattling around in the empty barracks by myself, I learned to become invisible. It happened that I was in the process of healing from an accident and was on light duty, so it was essential to avoid those NCOs and the tasks that they NCOs would heap on me if they could find me. It was under those conditions that I developed hiding into an art form.

The squad bays at the Marine Barracks in Portsmouth, VA, were painted an institutional bile green color and were filled with steel bunks without bedding that allowed a visitor an unobstructed view of the whole bay. Along the walls of the bays, there were lines of battleship gray steel lockers with ventilation louvers in the doors, interspersed with green wooden rifle racks.

At any moment of the day, some NCO could conceivably wander into the squad bays looking for the only remaining warm body in the barracks to do some dirty job. It was important to remain unseen from about seven a.m. until about five p.m. It would be foolish to even show up at noon chow, and so I didn't. It wasn't easy! But over time I discovered a solution to my dilemma. The answer, right in front of me all along, was one that Houdini or the Ringling Brothers would appreciate.

It occurred to me one day, as I nervously paced about the squad bays looking over my shoulder, that I might just be able to fold up my 6 foot, five inch frame and squeeze it into one of the many upright steel lockers. And even if they knew I was somewhere in one of the lockers, it would become a shell game to try to find me. After several attempts, I discovered that I had to back in and then very carefully fold up my limbs one at a time, but it was definitely do-able. And so I became invisible!

For the first few minutes of each insertion it was uncomfortable; jammed inside a steel box with no light, but by remembering the price of being spotted, I persevered. It may have been cramped and uncomfortable inside the lockers, but it was better than pealing a thousand potatoes, any day!

And once I was inside, what I'd do was to crack the door of the locker, just a little, and read a paperback in the small shaft of light coming from the squad bay. After a week of practice, I was able to stay inside the lockers for hours at a time.

This method of staying out of sight worked like a charm for many weeks. Years later, while watching Ensign Pulver in "Mister Roberts," I empathized with and thoroughly enjoyed the laundry and recreation officer's dilemma. I knew what it was like to hide out day after day, like some dysfunctional recluse, trying to avoid the inevitable confrontation with the commanding officer.

Then one fateful day, after a couple of hours in the locker and several chapters of a Western, I needed to step out of the locker for a moment and shake off a mean leg cramp. As I pushed open the narrow door and stepped out into the supposedly empty squad bay, I stepped on the spit polished arch of a shoe.

It just so happened that the commanding officer of the Sea School, who was deep in meditation and incidentally scratching himself at the time, had wandered into the squad bay and stopped just in front of that particular locker at that precise moment.

The mystical appearance of the wraith and the sudden pain in his foot as my 200 pounds landed on his instep caused the CO to jump about a foot in the air and let out a screech of surprise, landing his beautiful white, gold leaf cap on the dusty floor. For a moment I am sure the CO thought I was the ghost of all his past crimes. Then he recovered, and I had some explaining to do. And because I was equally surprised, my first attempt was to explain that I was inspecting the insides of the lockers.

This explanation, coming from a 6 foot-five inch marine with a Western paperback in hand, did not sit well with the CO, who was still hopping around rubbing his foot. Shortly thereafter, I was shuffling off to Boston for a tour of duty on the aircraft carrier *Wasp* with some new guy named Colyer tagging along.

Chapter 29:
A Slice of Watermelon

"The mark of your ignorance is the depth of your belief in injustice and tragedy"
- Anonymous

We had just returned from a cruise, and *Wasp* was laying alongside the dock at the South Boston Naval Shipyard, taking on fresh supplies. With a crew of 3,000 hands, the task was a logistical rubic's cube. The old saw "many hands make light work" simply wasn't true. Earlier, while at anchor, the Marines provided the muscle to hoist aboard barge load after barge load of bombs for the air wing to drop on some communist aggressor.

Life aboard *Wasp* was a frenetic 24 hour operation, especially when at sea. At sea, *Wasp* was in its element, doing what it was designed to do. The aircraft carrier provided a base for aircraft. The air wing would fly aboard, once we were at sea, and thereafter the level of activity would be nonstop. And since an army marches on its stomach, an extra meal was served at midnight.

The ambient noise level on board *Wasp* was constant, changing only in octaves and decibel levels. The steam catapult's hiss-bang as it launched aircraft was one of the loudest noises, only surpassed by the 5-inch guns. The ship's bell, another example, would tell us the time, clanging to the changing of the watch day and night using the ageless code that Lord Nelson used. The 1MC, the ship's public address system, was always announcing something or other; from the mundane "Heave out and trice up, make a clean sweepdown fore and aft," to those rare moments, "All personnel other than ship's company report to the flight deck immediately with all baggage."

That was the day we dropped them all, tinkers, tailors, soldiers, and sailors, on one of the destroyers and turned up the knots in a rush to Venezuela to save Vice President Nixon and his wife. Well, the fated day that changed two lives started like any other. It was at eight bells as the 1MC announced chow call, that down the ships ladder in a clatter of double-soled dress shoes came the duty supernumerary with a new prisoner for the brig.

As was the drill, I had him stand at attention with his nose tight against the steel bulkhead while logging him in; asking his name and particulars, and also assigning him a penal number. He would be referred to by that penal number during his stay in the brig.

"Slice of watermelon, *Sir*," I shouted, correcting him emphatically. Next, I ordered the prisoner to undress and logged him in with the supernumerary as witness, as being unmarked and unbruised, although it was hard to tell with his dark skin. The time was the mid 50s. Names like Medgar Evers and Martin Luther King were little-known. Events like the Democratic National Convention in Chicago would not unfold for years. The notion that another war could take place in Indochina was impossible. The French were just extricating their paratroopers and pride from that distant, verdant land. Khrushchev would not pound his shoe on the podium at the UN in New York, telling us that he was going to "bury us," for a while yet. And we hadn't moved very far from the "back of the bus" and separate drinking fountains, either. You could still find them in the South back then, small signs, "Negroes only," by the entrance to poorly maintained toilets. It would take generations.

And it was a time when the term W*asp* described a bug...or a proud, legendary ship.

Bill was the new prisoner's name. He was well muscled, about 6 feet, 180 pounds, and displayed good motor coordination. Bill's eyes were clear. He was quick to understand, and spoke well. Bill had a ready smile in those early days. His forehead was high and wide, confirming the intelligence within. Bill could have done anything he put his mind to. The potential was there.

Standing against the bulkhead answering my questions, he seemed confused. He wasn't angry, frustrated, or in a rage. No indication of a need for restraints or the straightjacket. He seemed calm—ok. The rage was incipient for the moment. In time it would burst into flame, consuming Bill. It would all come later.

For now, Bill thought that he was simply being singled out for an infraction. The process was probably something like a frat house hazing, Bill was thinking. In a few days, there would be a hearing and everything would be straightened out. "Sure I cut a slice of watermelon, it was hot working under the sun, loading all that fresh food aboard. What was the harm? To tell the truth, I was homesick for Georgia; all those miles away... home and family. Seeing that watermelon glistening with dew started me thinking of the family, of sitting on the rickety wood steps by the back porch with my brothers. Of ice cold watermelon juice running down my shirt front. Of seeing who could spit the seeds the farthest in the humid summer dusk, crickets singing, after a long day in the fields.... homesick."

In the beginning Bill was a model prisoner. "This mess would all be cleared up soon," he mused. But the days turned into weeks and the weeks into months. No date was set for the court marshal until almost 90 days had drained through the hourglass of time. Ninety days of "double drill and no canteen," of bone-weary labor, of a restricted diet, no time off for good behavior, maybe a single cigarette at the end of the day, no privacy, no communications, and no companionship or human warmth, curled up in a steel box at night, alone.

The day of the court martial finally arrived. A shipmate brought Bill his best uniform. The proceedings were swift and harsh. Bill was stunned as the escort marched him back into the brig. His sentence was four months, no consideration for the 90 days already spent waiting. His hitch in the Navy would automatically be extended by seven months, because brig time didn't count as time served, nor did the prisoner get paid. Like a reptile emerging from its shell, the realization came to Bill that he was well and truly in the belly of the beast.

The transformation from man to animal would begin now. Bill's dignity would slowly be peeled off like an onion's skin, layer by layer. The loss of each layer of itself would be deceptive because it would not seem to diminish the whole being. The cumulative loss would be devastating and irreversible. Kind of like peeling off repeated layers of skin damaged by sunburn. In the end Bill would be an ugly caricature of the expectant, hopeful young man who enlisted to serve his country two years before.

The brig on *Wasp* was on the third deck below the hangar deck. There was a locked, barred gate guarding the entrance to the brig. A Marine was always on duty, 24 hours a day. The Marine detachment of *Wasp* consisted of about 90 men and officers. They were the policemen, guards, prisoner chasers, gunners, and disciplinarians.

My recollection of the brig was of a stark gray painted steel interior with an oscillating fan and a medicine chest bolted to the bulkhead. The medicine cabinet had several bullet holes in it, the result of sleepy Marines firing their .45 caliber automatics at the changing of the guard. The furnishings in the brig were spartan, and consisted of a stool and a hinged shelf for the brig log. The air was stale and motionless, except when the fan droned. There was a chronic odor of disinfectant from the daily washdown, and a constant hum from machinery in an adjacent compartment. When *Wasp* was at sea, the deck would vibrate gently, especially when the hull was pushing through the sea at 30 miles an hour during the recovery of aircraft.

There were only four cells in the brig on *Wasp*. The cells were battleship-gray steel boxes, about six feet by five feet, with bars on the door. The accommodations were a thin mat that we threw on the floor at night so the prisoners could get a good night's rest. Lights out was 10 p.m. There was no natural light down there, nor were there any lights in the cells. All night long the Marine on guard duty would sit on the stool reading girlie magazines, practicing fast draws with his pistol or otherwise entertaining himself.

I enjoyed reading the huge library of field manuals the Department of Defense printed on every conceivable subject. One night I came across a discourse on a drug called "Spanish Fly." That subject piqued my interest, and I showed the article to Colyer. We agreed that having a supply on hand might be useful, but where to find it? Reveille in the brig was 4:30 a.m. We didn't want anyone around when we took the prisoners to the showers. The chaser would stand just out of range of the shower spray, keeping the prisoners under constant observation.

The prisoners wore dungarees and chambray shirts, buttoned to the top, with a large white P crudely painted on the back. They wore their caps with the brim turned down over their eyes and marched in lock step, shuffling along because they were not permitted to have shoelaces, creating a demeaning sense of being comic outcasts. The lead prisoner would begin a rhythmic chant, "Gangway, prisoners," whenever the shuffling caterpillar of prisoners approached anyone in the ship's passages.

The ship's company would all stand back against the nearest bulkhead to give clearance to the prisoners as though they were untouchables. Once in awhile some swabby would not make room, and the Marines would throw him in line and take the wise guy back to the brig for indoctrination.

The prison chasers carried a .45 cal. automatic and a night stick. Some of those southern boys seemed anxious to use their automatics. Looking back, there was always a latent suggestion of violence in the detachment. On occasion the violence surfaced for a few frenzied minutes. Something to do with the mindset of the Marines and the need to validate their martial status.

Late one night, as a bunch of us were telling stories in a dance hall, a drunk marine from the South told of hunting through his hometown one Saturday night looking for a "niggra." "Coon hunting," he called it. The car was loaded with drunk teenagers; good old boys. They found their prey and ran him down, killing him. The teller of the story, a blonde-haired, good-looking, apple-pie American boy, laughed as though remembering a great fishing trip. His dad, by the way, was the sheriff.

The prisoner's day was structured. Everything was planned. This was a necessary part of the punishment, and besides, handling prisoners in their day-to-day activities had its own problems. The Marines usually provided slave labor for whomever requested it. We particularly liked to provide labor for the cooks. The prisoners would do the dirty jobs in the galley, and we would sneak hot, fresh baked loaves of bread up to the marine quarters for the hungry troops.

The day to day activities were similar to boot camp during my watch. Boot camp was a yardstick that I could use comfortably, and it was easy to be consistent by falling back on my own experience. This approach helped eliminate excessive or reactive punishment and favoritism..

As an aside, on *Tarawa*, my second aircraft carrier assignment, there were 10 times as many prisoners as on *Wasp*. There were no cells, just a huge screened enclosure with so many offenders to house. It has been my conviction all these years that the two aircraft carriers were a classic laboratory study of societal leadership and discipline as it relates to lawlessness and the penal system. No amount of social worker hyperbole will ever alter my personal convictions in this regard. My convictions are the result of the thousands of hours spent in that abnormal environment, the equivalent of a degree in social work.

Discipline on board *Wasp* was strict. Liberty ashore was sparingly permitted. The food was wholesome and reasonably well prepared. The ship was clean and well run. The large "E" for excellence, painted on the superstructure for all to see, was well earned. And the brig rarely had more than a few prisoners.

Tarawa, on the other hand was dirty, undisciplined, poorly fed, free with 96 hour liberty passes, and unable to earn the "E." And the brig had an average of ten times the prisoners as *Wasp*. Yet both ships were sisters from the same country, Navy, language, rules, uniform, and so on.

Getting back to the tale, the certain knowledge that each harsh day of brig time did nothing to diminish the total enlistment time by so much as a second was probably the most painful punishment that the felon had to endure. The prisoners were in limbo, if not hell. When your brig time was served, your enlistment time resumed as if you had been comatose for those months. Bill's seven months of brig time counted for nothing, not so much as a heartbeat!

Wasp was frequently at sea. There was no escape at sea. Bill should have known better, but he wasn't thinking properly by then. Sooner or later we would find Bill and haul him back to the brig. The Marine who was prison chaser for the work party that Bill escaped from was disciplined. When that Marine and his pals were on duty in the brig, Bill endured. "Keep breathing, that's the most important, count time, let your mind leave your body...*endure.*"

It may not seem like it sometimes, but time does pass, and that distant day arrived when I signed Bill out of the brig and returned him to the racist chief petty officer who had engineered his ordeal in the first place. The chief was waiting for Bill back in his old division, like a black widow, in a dark corner of its web. The chief's hate had not been slaked in the least.

As soon as he could, Bill jumped ship and fled. Why he didn't head for the deep South I don't know, but in time we found him again. The police had arrested him for some misdemeanor. Bill had been hiding in some abandoned tenement in Boston's ghetto. The police turned him over to the Navy, and he was back in the belly of the beast by dusk, the whites of his eyes prominent.

Armies of body lice were in his hair, crotch, and arm pits. His body was thinner, and bruised, and several deep cuts were evident, festering. In his heart, Bill was festering too. There was no longer any willingness to submit. It was a classic management problem. Neither the carrot nor the stick would ever again move Bill to cooperate in any way.

Unfortunately, the young Marine guards had no management training. The following months will be left unspoken, other than to say that it was like beating a dead horse. Each refusal by Bill resulted in another countermeasure. Handcuffs, leg irons, bread and water, each day escalating further. One chaser couldn't handle him anymore. Several Marines were required. It was better for Bill anyway.

Ultimately, he was discharged dishonorably, though the question begs to be asked, "Who was dishonorable?" We marched him to the gate of the South Boston Shipyard, ejecting him much like we would put out the garbage. It wasn't long before someone else saw the potential in Bill and he entered the ranks of a militant organization, aptly named The Black Panthers. Bill would serve honorably and with distinction.

Chapter 30:
"That Crazy Horn"

"When first under fire and you're wishful to duck,
Don't look or take heed at the man that is struck.
Be thankful you're living and trust to your luck,
And march to your front like a soldier."

- Rudyard Kipling: "The Young British Soldier"

The "fog of war" has always been associated with combat operations, and has been described as the state of confusion which is induced by the sheer excitement of the moment. The confusion results, I believe, from the added anxiety caused by real bullets flying by, real anti-aircraft fire going off all around you, or real surface-to-air and air-to-air missiles roaring by your airplane. In carrier aviation it's a little different than it is in other services. The reason is simple. The end of the mission involves a carrier landing, which induces more excitement than enemy fire. So, the "fog of war" sometimes occurs around the carrier, especially at night.

There probably isn't a carrier aviator alive who has not heard the terrible sound of a fellow aviator in trouble. More often than not, the difficulty begins with a case of what is called "vertigo." Very simply, the balance system in humans is governed to a large extent by a series of semi-circular canals in the inner ear. There is a fluid in the canals. Also, sticking into the fluid are hair-like sensors which move with the movement of the fluid. Anything, body movement or movement of one's airplane, that causes the fluid to slosh back and forth in the inner ear is sensed and transmitted to the brain, where it is interpreted. We know that our senses can play tricks with us. When in an airplane without visual reference to the horizon, in the clouds or at night, our senses can convince us we are in a steep bank when we are not. The phenomenon, vertigo, has probably killed more Naval aviators than any other single thing. That is why the training in instrument flight is so intense. The motto, "Believe what your instruments tell you, not what your body tells you," is absolutely mandatory for a carrier pilot who wishes for a long career.

The event which comes to my mind is the case of the young Skyhawk pilot off the *Hancock* during a Tonkin Gulf deployment in 1968. He apparently had a bad case of vertigo on a particularly dark night. It didn't become apparent until the end of the mission when he attempted a night carrier landing. His first approach was so rough that he seemed to be all over the sky. The landing signal officer (LSO) waved him off, and he disappeared into the dark ahead of the ship. Carrier air traffic control center (CATCC) vectored him around the night bolter pattern and fed him into the next available slot for another approach.

Six minutes later he called the ball for another approach. The same thing happened again. His glide slope, line-up, and speed control were horrible. The LSO waved him off and sent him around "the penalty box," this time advising him as he again disappeared ahead of the ship that his approach was really rough and that he had to buckle down in order to get aboard. At this juncture fuel was still not a problem. I was passing "platform" about 15 miles behind the ship, and heard him as I switched to the carrier controlled approach (CCA) radio frequency. His voice croaked a little, there was a tremor in his transmissions, and he seemed to be holding the microphone button too long after each of his radio calls. I could hear him breathing during those brief intervals when he wasn't talking…just breathing. It was an eerie sound, and it made me extremely uncomfortable. I found myself wondering if I was listening to the voice of a young man about to die.

After the third waveoff, another LSO's voice took over. I recognized it as that of the air wing LSO. He spoke with the tones of a chaplain in the confessional. "Three Zero Four, you have a case of vertigo. I want you to stop moving your head around in the cockpit. Concentrate on the flight instruments directly in front of you. When I call ball, I want you to raise your eyes, not your head, and concentrate on ball control and line-up. Understand?" The young man's voice rogered the lengthy transmission a little shakily. By now he was on the downwind leg, and I could see his running lights as the CATCC controller turned him in ahead of me. It looked a little close, and I made a mental note to anticipate an interval waveoff if he didn't clear the landing area very speedily.

As luck would have it, he was again too rough on the glide slope, and the LSO waved him off again. The chaplain's voice came up on the radio, as soothing as can be: "Three Zero Four, this is Paddles. That was a little better, but still not good enough. Remember what I said about moving your head around too much. Now, let's see you get aboard next time. Got it?" The young man rogered.

I now had a clear shot at a trap and made it ok. I was taxiing forward and still listening to the young man, who was again on the downwind leg for his fourth attempt. Now, fuel became a concern. "Three Zero Four, this Rampage Approach. What state, over?" CATCC was asking him how much fuel he had remaining after three waveoffs. There was a long silence…and I knew why. The young man had begun to settle down; and suddenly they were asking him for information from an instrument which was not in his present field of view. Of course, it was right there on the instrument panel, I knew because I had flown the *Skyhawk* enough to know. But, it was not in his comfortable scan pattern, and I could tell he was reluctant to break into his newly acquired equanimity to shift his glance to the fuel quantity gauge, which was out on the lower right hand corner of the instrument panel. The CATCC controller repeated his question. Again, there was a deafening silence. This time it seemed like an eternity before the controller again asked for his fuel state…with a noticeable edge of irritation. "Three Zero Four, this is *Rampage* Approach. I say again, what state. Over?" This time the young man answered with authority, as though he had somehow figured out what his real priorities were.

"*Rampage* Approach, this is Three Zero Four. Ask me something in the middle!" He got aboard on that approach without incident. But, the legacy of his classic comment lives on, and will continue to do so for years. Anyone in the air wing, after that incident, who was asked a stupid question by *Rampage* Approach would feel free to give a version of that classic answer.

One evening after this event had faded into the background, I shared a "flight suit" mess table with the same young man. We reminisced for a while, and he finally revealed an earlier incident in his career of which I had heard as more of an apocryphal story. But it was definitely another "fog of war" phenomenon.

It seems the young man had been conducting carrier qualifications in a Skyhawk on *Ticonderoga* in 1966 just west of the island of San Clemente. This time it was in broad daylight. The young man had experienced failures of his gyro compass, navigational system, and radio and, because he was at bingo fuel, the ship decided to send him to NAS Miramar. He was given a vector of 089 degrees magnetic 148 nautical miles. The young man did the proper thing, added full power, sucked up his wheels and flaps, and started a climb to his maximum bingo profile altitude of 30,000 feet. The problem was that he used his gyro as a principal heading reference when, in fact, that instrument was reading 180 degrees out. He was already passing through 15,000 feet and climbing like a homesick angel before the ship's radar controller spotted him west of the ship and heading west, away from the continental United States at a ground speed of almost 400 knots! With precious little fuel remaining, the horrified controller tried in vain to establish radio contact with him. His radio, operating intermittently, had now seemed to shut down altogether. It was late in the afternoon and soon it would be dark. If they didn't get him to turn around in the next few minutes, he wouldn't even be able to make it back to the single emergency runway on San Clemente Island.

Things were frantic in CATCC until one of the controllers finally established radio contact and got the errant Skyhawk pilot to turn around toward the good old USA. A check of his fuel reserves told the controller that he could never make it to Miramar. In fact, we calculated that he would be lucky to make it to San Clemente. He finally made to that remote island 75 miles west of San Diego just about "on fumes," and refueled from the emergency Navy ground crew there.

The next day, back aboard *Ticonderoga*, the squadron executive officer was questioning him about the incident. Why, he asked the young man, knowing his gyro compass was inoperative, didn't he use the wet compass (the wet compass is a rudimentary emergency instrument mounted on the inside of the starboard canopy bow to be used only if everything else failed)?

"I couldn't see it!", the young man answered. The exec was stunned by this answer.

"I don't understand. Why couldn't you see it?" he pursued. The young man's response was made with perfect insouciance.

"Because the sun was directly ahead, low on the horizon, and was blinding me!" The dumfounded exec didn't have the heart at the moment to remind the young man that the sun sets in the west!

The young man and I had a good laugh over this incident, which only served to prove that distractions like high anxiety can cause even the most rational pilot to ignore the most obvious things. That was when he confessed to an even more monumental fog of war incident.

It seems that he was returning from a solo flight in the primary flight phase of the Naval Air Training Command. He experienced a rough-running engine in his SNJ and ended up landing at Whiting Field with his wheels up. In the process of dealing with the engine problem he had become distracted. There is a warning horn which goes off in the SNJ cockpit with deafening intensity whenever the power is reduced to near idle with the wheels up. It is there specifically to prevent pilots from forgetting to lower their wheels when they prepare to land. The young man came in, preoccupied with his engine problem, and simply forgot to put the wheels down. The tower operator ended up screaming at him again and again over the radio to "wave it off, your wheels are up." But he continued right to a touchdown, whereupon the airplane slid to an ignominious halt on the runway on its belly with the propeller blades bent back like spaghetti.

When the accident investigation board interviewed him, they asked why he didn't heed the tower operator's warning, his answer was stunningly insouciant: "I couldn't hear anything on the radio because of that crazy horn!"

Chapter 31:
Cocktale

"There is a devil in every berry of the grape"
- The Koran

When word came down that *Wasp* would be spending the next couple of months in the North Atlantic on maneuvers, Colyers' tongue started sticking to the roof of his mouth. Pete Colyer was his name, but he preferred to be called Don. He was fair haired, blue eyed, well built, good with his fists, and a natural salesman.

When I first met Don I was puzzled by the crow's feet and squint that made his otherwise youthful face look older. Then Don explained about his family's love affair with sailing, and the years of squinting across the ocean in search of vagrant breezes while under sail. Later on, in Narragansett Bay, Don taught me the art of sailing.

Tied to the dock behind the house was an assortment of boats. They were members of the local yacht club and raced in regattas each weekend. The Colyers entertained frequently, and that was what Don was used to; a cocktail in the evening, before dinner. Therein lay the problem. The Navy did not allow alcohol aboard their vessels, at least not knowingly.

As Don saw it, we would be living in an uncivilized fashion for the duration of the cruise. And so it was that sitting in our five inch gun tub, we discussed the problem and resolved to stock up on liquor before the cruise.

As an aside, the five inch guns, a pair of them, were the responsibility of the Marines. They were also Don's and my assigned responsibility. The two of us would chip and paint them, lube them, and so on. Whenever Wasp practiced firing the guns, Colyer and I worked the five inch guns.

My job was to load a 60 lb. projectile into the breech. Colyer sat at a console and made intricate adjustments to a bank of dials. Don wore one of those oversized helmets that fit over your head when you wear earphones. No one ever spoke to Colyer over those earphones, ever. And no one ever explained my job to me, ever. I just figured it out. After all, if I could fire an M-1, I could fire something a little bigger.

One day while we were resting after firing a zillion projectiles into the ionosphere, I asked Colyer just what it was that he did sitting there at the console. "I haven't the faintest idea" Colyer replied. "But you are very busy cranking the two handles attached to the console. Surely, you are following some rational plan," I retorted. Colyer grinned and shook his head sadly. "Gil, I just chase the dials around with the crank handles to ease the boredom." Neither of us knew what we were doing, aside from launching 60 lb. high explosive projectiles out into space. Fortunately, I never saw us hit a thing.

Getting back to our story, on our last Cruise, Colyer and I had consulted with a rebel moonshiner and had started our own still on board Wasp. The rebel's recommended list of equipment included many hard to steal items, for example, a pair of used red woolen drawers. According to the rebel, the drawers had unusual properties for filtering out the impurities in the moonshine.

The still project went pretty well for a while. Our biggest problem was that an active still has a distinct aroma; quite pleasant, actually, but pervasive. The Revenuers found our still and Colyer got me in trouble again.

Once before Don and I had managed to get alcoholic beverages aboard. On that occasion, *Wasp* had anchored off Hyannis Port on Cape Cod, and liberty launches were ferrying the happy young sailors to and from the sandy, summertime resort. The radios were playing favorites about love letters in the sand and sand dunes and salt sea air and lobster stew, by a window with an ocean view, but our two young marines were confined to the ship, again because of some misunderstanding. Colyer and I were as lonely as two chained up hound dogs. It's a wonder we didn't break down and bawl.

The weather was perfect; blue skies and azure seas. Small runabouts kept rumbling alongside as bikini clad young maidens smiled through white teeth and caramel tans at the sorry pair in the five inch gun tub. To keep us out of more trouble, we had been put to work chipping and painting the cannons.

Suddenly, we had an idea. Colyer ran off and stole a hundred foot hank of line. I think he unraveled the line from some poor soul's bunk, leaving the guy no place to sleep. We tied a loop in the end of the line and hung it over the side of the ship. It was bluefish season, but we were fishing for beers.

The happy vacationers in the runabouts took pity on two fatigue-clad young marines and tied cans of beer to our line. All afternoon, Don, the salesman, cajoled the boaters, and by sundown.... we were in trouble again. The two cannons looked like someone was trying to camouflage them.

On the forthcoming cruise, the two of us resolved to go First Cabin, and buy bottled liquor, good stuff. The problem was, how to sneak the alcohol aboard unnoticed. Now, as seems always the case, our sins came home to roost. Colyer and I had on occasions in the past taken great delight in stopping someone else from sneaking liquor aboard. Our method was simplicity itself. We both stood many hours of guard duty on the after brow. While standing guard, if some swabby had a suspicious bulge in his blouse as he started up the gangway, we would swat him in the midriff with our night stick, shattering the bottle hidden therein, sending shards of glass down into his jockey shorts. It almost made watch standing enjoyable.

Since we had made reputations for ourselves and a long line of people were waiting for a chance to get even, Colyer and I needed to avoid the enlisted men's gangway when sneaking our cocktail material aboard. Don and I had our usual boisterous liberty, and cracked a few cans of beer.

During the course of the evening, Colyer had purchased three bottles of JW Dant for the cruise. When we were ready to return to *Wasp*, I strapped the bottles against my stomach. There was still a distinctive bulge, however, so we had to be inventive. We decided that it would be necessary for me to remain doubled over, arms holding my stomach, as though sick, to hide the telltale bulge.

Our breath was heavy with alcohol fumes as we headed up the Officers' gangway. My job was to appear under the *influence* and sick. This I did with an ease that comes from much practice. Colyer was dragging me by the arm, cajoling and laughing uproariously, swearing a blue streak. Colyer could have earned an Oscar.

It so happens that enlisted personnel were not permitted to use the officers' gangway. The Watch Officer, a lieutenant (jg), was in such a state at our perceived mistake in coming up a gangway reserved for officers that he had trouble speaking. To make matters worse, we were obviously drunk and disorderly. As he stepped into our irregular path to personally stop this outrage, our plan called for me to vomit on his shoes. Colyer considered this the *piece de resistance* of the whole project. It was going to be a shoo-in, or more precisely, a shoe-on. As I began to regurgitate, the lieutenant danced away like Muhammad Ali. He was horrified.

"Why do these ridiculous things always have to happen to me?" the lieutenant was thinking. The duty petty officer was a salty old fellow who had been 'round the Horn a time or two. Out of the corner of my eye I caught him watching, amused, from a safe distance. The lieutenant, after ranting and raving, shouted for him to get us the hell out of sight immediately...mission accomplished.

Silently chuckling, Colyer and I scuttled below to the Marine quarters to hide our contraband. Our plan had worked like a charm thus far, but as is so often the case, overconfidence will get you. Don and I took the grill off of the big overhead exhaust duct in the marine troop quarters and hid the bottles up in the duct. No one would ever find them there. How prophetic. No sooner had we stowed the cocktail makings, than the exhaust system cranked up to a roar.

Now, it so happened that there was practically zero friction between the glass of the bottles and the metal of the duct work. As we stood looking up at the exhaust duct, the rush of air started slowly sucking our bottles through the ductwork foot by foot. Off through the maze of ducts the bottles slid; into the bowels of *Wasp*, never to be seen again.

For a time, the smugglers followed the progress of the bourbon by listening to the gritty sound and the occasional clink the bottles made as they slid through the duct. The sight of two young marines, moving crablike through the ship's passageways, staring intently at the overhead ductwork, swearing passionately, must have been bizarre.

After all our work and considerable expense, we were skunked. Colyer couldn't believe our bad luck. Two red blooded, squared away Marines deserved better than this! We were beside ourselves. Colyer and I were so upset that there were accusations on both sides. The two of us finally calmed down and resolved to get out of this chickenshit outfit as soon as possible, then hit the sack, disgusted.

A busy month went by, and after an astounding North Atlantic storm, Colyer and I again sat in the five inch gun tub chatting. The dream of an evening aperitif had not died. We were both feeling a bit liverish. After all, our normal intake of alcohol had been reduced to zero, up in the North Atlantic. Sitting there in the gun tub, we reexamined our options and resolved to try to recover our treasure.

Colyer and I reasoned that we would need to study the damage control drawings locked in the cabinet in the passageway outside the Marine quarters, so we devised another plan of action. On the quiet, in the following days, we got into the cabinet holding the drawings.

Problem solving so absorbs the mind that time flies. After deciphering the drawings, Don and I made several assumptions regarding where the bottles might get stopped inside the ductwork and decided to disassemble the entire duct system if necessary and retrieve our rightful property.

The following night the smugglers waited until most of the personnel were asleep, than set up cones and safety tape just like the damage control party did. The only odd thing that a casual observer would notice, was that this damage control party was made up of two thirsty young marines. There were a few odd looks, but we kept busy unfastening the hangers and removing the ducts, laying them all in the passageways, using our bayonets as tools. In the early hours of the morning, we finally were able to look into the end of the open ductwork and see our treasure, just a few short feet away.

Colyer and I were so pleased with ourselves, that the urge to rush off to sit in the five inch gun tub and have a well deserved cocktail almost tempted us to leave the duct work laying in the passageway for the real damage control party.

Later, in the gun tub, as we enjoyed our rewards, Colyer and I toasted each other and our futures. We also spent some time fine tuning our plan to buy an old sailboat when we were discharged, and sail around the world. After a couple of cocktails and some more discussion, we resolved to hammer out a workable plan; a far grander plan, to bring women on the next cruise. The last time we were in port, we had broached the subject with a couple of the hardier *Roses of Boston*, and they were enthusiastic. Looking back on those days, it seems like Colyer was always getting me in trouble.

Chapter 32:
"What Do You Mean, Old?"

" The Admiral rides in his motor barge;
The Captain, he rides in his gig.
It won't go a god-damn bit faster,
But it makes the old bastard feel big!"
- Old U.S. Navy sea chanty.

The main fleet anchorage at the atoll of Ulithi was the site, more than once, of the greatest assemblage of Naval power that the world has ever seen! On this particular occasion the 3rd and 5th Fleets were assembled for the purpose of preparing for a major assault on the Japanese homeland …4,000 combatant vessels of all shapes and sizes…from the battleships, to attack carriers, thence all the way down the tonnage scale to the lowly minesweepers. The aerial photos taken of the event show ships anchored in orderly rows and tiers from horizon to horizon. The year was 1945, and it was a glorious spring morning. World War II was in its final act.

Fleet Admiral Chester Nimitz, the senior officer present afloat (SOPA), called numerous meetings, and the goings and comings of gigs and barges carrying various fleet dignitaries to and from the flagships resembled a beehive. My brother, John, an ensign aboard the cruiser *Birmingham*, was a witness to it all. It was a sight never to be forgotten.

At the end of one of those innumerable meetings, Admiral "Bull" Halsey appeared on the quarterdeck of Nimitz' flagship, USS *Missouri*, and called for his barge to take him back to his own flagship, the fast attack carrier, USS *Enterprise*. The signal to come alongside the accommodation ladder was passed by the OOD's bullhorn to the crew of Halsey's barge, who were tied up to the boat boom extending outboard from *Missouri's* quarterdeck.

Halsey's boat crew sprang into action, started their engine, cast off from the boat boom, and made their way to the accommodation ladder under the watchful eye of more than a dozen captains and lesser admirals. Unfortunately, the prevailing wind was setting them onto the ship, and the bo'sun piloting the barge was forced to miss the approach and veer away rather than hit the accommodation ladder platform with a healthy impact. Halsey was leaning on the railing of the quarterdeck, watching the performance with a typical glowering expression on his face. The audience, not aware that it was a typical expression, immediately began to feel compassion for the fate of the boat crew who were appearing to be more than a little inept.

The barge boatswain rang the little bell on the stern of the barge whenever he wanted the engineman to change power. One bell meant all engines stop (idle), two bells meant all ahead one-third, three meant two-thirds, four meant full power, and five meant all engines back. With much ringing of the bells, the now nervous boat crew began a second approach and duplicated the earlier mistakes, causing them to veer off a second time. The audience on the quarterdeck held their breaths, knowing that this was now very serious for the two errant seamen…very serious.

The admiral cleared his throat and made a caustic comment which could be heard by everybody present over the sounds of the engine. "I hope this won't take all day!" he rumbled, causing several of the more junior officers present to quake in their boots. This was, after all, the same irascible Naval officer who could skin the hide off a junior merely with one of his withering glares. The bo'sun overheard the remark and was understandably stung by its sarcasm. Calling down to the engineman with a remark he never intended to be heard by anyone else, he said something he came immediately to regret.

"I suppose the old bastard thinks he could do better himself!" It was a foolish thing to say, but the boatswain felt certain no one would overhear the indiscreet remark over the sound of the engine. Unfortunately, the boatswain had just rung one bell. As the unwise remark escaped his lips the engineman pulled the engine throttle all the way to idle and a heavy silence ensued. The bo'sun's earthy comment could be heard across the intervening 50 feet of water as clear as a bell. The audience was aghast! No one uttered a sound as they waited for the explosion from Halsey.

In that pregnant moment at that remote spot in the western Pacific Ocean, amidst the enormous assemblage of men-of-war, time seemed to stand still. The crusty, four-star admiral stood there, hands on the rail, glowering at the boat crew for a few interminable seconds, then took in a deep breath and retorted to the boatswain the remark that was to make its way around all 4,000 ships in the anchorage like a firestorm. His voice came out like a roar!

"WHAT DO YOU MEAN, OLD?"

Chapter 33:
A Photographic Memory

"One picture is worth a thousand words"

Lowly young privates are not consulted when the Corps decides to implement a troop movement. And so it was that some of us were called out of a training class one day and told to pack our sea bag, and to be ready to leave the ship in an hour. Mild surprise was all that registered as we gathered on the dock with our gear and rifles.

A bus eventually arrived, and we all piled on and sat down. Experience told us that nothing ever happened fast in the Corps. The sergeant in charge was standing by the bus waiting for some signal to go. After a time, one of the office pogues trotted up and handed him a big manila envelope with all our travel chits and orders bundled together. The sergeant hopped aboard and we were off.

The last bus trip Colyer and I had been on was a ride from Portsmouth, VA, to Boston. That ride had taken forever, bouncing about on a yellow school bus like a football team. My imagination was in neutral, so I didn't even speculate on our destination. Some of the Southern lads were making quantum leaps to conclude the most unlikely of destinations.

Can't say I blamed them; we had done some odd jobs in the Corps. For instance, some time earlier, a few of us were called to the armory and handed submachine guns and trench guns, along with bandoleers of ammunition. You'd have thought that we were going to guard Fort Knox.

The lieutenant at that time was a tough Marine whom we all respected. When we were all armed and deadly, the lieutenant gathered us and explained that Wasp was about to go on a cruise, and the ship's pursar figured that we would need millions of dollars for the cruise.

Maybe we would need a tow or to pay a speeding ticket. It was no different than any family vacation. Go to the bank and get enough traveler's checks to carry you for the extent of the trip. The lieutenant told us that the pursar would be along shortly to go to the bank in the middle of Boston to pick up the loot. "Don't let anybody take the money from the swabbies," the lieutenant warned us. We climbed aboard a step van and a jeep, and drove to the bank in downtown Boston.

It was lunchtime on a Wednesday, and half of Boston was wandering the streets. We all felt personally responsible for the money, and each of us had made our own vow that we would not be easy pickin's. When the van stopped we all took up positions in doorways and store fronts, up and down the street, submachine guns cocked.

The Corps is right in picking young men with a sense of immortality and absolutely no sense of responsibility. Those young men will do just about anything, if told to do so, and quite often in spite of being told not to. Thank God no fool tried anything.

Anyway, our bus journey was hardly started when we stopped at the railroad station in South Boston. The sergeant collected the troops, and the next thing we knew, we were boarding a train. A holiday spirit overtook us as we sat back to enjoy the trip. Women were everywhere, and lonely young Marines were enjoying the proximity, the scents, and the largely imagined rustle of underwear as they walked the aisles of the train. Our necks were on swivels. Apparently, we were headed South. In due time the train stopped in Providence, so the passengers and troops could transfer to another train.

In past idle moments, my bunk mate Colyer and I had chatted about some of the fun times I had enjoyed in Providence before enlisting. As we saw it, here was a golden oppor-tunity to visit one of my old haunts for a crisp, frosty cold beer. *Ein voom fras grossen, bitte*!

The train wasn't due for half an hour, so Colyer and I had ample time for a brew. Naturally, the sergeant warned all to "Stay together, and by God don't leave the platform." As we saw it, sergeants were born killjoys and weren't to be taken too seriously, so off we went. Providence is a college town with lots of girls about. We had discovered over time, that some of those girls like uniforms and masterful young men. Hell, Colyer and I were willing to roleplay anyway they wanted.

Colyer and I somehow let time fly by and forgot about the station, the troops, the racks of M-1s, and the piles of seabags, and the sergeant, too. At some point in the evening, some college boys took exception to two lowly Marines keeping company with their girlfriends.

The upshot of the difference of opinions was that two innocent, misunderstood, young Marines were incarcerated. The Navy Shore Patrol was called, and we were eventually turned over to them. The ensign in charge was a Napoleonic little man without a proper sense of respect for Marines. After we were unable to produce proper paper work to justify our presence, we explained that the troops were at the station waiting for a train. The ensign marched us off to the railroad station, guarded by about eight swabbies. When we arrived, the troops were gone, along with all our gear and rifles.

Colyer's apple pie American face and sincere nature worked like a charm, and the ensign believed everything Colyer said. It was amazing! For reasons I never understood, Colyer said "The sergeant said something about the bus station." With that, we marched over to the bus station to find the troops. Once there, the ensign sent the Shore Patrol in all directions, looking for the troops. Colyer had the ensign thoroughly convinced that this was a total misunderstanding.

An idea suddenly popped into my head. We were standing a few feet from one of those photo booths. You know, the ones with the curtain. For a quarter, you can sit on a stool and have your picture taken. The ensign must have missed his supper, because he was fidgety. As he paced away from us, I grabbed Colyer's arm and pulled him into the booth. We pulled the curtain shut and both squatted on the stool so our feet wouldn't show.

Perhaps we had one too many beers that evening, but as we balanced on the stool, the ensign turned and suddenly realized we were gone. There was a lot of shouting, whistle blowing, and general running around going outside the booth. Colyer and I looked at each other and silently giggled. Then I put a quarter in the machine and took our picture. Still have that picture... and many other memories of the antics of two overactive, frustrated young Marines.

Gillcrist and Colyer on Liberty, 1958. (Bob Gillcrist Collection)

Chapter 34:
Big Brother

"One more such victory and we are undone"

- Pyrrhus of Epirus B.C. 297

When George Orwell wrote "1984," he introduced into the American lexicon a number of new expressions, like "double speak," and, of course, that omnipotent figure "Big Brother," whose attention nothing escaped, no matter how small the pecadillo that one of the new-world citizens may have committed. "Big Brother is watching you," is an expression for the ever-increasing watchdog roles which governments tend to assume in "protecting" its citizenry.

Now that I have no assets to manage and no people to lead, I believe I can reveal a few of the leadership principles which seemed to have been useful during my Navy career. One of them is an offshoot of Orwell's Big Brother. The rule is simple: If people in your organization are foolish enough to ascribe certain supernatural qualities to you...do not disenchant them. Let them think you are what they think. After all, what harm can it do?

To illustrate the point; when I arrived as the functional wing commander at NAS Miramar in 1979, I noticed that everyone seemed to be waiting to see if my management style was going to be as silly as my predecessor's. That was easy! But about three weeks after I took over what turned out to be the best job I ever had, my brother came to visit.

I took a day off to show him and his wife around the greater San Diego area. As luck would have it, one of the points of interest I showed them was the Cabrillo National Monument near the tip of Point Loma, not far from the old lighthouse. The monument occupies a commanding view of San Diego, the Pacific Ocean, and the Naval Air Station at North Island. In fact, it looks down on the air station and the main channel that runs from San Diego Bay to the Pacific Ocean...a great whale watching spot.

It was one of those glorious days in August..."another ho-hum day in Paradise," as San Diegans are wont to say. The sky was crystal-clear and blue, the temperature was a dry 78 degrees, and there was a slight ocean breeze of about 15 knots. What more could you ask?

After looking through the monument's interior exhibits, we went outside to the viewing terrace where there were a few of those large binoculars mounted on pedestals, the kind that are perfect for watching whales. It provided a spectacular panorama. I put a quarter into one of the binoculars and spun it around so that my brother and his wife could enjoy the scenery. My brother turned the scope in the direction of the Los Coronados islands, which lie off the coast of Mexico. I explained that the airspace above those islands was used frequently for overwater air combat maneuvering (ACM) training by Miramar's fighter squadrons, as well as Topgun. As I was talking my brother exclaimed, "I see some airplanes coming our way." He swung the binoculars around to me and I took a look. They were no larger than two specks, but they seemed to be at low altitude and coming directly toward us.

In a few seconds I was able to identify them as F-5s...they had to be from Topgun! I was now more than curious. Topgun's adversary airplanes were the only F-5s in the area and should normally be transiting to the ACM area and back at an altitude of say 15,000 feet. But here were two of them at no more than 1,500 feet, going fairly slow, and headed, apparently, for North Island, a base they never used! What in the world, I wondered, was going on? As I watched them about five miles away now, I saw the wheels come down on both airplanes...strange. The airplanes were now clearly going to land at North island. Not only that, but they were making a straight-in approach to Runway 36, the north runway. Runway 36 is too short for normal F-5 landings. In fact, the only runway long enough for routine F-5 landings is the east-west runway 08/26. Immediately, I decided that there must be some kind of emergency.

Adjusting the focus on the binoculars, I tried to ascertain what the problem was, but could determine nothing except that they were going to make a section landing...an evolution hardly ever done at Miramar. At this juncture, nothing about this whole evolution made any sense. I did know, however, that I was occupying a ringside seat for something that I didn't understand...but was getting more fascinating by the minute.

The two airplanes touched down smoothly and rolled speedily down the short runway. I found myself holding my breath lest one or both of them blow a tire trying to stop. They finally slowed enough to make the right turn off at the end of the runway onto the taxiway. Curiously, the lead airplane continued taxiing south on the taxiway, and the number two airplane stopped. Shortly, the pilot got out and stood alongside his airplane as an emergency crash truck sped down the runway toward him. That was when the lights came on, and I understood what had just unfolded before my eyes.

These two airplanes had come in to North Island because they were low on fuel. The lead airplane had enough fuel remaining to taxi back to the transient line parking area. The wingman had flamed out on landing and had been able to keep his speed up enough to turn off and clear of the runway! Mind you, Miramar is only 15 miles farther! I found myself furious that these F-5 pilots, Topgun instructors, supposedly hand-picked from the best in the fleet...these supposed role models, these instructors, could be so irresponsible as to almost lose a couple of multi-million dollar airplanes from fuel starvation...and on a perfectly clear day!

I walked to the pay telephone a few feet away in a cold rage, dialed Topgun, and asked to speak to the skipper. It was a tight-jawed conversation. "Skipper, do you know where all your planes are?" I asked trying to sound innocent.

"Yes, sir, Admiral. I sure do. Six are in the air and the rest are parked outside on the ramp. Why do you ask?" was his prompt answer. But, I detected a certain wariness in his voice. I set the hook!

"Well, Skipper. You evidently don't know that two of them just made a straight-in section landing on Runway 36 at North Island. The section leader is taxiing back, but his wingman has just flamed out on the runway and is sitting in the warm-up area at the end of the runway waiting for the crash truck to arrive." There was a long silence.

"You're right, Admiral. I'm not aware of that." There was a pause as I imagined the skipper was furiously waving for his operations officer to come running in to tell him what the f—k was going on. "Sir, can you fill me in?" By that he meant, how in hell do you know this and I don't? I wasn't going to give away my secret…not yet.

"Never mind how I know. Just be aware that both airplanes and pilots are okay. But, Skipper, they may not be when they have the opportunity to explain all of this to me in my office tomorrow morning at 0800!"

"Yes, sir," the Skipper said, his voice sounding dismal. By now I could tell that someone at Topgun had confirmed what I had just told him. Then he added the question which I knew he was dying to ask.

"Admiral, with all due respect, how did you find out about this so fast?" It was what I had been waiting for.

"Skipper," I responded, "That isn't important. What is important is that I know everything that goes on in this wing!" I hung up without waiting for a comment. Pilot discipline went up several orders of magnitude in the wing after that. The word went around the twenty-eight squadrons in the wing like wildfire; Don't f—k around with the "Old Man," he has some kind of crystal ball!

Topgun F-5E Tiger, NAS Miramar, 1979. (Robert Lanson)

Chapter 35:
Postscript

"The sins committed by many pass unpunished."
- Lucan

The reason why *"A Slice of Water Melon"* has been lodged in my mind like a fish bone in the throat all these years is because that incident took place at about the same time that Colyer and I committed a sin of our own. Our penance was equivalent to three Our Fathers and three Hail Marys by comparison.

Our incident took place at Fort Devens, an Army Base near Cape Cod. It so happened that the Marine detachment was required to shoot for record once a year. The reason for this was to maintain our awards for marksmanship as Marine riflemen, a Marine tradition.

Off we went in a bus one sunny day, leaving dreary South Boston behind for a summer vacation of shooting in the country at Fort Devens. One-half the detachment went at a time, and all the young Marines were in a holiday mood.

In order to keep us isolated from the Army personnel at Fort Devens, it was decided to park the detachment in some unoccupied barracks at the far side of the reservation. And since we could only shoot during daylight hours, our young Marines had a problem keeping out of trouble after sundown. Idle minds are the Devil's workshop, was apropos.

Adjacent to our barracks was a large Army motor pool where anyone needing a vehicle went (with proper authorization). Shohammer, a young man from Minnesota, took a stroll one evening, and upon returning to the barracks reported to all the young marines reclining in their bunks sipping warm beer that the vehicles in the motor pool were all fueled up with the ignition key in the ignition—*ready to go.*

Colyer and I digested the information about the motor pool and the ignition keys, and after a few minutes' discussion over another warm beer, decided to take "French Leave" in Boston in our fatigues. Getting to Boston would be no problem, since the question of our transportation had just been settled.

Perhaps it needs to be said that in order to keep the marines out of all Army base facilities, we were given permission to stock up on beer in the barracks. The detachment dunned each man five dollars to buy beer at the PX, stacking the cases of beer ceiling high in the barracks. After a day in the sun shooting, a body can build up quite a thirst. Colyer and I had been slaking our thirst on warm beer for awhile before arriving at the decision to go to the big city.

It seems that Colyer and I were a little cavalier about the manner in which we roared through the main gate of Fort Devens in one of the Army's olive-drab pickup trucks, Budweiser in hand. After the ensuing chase, in which our dog of a pickup truck failed miserably, we were invited back to the stockade by the truculent MPs to cool our heels. After a time, the Marines were able to reclaim their property (Colyer and me), albeit reluctantly, and Colyer and I were in trouble again.

So many of life's vicissitudes revolve around perceptions. The differentiation between a slice of water melon and a Ford pickup is an example. All those months, after Fort Devens, watching Bill's ordeal in the brig, I pondered the magnitude of the injustice of Bill's passage in the belly of the beast for stealing a slice of watermelon. When I compared it to our punishment for stealing a Ford pick-up truck, my spirit grieved.

Chapter 36:
Bon Liberte

"Liberté, Égalité et Fraternité*"*
- Motto of France

Compared to my brothers, I spent little time at sea— about a year and a half. They spent many years literally sailing the seven seas. But my time at sea was not without incidents and interesting ports of call.

And if I had to choose the best liberty port, it would be a difficult decision. Wasp's visit to Cherbourg and liberty in Paris organized by the laundry and recreation officer was a life experience, but so was liberty in Jamaica and Oban and a few other places. But one of life's truisms is that Paris is never a bad choice, so what follows is an arguable stretch of a sea story concerning liberty in Paris.

After months in the North Atlantic on maneuvers, with the loss of shipmates to the Arctic Sea, the crew was definitely ready for some R&R. And so it was that as soon as *Wasp* tied up in Cherbourg, the 1MC announced that any of the ship's crew who had 30 dollars to spare could enjoy liberty in Paris.

Colyer and I immediately pooled our resources and made the decision to go. If we were careful and stayed out of trouble, we could afford the trip. None of us had passports, just our plain vanilla liberty passes, the same yellow card we used everywhere.

The two of us lined up outside the paymasters compartment to exchange a few hard earned dollars for a fist full of colorful francs (*du mille*, or 2000 francs was 10 dollars back then) and to pay the 30 dollars for the junket. My mom had providentially sent me two 20 dollar money orders, so we were all set. Then we threw a change of underwear and our shaving kit into one gym bag and lined up again for the trip to Paris.

As we exited the shipyard, we passed sullen, middle-aged French sailors armed with submachine guns. The trip to the train station in Cherbourg was a short one— *Le Gare,* as I recall. The train we boarded was a typical European train with multiple compartments lining one side of each car; just like one of those Agatha Christie novels. As soon as we boarded, Colyer divined that there was a wine cellar within the line of cars. Once we were underway, Colyer went in search of the wine cellar and returned with some mean brandy that we couldn't drink, but did anyway.

After an hour of excited chatter and tippling in our compartment as the train rattled on through the night, we speculated on how long it would take to reach The City of Lights.

The train soon slowed to a halt to waiting for other traffic, and standing outside the window we saw a French railroad worker swinging a lantern. I asked if anyone in the compartment spoke French. Colyer, with a demi of brandy on an empty stomach, piped up that he could.

The whole compartment encouraged Colyer, so he lowered the window and shouted out, "Eh Pierre, ow fair ezz eet du Paree?" The switchman didn't even bat a gallic eye. I've suspected for a long time that the French people have some humor code missing from their DNA strands.

When we finally reached Paris, it was about 10 pm. Colyer and I were soon assigned rooms in a cheap hotel near the station, and we began a *non parille* of a liberty.

The hotel was *Hotel D' Ocean* as I recall. The two of us ran up to our room to drop off our bag and use *le toilet*. As I wandered anxiously about the room waiting, Colyer went into the bathroom.

Within a few minutes he called out, "Hey, Gil, how the hell do you flush this thing?" As soon as I entered the bathroom, I knew the problem. Colyer, the bumpkin, had used the *bidet* instead of the toilet. Every time he tried to flush, the water shot up in his face. Now, I've been told that some perverts like that sort of thing. Colyer definitely did not. Well, we took one last look at the mess, then at each other, and decided to "hit the beach."

The next morning, the chambermaid discovered Colyer's gaff and with her Gallic rage simmering, waited for days before Colyer returned, and then chased him around the room, swatting away, shouting *"Chacon."* I can't imagine who ratted on him!

Perhaps it was a harbinger, but on that first fateful night, with no map or prior knowledge of the city, the two of us unerringly walked through the balmy evening, across The City of Lights to *Place Pigalle*.

For the next week, The Blue Train in Place Pigalle was home base and our *rendezvous*.

This vignette is really about the mental change we underwent during the transition from the Arctic Sea to Place Pigalle. The difference between sea duty and liberty in Paris is of the magnitude of light years. *"Vive la différence"* was intended to honor sexuality, but I think it applies to our liberty in Paris as well. And isn't that what liberty is for?

Over the past months in the Arctic Sea we had lived through storms that would be hard for the landsman to imagine. At one point, I literally hung on with one hand from a steel half-inch cable that ran along the port catwalk, dangling over those frigid waters, and looking death in the eye. Colyer and I shouldn't have been above deck., but as usual we knew better than a Navy Captain, with 30 years of experience, and so we had disobeyed orders and ventured out onto the catwalk in the worst of the storms. Understand, we had to experience it, and so we did.

But all that was behind us now, and Paris was before us. We resolved that over the next week, we would look the women of Paris in the eye, instead of looking Death in the eye, and we also resolved to hue to the old Irish proverb, "It's time enough to bid the Div'l g'day when you meet him."

The Blue Train in Place Pigalle was interesting for many reasons. One feature that I recall clearly was the custom through all the wars of soldiers removing insignia and shoulder patches which identified their units and fastening the patched to the walls and ceiling of the bistro. I thoroughly enjoyed sitting quietly for hours, sipping a beer while examining unit patches that went back to before the Second World War.

There were patches from Scottish Highland infantry, and German SS, and Australian and Indian units. I'd sit there imagining all those other young men, far from home, full of life, invincible, resting, laughing, loving, before going back to their wars.

High up on the wall behind the bar, hidden in the musty shadows, is a globe and anchor, a gift from two young Marines. Alongside the insignia, you might still find an exuberant, youthful expression of life, inscribed with a shaky hand. The scribe had to stand on the bar to reach and write. Some day I'll go back; perhaps only to find musty shadows.

That memorable liberty in Paris was during a warm, dry, sunny October, and the weather couldn't have been better. Words like *insouciance, panache, savoir faire, bonne vivant, et je ne se que,* were not words invented by Webster. They were terms that characterized Paris that balmy October. Paris was a *bouillabaisse* of moxie cabbies, saucy shop girls, inflexible flicks, arrogant Algerian and gay gigottes— a feast for two young Marines.

All day long I'd wander through the streets, resting in the endless variety of small seductive parks scattered throughout Paris, watching nannies sedately pushing carriages and sharing their employer's indiscretions.

And if I wasn't walking, I'd sit in a sidewalk cafe and watch the passersby. The chic women riding sidesaddle behind their man on a motorbike; while trying in vain to look modest. My fellow voyeurs in the cafc were just as interesting to watch. The mixed couples, an oddity elsewhere in those days, were common in Paris. And all the while, the waiter would be watching me to see how many hard boiled eggs or croissants I ate from the pedestal serving plate on my table.

One memorable afternoon, I made a point of sitting in the Cafe de La Paix to see if it was true, as the legend told, that if you sit long enough in the Cafe de La Paix, everyone you ever met will walk by. Some faces definitely did start to look familiar, after several aperitifs.

Later, on another beautiful afternoon as the shops were closing and the sun was low in the sky, all of Paris seemed to be heading home, *baguette* under arm. I stood in the metro, watching, listening, savoring the moment, as a lone musician played "Under the Bridges of Paris" on a concertina. The melody wafted through the metro passages; inspiring the homeward bound to step along.

Those baguettes were delicious, by the way. For *petite dejeune* I'd enjoy espresso and bread. For lunch, I discovered a sort of steak sandwich served on a half baguette, which was delicious. I remember a little spot that was within view of the Eiffel Tower, where I'd sit and munch my baguette and sip rough red wine— a feast for body and core! That was the moment that began the *beguine.*

Upon turning a corner in my wanderings one morning, I found myself facing a huge building, that took up a whole block. Red flags were flying and a banner strung across the front proclaimed to all of France that this was communist headquarters. I was stunned. The communists had only recently humiliated France at Dien Bien Phu, and yet they had the effrontery to maintain headquarters in the capital of France.

Contrary to popular belief, the Parisians were charmed by the young men in uniform and expressed themselves in different ways. One night I was invited to the Opera House. Another night I was invited to bed.

Inevitably, Colyer and I were introduced to the *flicks, les gendarmee,* like metal filings to a magnet. Our particular flick swooped out of the night, black cape flying, silent as an owl on his bicycle and rasped out *"attencion."* He must have served his military time as well, because he let us go.

Back then, Paris still had its' *pissoirs*; *kiosks* on the sidewalks to screen *les hommes* as they relieved themselves onto the cobble-stone walks. You could stand there and lift your hat or salute, and greet *memselle, "bon jour,"* looking over the screen as you took care of business. I couldn't help falling in love with France.

One warm day, I wandered by a meat market that was open to the air, unrefrigerated and home to a million flies. The flies were all over the cuts of meat, turning them black. The hams and rumps were displayed by hanging them from steel hooks along the wall.

When we were in Paris, the government was in the midst of a campaign to stop the Gallic habit of feeding babies and young children with wine soaked sops of bread. The French saw nothing wrong with this even as breakfast.

It was also about the time that the French-Algerian terrorists, the OAS, were waging their secret war to kill *"Le General."* It was also the time when the Indo-China war was occupying the minds of the people.

One night I wandered into a movie and watched as lone French soldiers fought in vain from stone blockhouses, against silent Viet Minh rebels creeping through the Indo-Chinese night.

Those blockhouses were the same blockhouses that I passed many times in a place called Viet Nam, 10 years later.

The French papers were full of stories of soldiers who did not want to go to Indo-China. I recall seeing a photo in the paper depicting a group of maybe 30 pilots who staged a sitdown strike on the middle of an air field, refusing to go to their war. They sat cross-legged in a tight group, scowling at the camera, dressed in flight suits. Some things don't change.

The Metro was a real surprise for a moxie youngster from New York. My first surprise occurred when I heard the Metro entering the station below as I bought my ticket. At top speed I dashed down the stairs to catch the French version of the subway. The gate to the platform was just ahead, and the Metro was standing in the station, doors still open. Other passengers were running through that gate ahead of me. I could still make it, I thought.

At 20 miles an hour I hit the gate and almost knocked myself out. The French added a mechanism to the gate to prevent late arrivals from rushing the train. In the last seconds before the train pulls out, the gate automatically locks. I felt like I had run into a brick wall, but I had to admit that it was a good safety device.

When the next train arrived, I hopped on and grabbed the first seat I saw. The people all gave me a dirty look and I wondered why. In time, feeling uncomfortable, I stood and looked back at my seat. There was a message on the seatback. In time I deciphered the French words. The gist of the message was that this seat was reserved for pregnant women and disabled veterans. I felt like two *sou*, but I was learning.

The Metro beneath Paris, in the 50s, had so many advances over the subway in New York. And it still does!

It may seem strange to today's travelers, but I never visited the Eiffel Tower. If I had to pay, or it was a tourist site, I skipped it. I preferred to walk and walk and get to know the city. The Bois de Bologne, Bou Miche, Montmatre, the length of the Seine lined with the cupboards of the many art dealers who peddle their wares along the river, all provided memories. It was at one of those cupboards that I bought a print that I still have. I became a *Boulevardier*.

At night, Colyer and I would rendezvous and stroll the City of Lights. One night we pressed our noses against the glass windows of *Maxims*, near *The Arc de Triumph*. We could not afford Maximes, so we found a delightful place near by, called *Fouqettes*. I think I could still find it today.

One of the reasons why Fouqettes is a clear memory is that at one point in the evening, both Colyer and I decided to find the toilet. As we opened the door to the toilet, we saw a room entirely tiled in white. There was a large drain in the middle of the floor and oddly enough, a pair of imprints of shoes impressed in the tile floor. There were no urinals or commodes, and the room hadn't been cleaned in awhile.

Colyer grabbed the door jamb, measured the distance to the foot prints with a steely eye, and like a gazelle leaped a distance of maybe ten feet across the floor intent on landing perfectly on the two foot prints. Needless to say, the act took a far greater degree of self control and athletic ability than Colyer possessed at that late hour.

His approach looked good but perhaps windshear came into effect, because Colyer's feet barely touched the wet tile before slipping off. Sadly, Colyer ended up in an offensive heap in the corner of the room. No amount of cleaning would ever make that green woolen uniform whole again. Unfortunately, in his alcoholic state Colyer didn't take much notice of his extremely unfastidious state.

Back in the bistro, Colyer's success rate with the women went down to zero in an instant. Those young women who, moments before, were captivated by Colyer's charm were now fainting away. And because we were shipmates, I wasn't doing too well either. Every time I moved away and started up a conversation, Colyer would stroll over like a prince and chase away my potential conquest.

As the end of our liberty in Paris drew near, Colyer and I resolved to burn the candle at both ends, and let the devil take the hindmost. We were literally swept out the door of The Blue Train late one Homeric night, by the maid who slammed the door and locked it behind us.

It was about four a.m. and the two of us stood on the cobblestones chatting, and unwilling to give up. The sounds of revelers came from a bistro across the street and we strolled over to investigate. The place was still hopping so in we went. When the clock struck seven a.m., we were still there and again the broom came out.

Back on the street, we noticed The Blue Train's door open once again, so back in we went for breakfast... and stayed on into the next night. Perhaps I should write to the Guinness Book of Records.

Another subject that could be termed Homeric had to do with a *jeune fille* named Collette. I doubt the Guinness' would be interested though.

The French have a term: *malaise*. That term best describes my state as our train pulled out of the Gare du Nord. I think I might have broken something in Paris.

My memoirs of Paris would not be complete without Edith Piatt; dubbed the sparrow by all Paris. Within my memories of Paris, it seemed like Edith could be heard singing from almost any bistro radio, any day. La Vie en Rose, Pigalleur, Mi Lord, all evoke melancholy memories, even after all these years.

Paris was good to two young Marines from the crew of *Wasp*. It was good liberty: *Bonne Liberté*!

Chapter 37:
The Backbone of the Navy

"The backbone of the Army is the non-commissioned man!"

- Rudyard Kipling: "The 'Eathen" 1896

Chief petty officers are frequently referred to as "the backbone of the Navy" for good reason. It has long been a basic element of Navy lore that the newly minted young officer arrives for his first assignment and is immediately placed under the tutelage of a crusty chief petty officer to "square him away." In my case I was given the best possible assignment in that category in Fighter Squadron 191. They made me the "line officer!"

The line was a division of the maintenance department and was the largest one in the squadron in terms of people. The division included all plane captains and personnel whose job it was to service aircraft with fuel, oil, hydraulic fluid, oxygen, nitrogen, pneumatic air, and, in general, prepare the airplanes for flight. Most important, however, the line contained all of the most junior enlisted men in the organization, the least experienced and least desired by the other divisions. So, it was simultaneously the biggest personnel headache in the squadron and at the same time the greatest opportunity for a junior officer to learn leadership.

I spent a great deal of time bailing my troops out of jail in all of the watering spots of the western Pacific; and standing beside them at captain's mast. It was a great learning experience. The division leading chief was David Johnson, a crusty veteran of 30 years or so. His language was as salty as his appearance, which included a CPO's bridge cap crushed to the proper droop and always perched on his head at the correct "salty" angle. Chief Johnson was the perfect tutor for Lieutenant (junior grade) Gillcrist…and one day he saved my career (but that will come later).

The second-tour pilots in the squadron had all come to respect Chief Johnson as a man of his word. If he said something was going to happen to your airplane, you could bet on it. Unfortunately, I had not yet developed that level of faith in the man. So, when I went up to the flight deck one day on USS *Oriskany* steaming in the Sea of Japan to man my airplane,

I was unprepared for what I found. There, parked among all of the other squadron airplanes, was mine…without a canopy! I was surprised, chagrined, and outraged all at the same time. When I had left the ready room headed for the flight deck, my airplane, side number 108, was labeled "up and ready." Now it was not. What had happened?

Chief Johnson was standing there watching the expression on my face with a knowing look on his own. Before I could open my mouth to berate him he said, "Relax, Lieutenant, the canopy is on its way up from the hangar deck." He further explained that it had developed a hydraulic leak, and they pulled it to replace a seal. Somewhat mollified, I proceeded to do a pre-flight inspection of my airplane, all the while keeping a weather eye out for my canopy to appear. It didn't appear by the time I finished my inspection. Looking up to the island structure of the carrier, I could see dozens of people watching from the captain's bridge, primary flight control, and even observers from the catwalks. I imagined they were snickering at me…and it ticked me off. Finally, I couldn't stand to wait any longer, as everybody else on the launch had already climbed into their cockpits and were strapping in.

"Chief," I shouted over the ambient flight deck noise, "Where the hell is my God-damned canopy?"

"It's coming, Lieutenant. Go ahead and man up."

Lt (ig) Gillcrist in his Cougar VF-191, U.S.S. Oriskany, Sea of Japan, 1955. (Paul Gillcrist Collection)

"Like hell, I will," I responded hotly. "I am not climbing into this airplane until there is a canopy on it. Jesus, I feel like an idiot!" His answer came couched in the soft, soothing tones of a chaplain.

"Go ahead. Get into the airplane, Lieutenant. The canopy is on its way. Everything is going to be all right." Muttering obscenities to myself, I reluctantly climbed the boarding ladder and, sitting down in the ejection seat, began strapping myself in. It felt odd sitting there without a canopy. I looked up into the catwalk above me several levels and recognized some air wing pilots pointing at me and laughing. I felt angry, stupid, cheated, abandoned, and foolish. Then came the voice of the air boss over the bullhorn.

"On the flight deck. Check chocks, tiedowns, and loose gear about the deck. Standby to start the jets." Turning to look at Chief Johnson, I shook my head emphatically and shouted, "Chief, I am not starting this engine without a God damned canopy! No God damned way!" He merely smiled and gave me a thumbs up signal…meaning go ahead and start your engine. Now I was really mad! The voice of the air boss came over the bullhorn again, this time with an electrifying directive.

"START THE JETS. START THE JETS!" The noise level on the flight deck trebled as engines began to wind up. The emphatic way I shook my head toward the chief prompted him to climb up the boarding ladder and shout into my ear.

"Go ahead, Lieutenant. Start the engine. It's all right. The canopy will be here any second." I grimly shrugged my shoulders and started the engine. Now I didn't even dare to look at my friends observing from Vulture's Row. I knew they were laughing their heads off. Seconds ticked by as I went through the post-start procedures of turning on my generator, radio equipment, and checking the readings on the oil and hydraulic gauges. Where, I asked myself over and over, was that frigging canopy?

Everyone on the flight deck seemed to be oblivious to my plight. I could only assume that they all had more faith in Chief Johnson than I did. A yellow-jerseyed flight deck director walked over to my airplane to give the plane captain the signal to remove the chain tiedowns preparatory to taxiing me forward to the catapults. This time I had had it. No God damned way was I going to taxi this airplane one frigging inch without a canopy. The vehemence with which I shook my head at Chief Johnson must have convinced him to make the trek up the boarding ladder again. When he leaned close to shout in my ear, I beat him to it and shouted back…our noses just inches apart. "God damn it, Chief. Do I look like an idiot? That frigging canopy must be coming from China! This has gone far enough. I want to know were that canopy is." He smiled broadly and confidently and leaned forward to shout in my ear.

"Lieutenant, I wouldn't kid you. The canopy will be here any second now. You gotta have a little faith! Now, go on and taxi this airplane or I am going to be in a heap of trouble with the air boss!" I couldn't stand it.

"*Going to be? Chief, you are already in trouble with me!*" I shouted. But it was too late. He never heard me, having already climbed back down to the flight deck and nodded to the flight deck director, who was now giving me the taxi forward signal. Almost in tears of frustration, I added power and felt my airplane begin to move forward towards the catapult. Jesus! I said to myself. I must be crazy. How embarrassing! The flight deck director gave me the stop signal directly behind the port jet blast deflector. The airplane just ahead of me was already hooked up on the port catapult and was coming up to full power.

Just then, a movement in the port deck edge catwalk caught my attention. It was two sailors and Chief Johnson carrying a canopy and struggling against the 30 knot gale blowing across the flight deck as they staggered toward my airplane. I don't know how they did it, because the canopy must have weighed two hundred pounds and was very unwieldy. But they clambered up the side of my airplane with it and popped it on top of me. The chief whipped out an open-end wrench and took a few deft turns with it. Then he reached into the cockpit, grabbed the canopy control handle and moved it to the forward position…letting the canopy move forward about three inches, and stopping it there. He moved the handle backward and the canopy opened to the full open position. He thumped me hard on the shoulder, flashed me the thumbs-up signal, and the most triumphant grin I ever saw crossed his face. He had done it! The port catapult fired and, as the jet blast deflector descended, I was taxied onto the catapult. The rest is history!

An hour and a half later, after I landed, my irritation at the chief had turned to admiration, and I almost forgot the whole incident. Then, three days later he must have figured out that I was worth saving…and he saved my Naval career!

The task force was steaming in the northern Sea of Japan, and the air wing was scheduled to give a firepower demonstration to a group of dignitaries from the SEATO Alliance countries that had come aboard for an orientation visit. It had been decided that the skipper's flight division (my division) would put on a strafing demonstration by firing at a spar towed behind a cruiser steaming alongside the carrier. The observers, gathered on the flight deck to watch, had a ringside seat for our demo. The skipper gave us an extra-long briefing to cover safety aspects about the strafing demonstration.

The target spar was towed at the end of a long steel cable behind the cruiser. The spar, as it passed through the water, created a geyser which shot up about 10 feet into the air. The geyser was our target. Our firing passes would be done at 450 knots in a 20-degree glide oriented 90 degrees to the course of the task force. We would fly a standard race-track pattern. All turns were made away from the ships so that if our guns went off accidentally in the pattern, no harm would be done. The other safety aspect which our skipper, "Butch" Voris, stressed was the danger of a phenomenon called "target fixation." "Squeeze off a two second burst," he told us, "and pull out immediately. It will put you level at 100 feet over the water. If you try to observe your bullet stream hit the target you will fly into the water at 450 knots and you will be history!"

Of course, I had heard all of this before and thought I was pretty good at strafing. We had been chosen to do the demonstration because our division had all done well in our recent competitive exercises. No sweat, I thought as we launched…this will be a "piece 'o cake!"

The demonstration went fairly well until about my fourth strafing run. During my firing burst I felt that I was getting great hits, and waited just a split second longer before pulling out in hopes of seeing my 20 millimeter rounds hit the target. That was all it took…a half a second…and then it was too late!

Realizing what I had done, I yanked back hard on the control stick and the airplane leveled off. Then, as the airplane settled, I waited for the impact and certain death. Just as the airplane bottomed out I felt a loud THUMP, and the airplane shook momentarily…then it was flying again. I was in a state of shock at what I had done. But I was also perplexed. Why wasn't I dead in a horrible ball of fire? Why was the airplane still flying? What had happened? What was that loud noise?

It is difficult to explain the emotions which ran through me for the remainder of the flight and the return to the carrier to land. It was with deep regret and horrible expectations that I crawled out of the airplane and motioned for Chief Johnson to follow me as I crawled under the belly of the airplane to look for damage. We found it! There was a deep depression in the belly of the airplane about four feet long, eight inches wide, and perhaps three inches deep. The geyser of sea water had all of the characteristics of a titanium rail when my airplane hit it at 450 knots. Fortunately, the airplane had been built by the Grumman Iron Works, and the keel area was heavily reinforced. Chief Johnson whistled when he saw the dent, and said only two words which startled me, "Bridle slap."

In those days, airplanes were catapulted by attaching the airplane to the catapult shuttle with a heavy bridle made of steel cable. At the end of the catapult stroke, the bridle fell away from the catapult shuttle and the airplane nearly simultaneously, and was retrieved by something called the bridle arrestor. Since the bridle was traveling about 150 knots, the arrestor was a fairly powerful piece of equipment. On occasions, the bridle would make contact with parts of the airplane as it fell away. This phenomenon was called bridle slap.

"No, Chief," I countered. "I flew into the geyser of water." Chief Johnson and I were squatting together under the wing of my airplane, separated from other people in the area. He repeated his statement.

"Lieutenant, that is bridle slap." Then he straightened up and walked down to the ready room where pilots were filling out maintenance reports and describing things that needed to be fixed on their airplanes. Once inside the ready room I again corrected him.

"Chief Johnson, I flew my airplane into that column of water!" I was still in shock and felt terrible about what I had just done. I realized that I had violated one of the most basic rules about strafing…one that had already killed scores of other tactical pilots. I also knew that I would probably be given some kind of flight violation and be evaluated by a board with the purpose of taking my wings away from me. My Naval career was over, and the realization sickened me. I felt desolate and must have looked it! Then, I was startled to hear his words for a third time. This time he stood very close to me and lowered his voice as he looked me square in the eye.

"Lieutenant, that was bridle slap. Do you understand...bridle slap!" Then I really understood what Chief Johnson was telling me. We looked at each other for a long two or three seconds in silence. Then I picked up the maintenance form and wrote two words, "bridle slap."

I do not know where Chief Johnson is today...or whether he is even alive. But, wherever you are Chief, I salute you!

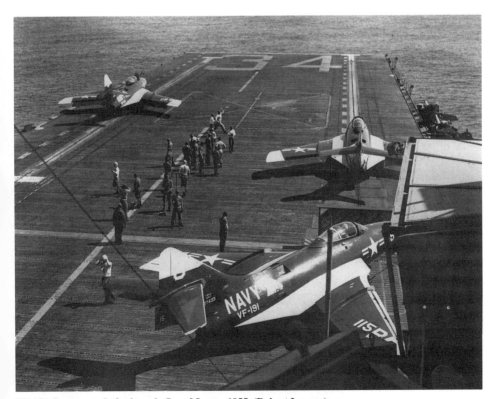

VF-191 Cougar ready for launch, Sea of Japan, 1955. (Robert Lanson)

Chapter 38:
Caribbean

*"Where the flying fishes play and the sun comes up like
thunder.... 'cross the Bay"*
- Rudyard Kipling

It was early morning after a restless night, and like a kid on Christmas morning, antici-pation had kept me awake. Just two days before, *Wasp* had stolen away from Boston during a blizzard. The wind had been nor'east, bitterly cold, and it cut like a knife, and brought tears to the eyes. It had been so cold that as Colyer and I stood in Scully Square in the prime of louthood, saying a melodious goodbye to Boston before slipping the lines, the beer had frozen solid in my mug.

By afternoon of that first day out, as I worked in the 5-inch gun tub, a change had come in the weather. As soon as I had noticed this, I had walked to the steel splinter shield and looked down into an azure sea and felt the caress of a balmy breeze.

It was that noticeable. A distinct line could clearly be seen in the sea below, separating the Gulf Stream from the cold North Atlantic. Wasp knifed through the phenomenon arro-gantly. That first sighting of the Gulf Stream is something that I will always remember. During my night watch in that steel tomb, the brig, I mulled over my forthcoming visit to the Caribbean. Novels and movies had given me some notion of what to expect, but as usual I needed to see for myself.

That was how I happened to be high up on W*asp's* island in the early hours of our second day out, standing on the catwalk, with a grey dawn looming in the east, washing away the stars. The first thing I noticed as I stepped over the coaming was a small island to starboard. It was a distant sighting, but I could make out a golden sand shore and the green of the palms as they stretched their trunks out over the water, as if protecting the island from the sun and weather. There was a hint of muskiness in the air, too. A piquant perfume, a compound of sun, vegetation, and animal life gently stirred by the trade winds.

Through the years, having been drawn back time after time to sail the Caribbean, I've concluded that the odor of musk was of land crab burrows and breadfruit, dead coral drying in the surf and climbing hybiscus, sugar cane, and charcoal. The odor was also of the sub-liminal scent left on the surface of the sea by the life hidden in the depths below, and of precious, punky, sump water captured by tile roofs and stored in secure dark cisterns like gold doubloons. It was a melding of all the scents that made up the islands. A musk out of the tropics—its' essence.

Had *Wasp* been close enough to the island to listen, we would have heard above the ambient hum of blowers, pumps, and turbines, all those early morning sounds peculiar to the islands—the first cock's crow and thirsty donkey's bray, the splash of pelicans as they fished for breakfast, the rustle of the fronds as the persistent trade winds upset the palms, the thump of ripe coconuts in the groves as they hit the sand, and the natives calling from the hills in their peculiar cadence as they gathered before the heat of day.

Closer to shore, the colors of the islands would have captured our eye. The sea itself can't make its mind up what color to be. Close to the shore it's as clear as air. A little farther out, the sea begins to turn azure, and then finally makes its mind up in its deepest, dark-blue. The colors of the island are as varied as its fruit. Banana yellow and lime green and plump kelly-green mangoes, and the natives themselves of a glossy brown with a brilliant white flash of a smile.

On that memorable morning of my first cruise to the Caribbean, the feast of the island sighting occupied my thoughts for some time before I walked to the forward end of the ship to look philosophically toward the future. It was while looking at the calm seas before the Wasp's bow that my eyes caught a flickering motion. For some reason, at that sleepy hour, *Wasp* was making gentle turns, moving through the sea as if afraid to disturb the tropical tableau.

The flickering resolved, with the help of borrowed binoculars, into dozens of flying fish. They sprouted from the sea under W*asp's* bow, millimeters ahead of the brutish steel bow plates, like apparitions. Their pectoral fins would blossom, and the flying fish would glide for hundreds of yards, then dip into the sea in a blink, leaving a sense that the imagi-nation had been playing with the eye.

It was a durable gift, a souvenir—the flying fish, the peaceful silence before dawn, the balmy trade winds, and the whisper of the tropical seas as they greeted the giant intruder from the north. Is it any wonder that many sailors from the cold, stark, disciplined northern climes have been enchanted by their first visit to the sleepy Caribbean, and jumped ship in their exuberance?

The time was February, 1958, and we were on our way to Guantanamo Bay, at the foot of Oriente Province, Cuba. Wasp had been ordered to Gitmo, to earn our "E" for excellence as a proud ship of the line. Within an impressionable young Marine's recollections, the cruise to Gitmo is just a vague memory, but the gift of the flying fish, the island, and the Caribbean Sea is a treasured mind picture, one that keeps calling me back.

Chapter 39:
Degree of Difficulty

"Where do we get such men?"

- James Michener: "The Bridges Of Toko Ri"

I will never forget his name or his smiling face or his ever present attitude of geniality. Epecially, I will never forget the backward triple somersaulting dive that Airman John Hemming executed from the flight deck of the USS *Bon Homme Richard* (CVA-31) into the Tonkin Gulf one warm spring day in 1968. Technically, his water entry was not perfect…far from it. However, I would have awarded him a "ten" for degree of difficulty had I been an Olympic diving judge.

For reasons I cannot recall our flight of four F-8s was parked side by side on the ramp (the rear edge of the flight deck) with their tailpipes extending out over the water. My airplane was on the extreme port side of the foursome nestled up against the port deck-edge catwalk. In other words, my F-8 was in the farthest left rear part of the flight deck. Obviously, it was the first launch of the day, and we were the last of the airplanes to be launched. As I strapped myself into the ejection seat, Airman Hemming busied himself immediately to remove the port jury strut, knowing it would be a problem.

Jury struts are devices clamped on to the wing-fold mechanisms of carrier airplanes that keep the wings from spreading after the hydraulic pressure has bled off following engine shutdown. The outer wing panels of the F-8 fold straight up. Without the jury struts installed, the wings tend to slowly fall back to the horizontal position, often coming to rest on some vulnerable part of an adjacent airplane. The port outer wing panel of my airplane would be out over the water if it accidentally spread, so it wasn't a problem. The problem was that, with a wind blowing and the jury strut installed, it was extremely difficult to remove it because the wind force against the wing panel would cause the strut to bind. Airman Hemming knew this, and was trying to remove it early.

But Hemming was short and couldn't reach the jury strut without standing on something. The only thing available on the flight deck was a wheel chock stood on end…a very precarious arrangement! I took a long look at the chock that was only a few inches from the scupper marking the edge of the flight deck. Beyond the scupper was a 68-foot drop to the water. I should have known better than to let him try to stand on that precarious perch. But I had seen plane captains do the trick hundreds of times before and with never a slip.

So there I was, strapping in…aware from the corner of my eye that Hemming was balanced on top of a chock pulling backward mightily at the reluctant jury strut. The wind was gusting, and every time it blew the jury strut would bind. Hemming was lunging backward with both hands on the jury strut, hoping that it would come free when the wind abated momentarily…and it finally did so!

Hemming gave one final heave backward, and the strut came free. He fell backward, both hands still grasping the strut, and gave a small yelp of fright. I glanced to my left just in time to see him tumble over the edge of the flight deck…end over end, falling the equivalent of a six-story building into the turbulent waters of the Tonkin Gulf. I counted the backward somersaults as I watched, horrified. He made three complete turns and luckily entered the water feet first with a resounding splash…still holding on to the damnable jury strut. Water geysered 20 feet into the air, and a few seconds later I saw his head reappear on the surface, drifting rapidly astern. Since my engine wasn't running, my radio wasn't working. I did all I could do, screaming at the top of my lungs, "Man overboard, port quarter. Man

Commander Joe Salin's Skyhawk coming aboard the U.S.S. Hancock, Tonkin Gulf, 1967. (Robert Lanson)

overboard port quarter!" Several other people saw Hemming fall and picked up the cry: "Man overboard. Port quarter!"

Word went quickly to the air boss, who dispatched the helicopter hovering a quarter mile off the starboard quarter. Within a minute or two the helicopter, now a mile astern of the ship, was hovering over Airman Hemming. I could still see him by craning my neck as he was lifted out of the water in the rescue sling. Of course, the launch had been delayed while this operation went on.

Finally, my plane captain was deposited, soaking wet, but otherwise all right, onto the flight deck a few hundred feet forward of where I was parked. A flight surgeon and two corpsmen with a Stokes litter came out on the flight deck toward the helicopter as soon as it touched down. But Hemming did a strange thing after he stepped out of the helicopter.

Completely ignoring the flight surgeon, he turned and sprinted down the flight deck in my direction. I couldn't believe what I was seeing! Ten seconds later Airman Hemming was standing by the left side of my airplane, panting and smiling. "Sorry, Skipper," he said, "I guess I need to be more careful with those jury struts!"

I sat there looking at him in utter disbelief. He had just fallen backward a full six stories into the water. The fall itself could easily have killed him. Finally, I shouted. "Hemming, for God sakes. Go down to sick bay and have them look you over. By the way, young man, I am really glad to see you back in one piece. Now, go!" He smiled again and saluted. Then he walked toward the two corpsmen carrying the litter. He refused to get in the litter, and followed them to the hatch in the island into which he disappeared.

The flight went okay…I think. During most of it I found myself thinking about the young man who had nearly lost his life. It took positive effort to keep putting thoughts of him out of my mind so I could concentrate on my mission. But, I kept asking myself the same question over and over, "Where do we get such kids?"

Airman Hemming's famous dive was only the precursor to another dive taken two nights later by none other than the colorful commanding officer of Attack Squadron 93, Commander Joe Salin. Joe had taken off with a wingman on a night coastal interdiction mission; their A-4s loaded with flares and 500 pound bombs. They reconnoitered the coastal highway from the North Vietnamese city of Vinh southward to the DMZ. There had been coastal truck traffic reported on the narrow highway paralleling the coast the night before. Their tactic was simple…to go to a particular stretch of the highway, illuminate it with a flare, then bomb any target which the flare might reveal. They had modest results for their 45 minutes spent doing the actual interdiction…a few trucks set afire and assumed destroyed. Joe's wingman later revealed that his skipper had become more and more erratic as the flight wore on. His airplane seemed to weave around, failing to stay on altitude en route back from the coast to the ship. Joe's voice transmissions on the radio became slurred. In his wingman's words he acted a little drunk.

Finally, when they let down to the ship for a recovery, Joe couldn't get his Skyhawk aboard. In fact, he couldn't get his airplane even close to a reasonable start for a night carrier landing. Fortunately, his wingman had let air operations know that his skipper was behaving strangely. Air operations had the native intelligence to keep the wingman airborne in case he was needed.

Finally, the captain of the ship got into the act and ordered them to "bingo" Joe and his wingman to Danang. Of course, it was also decided to give the two some fuel before they departed for Danang, and a rendezvous with the duty tanker was accomplished. By this time I had gone down to air operations to listen on the radio. The first thing I heard when I entered the space was, "Skipper, push over, push over, push *over!*" This was followed by some heavy breathing and then, "Skipper, pull up, pull up, *pull up!*" I found it very difficult to listen to this. After all, Joe was a close friend, and I felt as though I was listening to the end of his life…literally.

The wingman finally called the ship and said that the skipper was not answering his calls on the radio and asked permission to head for Danang without the refueling. He said the skipper was acting in an extremely erratic way…and any attempt to aerial refuel might cause a mid-air collision with the tanker. Then the terrified wingman, for whom I felt equally sorry, switched radio channels to contact Danang approach control.

The rest of the story unfolded after Joe and his wingman were debriefed the following day upon their return from Danang. It seems that Joe was suffering from hypoxia, having been breathing from a supply of tainted oxygen. Joe was slowly being poisoned as he flew, and there was nothing anyone could do about it…because Joe was not responding to external commands. With his wingman's help, Joe flew his Skyhawk all the way to Danang and landed safely…a minor miracle in itself. He taxied into the transient parking ramp and shut down his engine, and began unstrapping himself preparatory to climbing out of the airplane.

The canopy rail of the *Skyhawk* stands about ten feet above the concrete, and there is a well-defined way of climbing down a set of boarding steps. What Joe did at this point absolutely astounded the Air Force personnel who were standing at the foot of the ladder. He simply stepped off into space!

Joe's limp figure described a three-quarter forward flip, and he hit the concrete ramp flat on his back. The impact knocked him unconscious. An ambulance was summoned, and it trundled off to the base hospital with Joe snoozing comfortably on the stretcher inside. After considerable effort, the doctors revived Joe, examining him carefully and concluding that he had been poisoned by "bad oxygen." Messages flew back and forth between the ship and Danang, after which the ship purged the tanks in its liquid oxygen production facility and all airplanes on board. The ship stood down from flight operations to accomplish this, and an expert was flown in to trouble shoot the oxygen generation plant. After about 18 hours the problem was found and fixed, and the oxygen plant was tested and put back into operation. Oxygen is a very important element of carrier operations.

The following morning Joe awoke to a world completely foreign to him. He remembered nothing about the events of the previous evening. After his wingman debriefed him on the whole evolution, he was horrified to see his skipper get out of the hospital bed and put on his flight suit. The doctor's orders called for complete bed rest for several days while

Joe was kept under close observation to see if any brain damage had been done by his extended deprivation of good oxygen.

Despite the strenuous protestations of Joe's wingman, the skipper sneaked out of the hospital and hitched a ride to the flight line. Both of the Skyhawks had been purged of oxygen and refilled. They climbed into their airplanes and launched without further ado for *Bon Homme Richard*. After all, he was the skipper of the squadron, they had a job to do and it didn't include "screwing around in some stupid Air Force hospital!"

In the days following Joe's incident, there was a great deal of discussion in all of the squadron ready rooms about the hazards associated with oxygen; hypoxia and anoxia among others. The question continually arose from the junior officers as to how Commander Salin ever managed to complete a night bombing mission, several night carrier landing attempts and then bingo safely to Danang...all in a semi-conscious condition. It just didn't seem possible!

My conclusion, finally, was that in the midst of Joe's difficulties, the survival instinct and 20 years of intense carrier aviation experience kicked in and combined to bring him home safely. There just isn't any other explanation. But, as far as Joe's dive off the Skyhawk and Airman Hemming's dive off the flight deck of *Bon Homme Richard*, if I were an Olympic judge, I would have to assign them an equally high score for degree of difficulty.

Chapter 40:
Pignano

Just once before I die, I'd like to turn on the TV or open a newspaper and read about someone who openly admits to the crime he is accused of. Just once! But my conviction is that it will never happen. Having served on more jury trials than is reasonable, I've seen too much bold-faced denial.

Maybe people forget. Maybe they honestly don't recall committing their crimes. Perhaps they are crazy and don't know what they are doing. They will look into the TV camera or the interviewer's eyes and deny ever having been at the crime scene, despite their finger prints left all over the place. There is another explanation for this phenomenon. Some people do not think what they do is criminal, or worthy of punishment, or they think that they are justified.

In Pignano's case, he knew that he was guilty. I knew he was guilty. Where the hell was this sense of outrage coming from? What makes a cornered thief fight so righteously? Pignano, one of the Marines aboard *Wasp*, was a classic example. After all these years I still recall the incident and the impact it had on this naive young man.

Pignano was a tall, well built young man from an Italian neighborhood in Philadelphia. He had an engaging smile, an effusive manner, and an explosive temper. Pignano was olive-skinned, had a mellow, outgoing voice and thick, glossy, raven hair. The women went into a sort of meltdown whenever Pignano entered the room. As a result, we enviously called him "Killer" Pignano.

When Pignano came back from liberty once, he sat on the edge of my bunk, late at night, and spoke in wonderment about the woman he'd been to bed with. The tale was so bizarre that I didn't believe him at the time. And, as worldly as he was and as successful with women, Pignano didn't appear to fully comprehend his interlude, either. Unfortunately, my lasting remembrance of Pignano is of a raging man being dragged away in such a state of apoplexy that his rational mind was about as far away as the planet Pluto.

It was a nightmare come true. Another brig guard dragged him off to a meaner brig, a notorious Marine disciplinary battalion in the South—truly your worst nightmare. I really felt sorry for him, but I learned a valuable, indelible lesson from Pignano. The lesson was that people will do something so often that they will no longer view it as unacceptable conduct. There is no doubt in my mind that Pignano had many times in his early life stolen things. It was probably part of his passage into manhood in his Philly neighborhood.

And I can imagine Pignano's dad telling him that life is a street fight. That you "gotta fight" for every advantage and grab all you can. "Grabba wid boat 'u aans, and efa theys mo, grabba da resta wid da cheeks a' you ass efa 'u gotta," said in a voice filled with frustration at his own inability to get an edge on life. We never saw Pignano again; a young man who was as normal as anyone else on board. To see him screaming "I didn't do nothing" over and over, as they took him away, was memorable. What ever became of him, I wonder. It is most unlikely that he came away from his time in the disciplinary battalion a better man.

Up until then, Pignano had enjoyed his time in the Corps. The uniform, the travel, the sense of being in an exclusive club, all worked for him. The daily drudgery and discipline were water off his back. He could laugh it off and find an advantage in everything. And then one day as he was guarding a work detail of prisoners in a storage locker on Wasp, he discovered some parachute canisters. They were made up to give a downed pilot the food, clothing, and shelter he would need to survive in the Arctic.

The canisters contained down jackets, boots, and canned food that would heat itself if water was added to the outer tin can. There was a unique folding survival gun that fired shot shells, .22 cartridges, and .45 shells, too. The canisters were cornucopias. Pignano took many things, including a down jacket. All the other Marines envied him the jacket since we were always cold; wearing only an unlined field jacket all winter. We would all have liked to have a down jacket.

I remember asking Pignano where he got the down jacket. Pignano was straightforward about the theft. He even asked if I wanted one, too. Pignano wore the stolen down jacket openly about the ship; further evidence that he saw nothing wrong. However, the Navy finally discovered the theft and viewed the pillage of the survival canisters as the worst kind of theft a shipmate on an aircraft carrier could commit, and rightfully so.

And I learned about people from Pignano.

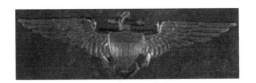

Chapter 41:
Sierra Wave

*"Mackerel skies and mare's tails,
make tall ships carry short sails"*

- Old seaman's weather warning.

Mother Nature has a way of taking us down from time to time, whenever our egos elevate us to a point at which we no longer respect her. Never, in over 40 years of flying, have I ever been so abruptly brought to earth as the day Dave Hancock and I flew a Beechcraft to China Lake and back.

The year was 1956. I was a lieutenant (junior grade) serving a tour of duty as an aerial gunnery instructor at the Fleet Air Gunnery Unit, Pacific. Lieutenant Commander Dave Hancock asked me to fly with him from our base at Naval Auxiliary Air Station, El Centro, California, to Naval Weapons Center, China Lake, CA, and return. It was to be an administrative run to pick up a small package, Dave explained, and would involve some night flying. This was an incentive, because we got very little night time as instructors...and, therefore, had to scratch to get in our minimum annual requirements.

Our mode of transportation was to be one of the two ancient SNB twin propeller-driven Beechcraft assigned to our unit for administrative support. I accepted, and had the foresight to call Nancy in the early afternoon to tell her I would be getting home from work late that night because I was going night flying. As soon as I had finished debriefing my afternoon gunnery flight, we launched for China lake. It was, Dave reassured me, going to be a "milk run!"

The flight to China Lake was about 400 miles each way and would take the old "Bugsmasher" about six hours for the round trip, not counting the 30-minute refueling and cargo pick-up at China Lake. The route of flight would traverse the Sierra Nevada Mountains going and coming...and the weather promised to be clear all the way. I reasoned that it really would be a "piece 'o cake"...and, of course, I had never even heard of the Sierra Wave. But, afficionados of soaring know all about that meteorological phenomenon. In fact the small town of Hemet, in the high desert, had been the launch point for most of the altitude records set in unpowered gliders. The Sierra Wave had carried many soaring enthusiasts to heights of over 40,000 feet!

The Sierra Wave is caused by thermal heating of air masses carried east by prevailing winds and pushed up against the slope of the Sierra Nevada mountains. Hot air rises. When it experiences the effects of thermal heating as well as the push from below caused by the slope of the mountains over which it passes, the effect is magnified. At certain times of the year and under certain meteorological conditions, the Sierra Wave generates enormous lifting power. This is when soaring records are set. It is also when Mother Nature can deign to teach unwary aviators a lesson in humility.

The weapons center at China Lake sits in a natural bowl in the high desert surrounded by mountains. There is no lake…just dust and sand, at an elevation of about 4,000 feet above sea level. The southern edge of the bowl of surrounding mountains is the lowest part of the rim and extends no more than 3,000 feet above the valley. Hemet lies to the south and east of China Lake about fifty miles.

Our flight to China lake was uneventful. We cruised up there at an altitude of about 9,000 feet (about all the ancient Beechcraft could manage), picked up our package, took on a tank of fuel and headed back, having been on the ground all of 30 minutes.

One event occurred during our brief stay on the ground which should have caught our attention, but unfortunately did not. Dave and I were in the Operations building filing a return flight plan, and had stopped in the weather office for our weather briefing. While the aerologist was back at a bank of teletype machines copying the weather onto our flight plan, we overheard a Marine jet pilot calling in a PIREP (pilot report) over the radio. It came through on the loud speaker, so we could hear what he reported to the aerologist. He said he was 50 miles northeast of China Lake and wanted to report upper winds in excess of 250 knots at his flight level of 40,000 feet. Both Dave and I simultaneously burst out laughing. Our Navy bias told us that all Marine pilots were notoriously poor navigators. Furthermore, his airplane wasn't equipped to measure wind velocity with any degree of accuracy. It would take a very thorough and experienced pilot to correctly calculate upper-wind velocity. He was, we concluded after our laughter subsided, just another incompetent boob cluttering up the in-flight weather reporting channel with nonsense. Neither of us had the slightest notion that he could possibly be right!

After takeoff we turned southeast and headed for the low point in the rim of the basin, climbing as fast as the old airplane could manage. The sun had already set, and twilight was fading fast as we passed over the ridge line, still climbing. The poor airplane was struggling when we leveled off, throttled back, and set cruise power for the trip back to El Centro. Since Dave had flown the left (pilot's) seat on the way up, I flew it on the return leg. The power setting I established with the throttles should have given us an airspeed of 120 knots at that altitude. It didn't! The airplane began to settle, and I added up elevator trim to correct for it and get back to our assigned altitude. When I got back to altitude the airspeed read 110 knots, and the plane began to lose altitude again. Irritated, but not particularly concerned, I commented on the engines and added a few more inches of manifold pressure by nudging the throttles forward a bit. I crept back to altitude, and noted with increasing irritation that my airspeed was now 105 knots. By this time Dave had stopped navigating and begun paying attention to our power anomaly. The airplane settled again and the same thing happened. We were at 95 knots when I said to Dave on the intercom, "This is beginning to be not very funny!" He agreed.

We were both jet pilots with not a great deal of propeller experience. Was it possible we had done something terribly wrong? What could possibly explain the airplane's sudden loss of flying ability? Were the engines failing somehow? By now it was pitch black, and darkness merely added a sense of the eerie to our discomfort. What in hell was wrong?

By now I had advanced the throttles to nearly take-off power and we were still decelerating. Dave called the air route traffic control center and told them we had a power problem and were forced to descend. We were on a VFR flight plan and were therefore allowed to descend to a lower altitude. Fortunately, the desert floor was falling away beneath us as we headed across the high desert of Antelope Valley. By now the airplane was settling much too rapidly for us to ignore. In all of my subsequent years of flying I have never felt so helpless. Somewhere out in the darkness ahead of us was the spot on the ground where we were going to crash…it was that simple!

Dave was preparing to declare an emergency when I looked ahead and saw the runway lights of an airfield flickering off. I quickly checked my chart and realized it was Marine Corps Auxiliary Air Station, Mojave…and they were in the process of shutting down for the night. "Dave," I announced, "we are going to land at Mojave whether they like it or not!" He nodded agreement as he frantically dialed up the radio frequency and called for landing clearance. This airplane was going to impact the ground in a very short while, and I preferred that it be on the nearest runway. By now I was in a panic. The airplane was descending, and we were at full power holding 95 knots in the descent. Nothing I could think of doing was changing the unalterable fact that our flight was about to end in a matter of a few minutes.

"Marine Mojave Tower, this is Navy 23478, ten miles northeast. We are experiencing power problems and request immediate landing clearance. Over." Dave's voice on the radio sounded unbelievably calm considering the circumstances.

"Roger, Navy 23478, you are cleared to land Runway 32. Cleared to enter the downwind from your present position. Be advised there are some shear winds of unknown velocity at one hundred feet AGL. Over." We couldn't do it that way, and I knew instinctively that Dave understood that as well. He responded like a trooper, looking over at me as he spoke.

"Sorry, Tower. I believe we will have to land downwind on runway 32 immediately. We are barely able to control our rate of descent. Out." It should have been clear to the tower operator that we didn't have time for any more conversations…but it wasn't!

"Navy 23478, are you declaring an emergency? Over." Dave and I were too busy going over the landing check-off list to respond. We were fast as a fox when we passed over the fence, and I chopped power completely. We didn't want to run off the far end of the runway. Touching down two-thirds of the way down the runway, I got on the binders and rolled to a stop with maybe a hundred feet of concrete left ahead of us. As we sat there in the dark for a moment, I realized that my body was bathed in sweat, and I must have been holding my breath, because I left it all out of my lungs in a huge gasp.

"Christ Almighty, Dave. We made it!"

Ten minutes later there was a Marine mechanic in the cockpit of our airplane running the engine up to see what was wrong. His conclusion when he finished was unbelievable. "There's absolutely nothing wrong with your airplane, sir," he told Dave with a wry grin. He obviously thought we were a pair of cretins. The weatherman came out of the tower building to tell us that something funny was going on. A helicopter which had landed just before us had reported hovering at 100 feet over the taxiway with an indicated airspeed of 75 knots! That was the shear wind which the tower had mentioned to us just before we touched down!

Dave and I looked at one another knowingly. We had had enough for one day. "Dave," I told him, "I am not getting back into that frigging airplane again tonight."

"Neither am I, Paul," he responded. "Let's go find the BOQ." I called Nancy five minutes later with news she didn't appreciate very much. I told her we were spending the night at MCAAS Mojave and gave her our telephone number, just in case.

In reviewing the bidding the following morning as we prepared for takeoff, we came to some startling conclusions. We had been caught in the aftermath of an enormous Sierra Wave. The large mass of cooling (descending) air which was flowing out of the southern exit of the valley had generated cold, gusty surface winds of up to 100 knots throughout Antelope Valley. Aerologists have since reassured me that as we had gotten closer to the surface we would have regained our ability to maintain level flight. That sounds very reassuring in the cold light of day. But at 8,000 feet over the Antelope valley on an inky black night in the cockpit of an SNB, the Sierra Wave had an unforgettable and almost surreal effect on both of us that I will never forget!

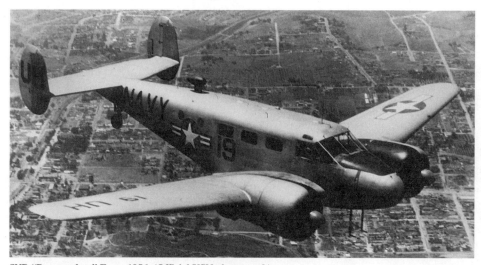

SNB "Bugsmasher," Fagu, 1956. (Official USN photograph)

Chapter 42:
Life on the Roving Sea

"...Of ships and socks and sealing wax... "
- The Walrus and the Carpenter, Lewis Carroll

Watching from the island on *Wasp* one day, I spied a small plane, a Piper Cub, I think, lazily circling over the arid mountainous coast of Oriente Province, Cuba. We were close in, and the pilot or his passenger appeared to be dropping either mortar rounds or slow-fused grenades on some people, probably Castro's rebels, running through the hills below. Leaning against the splinter shield, I felt like a spectator at a sporting event.

Remember, back in the 50s, Castro was just another raggedy-ass young rebel running around the hinterlands of Cuba. It wouldn't be until February of 1959 that he would oust Batista and triumphantly enter Havana. And it wasn't much later that he would introduce his own brand of tyranny.

One clear day in the Arctic Sea, as *Wasp* and the oiler struggled to maintain station and refuel in heavy seas, and the huge swells caused the fuel lines to stretch and part, spilling oil. As the lines parted, the heavy oil lines swept several sailors overboard into the frigid water.

Wasp put up a helicopter immediately, but the water was so cold that when the 'copter attempted to drag a horse collar to the first sailor, he didn't respond. They then snagged his lifejacket, but he had neglected to fasten it properly. As they attempted to lift his body, his life jacket slipped off, making matters worse. The ship's company held an impromptu funeral service then and there. I envisioned one of those souls coming to the top of a giant sea and spotting *Wasp* a mile off, slowly searching. What exquisite despair he must have felt before the numbingly cold sea claimed him.

There was once a sergeant aboard whom we all called Sergeant Beno. I don't think I ever heard him called anything else. For a time when I first joined the detachment, I thought Beno was really his name. But, alas, no! The real story was that after spending time at sea and after arriving at an exciting port, and having put on our best uniforms before going on liberty, Sergeant Beno would stroll through the compartment inspecting the state of neatness and declare in a loud voice, "Beno liberty."

Whenever we were given liberty in Guantanamo Bay, Cuba, I'd grab my mask, speargun, and flippers and hike out to a remote area of the base by the shore. The shoreline was bounded by coral cliffs. After some exploring, I found a way down the cliff to the water. Once in the water, it was necessary to work my way over the coral shallows for about a hundred feet to reach deep water, where the world opened up into a botanical and zoological wonderland. For a diver who had learned his skills in the cold, murky waters off Long Island, the Caribbean Sea was heaven.

While following the reef one day, I spotted a dark opening in the coral, maybe 15 feet down. After diving and poking my head into the opening several times, I finally dived and swam into the dark cave. Once inside, my eyes acclimated, and I followed the cave inward and upward. In a moment my head broke the surface, and I was floating in a small grotto. All around me were spiny sea urchins. No matter which way I turned, the urchins were waiting for me.

After some thought, I realized that I was going to get punctured all over my back and legs when I dove out of the cave. Finally, I made as tight a dive as I could and swam out and up to the surface. There were many spines embedded in my back and legs. Knowledgeable divers will tell you that the spines will cause painful infections. They never did. In Gitmo, there was a little cantina. Whenever I had the time, I'd go there for lunch. It was always a treat, because I enjoyed the damp humid heat and the island atmosphere.

My lunch invariably consisted of a sizzling steak served on a wood platter, a half head of fresh lettuce, and a number ten can of chilled pineapple juice. A meal fit for a king. One day as I strolled into the cantina, a voice called out, "Hey, Gil." I looked at a fellow whom I did not recognize at all. He saw my confusion and said, "It's me, Franklin Van Ardoye." Looking again with this added intelligence, I realized that it was indeed my classmate from grade school.

Franklin and I enjoyed a good chat. His brothers Caesar and Conrad had also been in my class. Come to think of it, they were also my older sister Frances' classmates, and later on, probably my younger brother Dan's classmates. The Van Ardoyes were definitely not rocket scientists. When we were in Gitmo, we liked to go to the "slop chute" for a beer whenever we had the chance. One night there was a fight with the Marines who were permanently stationed at Gitmo. Colyer found himself matched up against a streetfighter who was better than he was. The outcome was that Colyer was hurt and complained of dizziness and blurred vision, which still haunts him 40 years later.

One of the lasting memories of Gitmo was the anchor watch. The reason was the obvious, but it was also a subtle unspoken reason. You see, it was considered fair game for the UDT teams to sneak through the night and attack *Wasp*. It was good practice for the UDT teams and embarrassing for *Wasp*. The UDT considered it good fun, and *Wasp's* Marines did not. We were in charge of security, and had no intention of being humiliated by a bunch of sailors in tights.

And so it was, while making my rounds on the midnight to four a.m. watch one night, that the Marine on the anchor watch told me he had seen some movement in the sea on the very edge of the anchor light's aureole. Together we began a search of the waters alongside, looking for those rascals in rubber suits. In time we spotted movement and decided to give them something to think about. I must have been imbalanced by that time in service, because I remember unhooking a 40 pound fire extinguisher and dropping it on the shadows lurking below, with the instructions to the Marine guard to do the same again if the UDT came back.

The anchor watch in Gitmo was fun. This may sound strange, but I thoroughly enjoyed the late night watch because I would lean over the side, watching the amberjack and barracuda racing in the thousands through the glow of the anchor floodlights. It was a sort of kaleidoscope of marine life as they frantically struggled to survive the savage tropical night. Imagine the stark terror they must live with each time the sun goes down, until the inevitable happens, when out of the darkness, a maw with a snaggle of jagged teeth erupts with an abruptness that stuns.

On rare occasions, particularly on a warm summer Sunday at sea, *Wasp* would heave to and shut down all operations for a few hours of absolute inactivity. I'm sure someone on board was sitting watching a gauge, but the rest of us lay on the flight deck in our skivvies, getting a tan and catching up on sleep. As I said, those occasions were rare, because they inevitably validated an old, tried and true expression, "Idle minds are the devil's workshop." And so it was that on one balmy Sunday that as some idle sailors were leaning over the fantail, flicking their cigarette ashes into the sea, they spotted a huge shark coasting along as if he owned that particular neighborhood. In a moment, the sailors rushed off to steal line, fashion a sharpened steel dowel shaped like a giant fishhook, and retrieve a leftover steak from breakfast.

The shark was nosing around, cutting lazy circles as if waiting for the next train to pull into the station. We all hung over, watching the sleek, powerful monster in an environment that we feared, but one that the monster lived in all its life. Finally, with an excited clatter of shoes and shouts, the shark hunters returned and assembled their makeshift gear. Over the side the hook went, with the steak skewered in place. The splash didn't frighten the monster in the least. It orbited a few more times before swaggering over to check out the steak. After we all had held our collective breath for minutes, the shark inhaled the steak and hook and started to swim away.

There was a roar of satisfaction, and the crowd gathered closer as a team of sailors began hauling the monster up the thirty five feet to the fantail. The monster was frightening to watch as it snapped, rolled, flipped, and lunged in a fight to spit out the hook. In through the massive hawser hole they pulled the shark. It must have weighed close to a thousand pounds. The crowd surged forward to see the shark, pushing the onlookers right up to the thrashing monster. And as it lunged, the nearest sailors dodge about and danced out of range of those gnashing rows of teeth.

I stood, mouth agape, watching the irresponsible, idiotic, and dangerous conduct, expecting someone of authority to call a halt before the shark grabbed a victim. Why I was concerned, I don't know. My brother and I had done the same foolish thing a few years before while spearfishing off Short Beach. It certainly got those sailor's minds off other things for awhile.

When we were at sea, *Wasp* had an enormous task in feeding the crew. The normal routine of three meals a day changed to four because we were launching and recovering aircraft in simulated combat conditions which required 24 hour a day operations. With that much activity, a fourth meal was served at midnight.

It must have been during the service that I developed a deep-seated hate of standing in line. I remember one line in Camp Lejeune that stretched for about a half mile. We were transferring out, and so many troops were involved in the transfer that the line was out of sight. It was a rainy January day, and we had been in the field sleeping in water for days. I was in a bad humor, and after maybe an hour in line, I walked to the head of the line and found a sergeant collecting tent pegs, slowly counting the pegs and recording the return on a clipboard. I took my gear and threw it into the Quonset hut and stalked off with the sergeant staring at my back. The long line of obedient Marines saw this, and there was suddenly a rush and an avalanche of gear thrown at the sergeant.

Getting back to the chow line on *Wasp*, the chow line was so long that Colyer and I would simply buy a can of peanuts and sit in the gun tub and gab, munching on nuts rather than spend an hour or more on that chow line. One of the unofficial duties of the Marine guard who stood watch on the after brow (the enlisted gangway) was to referee fights that took place at the foot of the brow. Another unofficial duty was to accept delivery of the unconscious Marines the shore patrol trucked in whenever we were in a good liberty port.

What we did was to drag one or two at a time up the brow, across the hangar deck. And since we didn't get to enjoy liberty, we might drag the carcasses through as much grease and oil as possible, en route to the hatch leading to the Marine quarters, one deck below the hangar deck.

All the while we were trudging along, pulling the dead weight of the foul-smelling drunks, they made complaining noises and flinched whenever we dragged them over a pad eye say. And when we finally reached the hatch to the deck below we'd simply dump the bodies down the ship's ladder, a drop of maybe ten feet. They never seemed to suffer any serious damage. Maybe the first one would bleed a little, but each successive drunk would land on the bodies below. It worked reasonably well.

I was standing duty on the after brow, one night in Cherbourg, when the shore patrol pulled up with their vehicle filled to the brim with drunks. They backed up and began to pull them out, one at a time. Things went pretty well until they came to one feisty sailor. He just wouldn't get out. He had sobered up a little during the trip and wanted to go back into town. As they struggled, trying to pull him out of the van, they dislocated his arm. This made the sailor mad, and he came out fighting, with one good arm. The guy was a real tiger. First one shore patrolman took him on, then two, and then three. As I stood, leaning against the brow, my turf, the melee continued.

When all four were rolling around in the dirt, along side the van, in their white uniforms, the next drunk sailor to come out of the van pushed open the window of the van, stuck his groggy head out, and vomited all over the foursome rolling around on the ground below. This really incensed all four, and they each put all they had into the match. It was one of the best fights I have ever seen.

Earlier, I mentioned that the brig rats were used for manual labor all over the ship. Whenever we received a request for a work party, we scheduled the prisoners and a chaser would march them off to a new assignment. The bakery was the best spot, because we'd scrounge fresh bread for the detachment. *Wasp* was a small city, so there were compartments for just about any necessary service needed in a small but warlike city.

One compartment that came up in conversation recently while visiting with Colyer was the photographic compartment. The topic came up when I discovered a group photo of the detachment in a drawer at home. Colyer asked where I got the photo, and I remembered looting it from the Photo compartment one night while prisoners were cleaning the place.

The photographers were a lascivious group who took photos in every port. They had a file of photos of their conquests hidden away where no one could find them. The Marines, possessed of inquiring minds, knew about the hiding place and entertained themselves whenever we took prisoners to the photo compartment. It was as good a way as any to spin out a midnight watch.

The armory on *Wasp* was a treasure trove of out-of-date weapons. We had carbines, Thompson submachine guns, trench guns (short, pump shotguns), water cooled .30 cal. machine guns, air-cooled machine guns, 60mm mortars, 81mm mortars, springfields, BARs, .45 cal. automatics, and who knows what else that Marines had Squirreled away since 1942.

We decided one day to get rid of all the old ammunition, borrowed some pickup trucks, and drove up to Fort Devon. A range was set aside for us, and we proceeded to try to shoot up all the ammo in a single day. We all brought our M-1s along, but discovered that after 100 rounds that the linseed oil we had so lovingly massaged into the wood stocks started to boil off because the rifles got so hot.

I remember sitting for an hour loading magazines for a Browning automatic rifle. When I had about 300 hundred rounds loaded, I sandbagged the BAR and tried to cut down a tree that was about 300 yards out on the range. Then a truck drove by on a hidden road about a thousand yards out on the range, and I borrowed a machine gun and kept adjusting the sight until I was dusting that road. Fortunately for the truck, it did not return along the road while I was dusting.

All in all it was an interesting day. To top off the day, the Army dropped off hot chow at noon. This was amazing, because none of the Marines had ever had the pleasure of hot chow in the field in all our combined years. In the Corps, they threw boxes of C-rations at you with a warning not to start fires in an effort to at least heat up the food.

U.S.S. Wasp (CVS-18). (Official U.S. Navy photograph)

One night, Tackhammer was standing the dog watch on the nuclear weapons and got bored. As he later told me, he began practicing a fast, western-style draw. He would whip out his .45 cal. automatic and slap the slide back, jacking a round into the chamber. In time his draw became a blur of movement, and finally the moment arrived when his finger nudged the trigger too far and the automatic exploded, slamming a slug into the steel bulkhead a few feet in front of the steely-eyed Tackhammer. As he stood there explaining the story to me as sergeant of the guard, blood oozed out of dozens of minute punctures in his face and body. The ricochets of the splattered lead bullet had missed his eyes, but sprayed "Wyatt Earp's" body with fragments.

While on maneuvers at Camp Lejeune, we found ourselves one night, bivouacked in a gully. It was January, and we all slipped out of our clothes and slid into a cosy, down sleeping bag. Fortunately, I rolled my clothes up in a ball under my head. It had been a long day, and we all fell into a deep sleep. During the night, the rains came, and at four a.m. the gully had about a foot of water in it. What awoke me was a sort of patting on my rump. At first I was puzzled, and then I realized that I was afloat except for an occasional bump on the rump.

With great reservations, I unzipped the bag and let the cold January rain pour into the cosy warm sleeping bag. It was definitely a "waker-upper." My clothing was in the bag, so I was able to force my limbs into the soaked fatigues. My M-1 was by my side, so it wasn't lost as were many rifles.

After a couple of hours of standing around, soaking wet and cold, in the rain, the trucks showed up, and we fled in full retreat to the warm dry barracks back at Camp Lejeune.

All in all, I made out alright. Many Marines were wandering about in their skivvies out there in the boondocks in January. They lost everything. Is it no wonder that we had about 80 percent of the battalion on sick call with pneumonia?

Chapter 43:
"Narssarssuaq"

*"Oh the north country is a rough country,
That mothers a bloody brood;
And its icy arms hold hidden charms,
For the greedy, the sinful and lewd."*

- E.E. Paramore, Jr.: "The Ballad Of Yukon Jake"

There were seven telephones on my desk. To be more precise, there were four phones on my desk in front of me and three phones on the credenza behind me. Two of the three on the credenza were colored bright red. They were "hot lines." The plethora of telephones was an indicator of the vast domain of the Atlantic Command, the Atlantic Fleet, the Western Atlantic Allied Command and, finally, the Supreme Allied Command, Atlantic. The span of control was enormous.

Whenever the CinC (Commander-in-Chief, Atlantic; Commander-in-Chief, Atlantic Fleet; Commander-in-Chief, Western Atlantic; and Supreme Allied Commander, Atlantic) wandered into the command center, I would get a call either on one of the phones or on the squawk box. The simple message, "The CinC is in the command center," was all I needed to get me moving. Letting myself in through the back way was always easier in the long run. I had memorized three different cipher lock codes and was able to sneak into the command center via the back without anyone knowing…not my secretary, not the Marine sentry outside my door, nobody. It was like the magic act where the prestidigitator disappears from one place in a puff of smoke and reappears in another in an equally mystifying puff.

By the time I got to the command center the CinC was standing by the main panel of motorized wall maps (they were 20 feet tall and 15 feet across) looking at Greenland. "How many fighters," he asked, "could we operate out of that base at the southern tip of Greenland?"

I was dumbfounded. What base? I hadn't a clue what he was talking about. Losing patience in me, he turned to one of his favorite assistants, Captain Jim Kramer, and asked, "Jimmy, what's the name of that base at the southern tip of Greenland?" Jim's greatest gift was that he always knew the answers to the CinC's questions. God, how I envied him!

"Narsarssuaqq," Jim responded in his omniscient voice.

By now I was standing by the CinC's side, examining the craggy coastline of southern Greenland as displayed by the wiggly line on the chart. I gave the CinC the only answer that was appropriate. "I'll find out, sir!" The four-star admiral walked out of the command center, confident in the knowledge that someone in his vast command was going to come up with some kind of answer.

The reader might conclude at this point that I may have been reduced to despair. How in the world could I ever answer such a question? Far from it! If I had learned anything from my two or three months in the J-3 job, it was that the talent embodied in the hundreds of officers on the staff was almost limitless! After two phone calls, I learned that a VQ-4 C-130E flight could be arranged to fly me to Narsarssuaqq the following day on a regular TACAMO mission, and get back the following day on a return flight, which would be a second mission. All I had to do was appear at the airplane before it took off from its home base at Naval Air Station, Patuxent River, Maryland. After all, my staff reasoned, wasn't I the one who tasked all TACAMO missions in the first place? Why then, couldn't I schedule a mission which went to Narsarssuaqq, with a remain overnight (RON) at Sondestrom Air Base, Greenland, and a return home the following day? I would simply be altering the schedule slightly to accommodate my plans.

Normally, I would never consider leaving the environs of the Norfolk area without special permission all the way up the chain of command to the CinC. Even then there would have to be a qualified relief standing in for me. Indeed, I was required to carry one of those two-way radio devices we called "the brick," anytime I was out of the command center building. However, the TACAMO airplane was a remarkable airborne command center. As such, it carried enough communications equipment in the back for me to carry out much of the routine business of the J-3 as though I were sitting at my desk at CinCLant headquarters.

Probably, the reader ought to get a brief explanation of what the TACAMO mission was. TACAMO stands for "Take Charge and Move Out." I never did understand how that expression fit the mission, but that doesn't matter, I suppose. The TACAMO C-130E was the link to the deployed, submerged ballistic missile submarines assigned to the operational control of CinCLant.

If a decision to engage in a nuclear war with the Soviet Union were made by the national command authority, the primary communications link between the decision-maker and the nuclear powered ballistic missile submarines on patrol would probably be the TACAMO airplanes. I use the word "probably" because I assume that the normal mode of communications, the huge radio antenna farm at Cutler, Maine, would have been turned to nuclear dust. At any rate, the actual launch message to the submarine would come from the command center at CinCLant headquarters…either by normal means or TACAMO.

The TACAMO concept of operations was a 24-four hour-a-day, seven days-a-week system whereby an airplane was always "on watch" on airborne alert out over the Atlantic or Pacific Oceans, where it could communicate with the submerged SBNs. This was done by deploying its antenna and transmitting the message. The antenna was a tapered wire 25,000 feet long with a cone-shaped drag device at its end. There was another antenna, a shorter tapered wire about 1,500 feet long, called an exciter antenna. In order for the pair of antennas to broadcast to the submerged submarines, the TACAMO airplane had to fly a tight circular pattern which generated a helical shaped antenna. With the wire in a standing helical shape and stationary over the water's surface, the TACAMO system achieved what is called "verticality," and the radio transmissions impacted the surface of the water in such a way that the message it carried was transmitted hundreds of miles through the water and picked up by the receiving antenna that the submarine trailed behind itself as it patrolled.

Once the launch message was received, the target coordinates which it contained were inserted into the missiles. Then the ship's commanding officer and executive officer (at two points in the submarine's control room) each had to insert launch keys worn around their necks. The two key receptacles were far enough apart that one person could not reach both of them by himself (if somehow he got both keys in his possession). Once the keys were inserted into their receptacles, they had to be turned simultaneously to launch weapons.

Of course, the final link in the chain was what was called the "O-sub Broadcast," a radio transmission that was on all the time. Whenever the submarine was on patrol the O-sub broadcast was being copied by a radio operator. A launch message, if sent, was received, and the ship went to General Quarters," ascended to launch depth, opened its missile doors, and launched missiles. Once the missiles were launched, the submarine went back to whatever depth the operations order called for…and the war was on…irretrievably, inexorably, and irrevocably.

Saturday morning, bright and early, a CinCLant helicopter on a routine flight to the Pentagon in Washington, D.C., dropped me off at NAS Patuxent River en route. The airplane was waiting when I arrived, and we launched on schedule. We headed north and then, once past the New York area, turned northeast and went out into our operating area in the North Atlantic east of the Canadian coast. For four hours we conducted TACAMO opera-

EC-130Q TACAMO airplane, Norwegian Sea, May 1977. (Tailhook Association)

Narsarssuaq on a sunny day, May 1978. (Paul Gillcrist Collection)

tions with me seated in the pilot's seat, flying the tight circular pattern and trailing the long antenna.

The first thing I learned was that it is not an easy pattern to fly—requiring considerable concentration. The second thing I learned was that antennas are expendable. There was a gauge on the pilot's side of the cockpit that read tension in pounds. When I asked about it I was told that the tension in the trailing wire antenna needed to be constantly monitored. At that moment, as if by design, some lower clouds drifted by beneath us, engulfing the antenna inside. Immediately, the tension on the wire began to increase and the needle on the meter began to show a steady rise. It seems that the wire tended to accumulate ice when in clouds, gradually increasing the tension to the point that it failed. We spent the next 15 minutes reeling in the wire, splicing new wire and a new cone on its end, and redeploying it.

After our stint in the circle was over, we set a course for Narsarsuaq, arriving there about one o'clock in the afternoon. It was quite an experience, as the letdown plate for the airfield was labeled "VFR ONLY." This meant that airplanes were not allowed to attempt to land there in bad weather. It turned out that there was an overcast shrouding the southern tip of Greenland that began at about 1,500 feet. The pilot of the airplane asked me to vacate the pilot's seat, offering me instead a jump seat between the pilot and co-pilot, where I sat during the approach to our destination. It was eerie! At an altitude of 1,000 feet we made landfall at the opening of the fjord leading to the airfield and proceeded up it, following its sinuating trace. The mountains on either side rose steeply into the clouds. The fjord was filled with ice, which was beginning to break up in the early spring thaw. The pilot realized that if anything went wrong, it would be impossible to turn around in the narrow confines of the fjord and stay below the clouds. If the weather worsened and/or the overcast lowered, we would have no recourse but to pull up into the clouds and hope we didn't hit a mountain before we got above it. Fortunately, the weather stayed about the same. It was an ominous experience to be flying into that forbidding wasteland like that.

About 50 miles up the fjord the letdown plate had a notation on it saying cryptically, "Lower gear at the wreck!" In a moment we came to the wreck of an old sailing ship, its wooden mast sticking up at an odd angle through the ice. The airfield was nowhere in sight, and my stomach developed a queasy feeling as we lowered our landing gear and flaps. Just past the wreck the fjord took a sudden hard turn to the right. We turned the corner around the sheer rock wall of the mountain and there, right under us, was the approach end of a 6,000 foot concrete runway. There was no overrun, just the concrete lip of the runway and deep water. The Danish engineers had fit this runway into the end of the fjord with deep water at south end and an enormous glacier at the north. It was a shock!

The pilot instinctively pulled all four throttles way back and started down before we realized that there was a huge iceberg sitting at the very end of the runway, its tip rising several hundred feet above the water. The throttles were shoved up enough to clear the top of the iceberg, then yanked back as we all fixed our eyes on the glacier at the far end. Vigorous use of reverse thrust stopped us just before we reached the end of the runway and the glacier's edge.

Taxiing back to the tower building, we were able to examine this most peculiar portion of the world. I had the sense of almost total desolation. The single runway ran in a north-east-southwest direction. To the east of the runway was the steep slope of the mountain that marked the east wall of the fjord. To the west of the runway was a flat area perhaps a half mile wide whose western edge dropped off sharply into the fjord. The fjord was a half mile wide at this point. On the far edge was the declivity that marked the other side of the fjord. The base was a small flat spot at the base of the glacier, surrounded by fjord and steep mountainsides. Our airplane was parked on the transient mat area near the tower. Three men were waiting there for us as we disembarked.

The men were all dressed in anoraks with fur-lined hoods. One of the men, a small, blond-haired fellow, extended his hand and a smile of welcome. "Hello, I am Major Eigel Schmeltz, Danish Air Force. I am the base commander. Welcome to Narsarssuaq!" We exchanged pleasantries and handshakes, and I explained that I had come along to supervise the airplane and observe an operational mission. He knew what the TACAMO mission was. He also knew that we weren't allowed to discuss it. Naturally, I didn't dare mention why I was really here. I knew I could find out everything I wanted to know by asking for the one thing I knew no base commander could refuse.

"Major, I'm Captain Gillcrist, U.S. Navy. While we are gassing up, would you mind giving me a tour of your base?" He grinned broadly and complied. The tour only took 15 minutes.

The tower building was one of half a dozen small, single story structures made up of pre-fabricated concrete slabs. The north and east sides of all of the structures were window-less. When I asked the major why he answered somberly, "The firn wind!" When I asked what that was he told me. During the spring season, prevailing winds and the topography of the fjord cause warm air (relatively warm) to rise over the northeastern side of the moun-tains and be carried in a southwesterly direction, cooling as it passed over the glacier. This mass of air accelerated as it descended and was forced into the funnel of the fjord. When I asked how hard the wind blew, he looked at me somberly and said 120 knots! Since every-thing around the area was rock and gravel, one didn't dare venture out in it for fear of being killed. Being hit by large pieces of gravel flying through the air at 120 knots would be fatal.

On the way back to the airplane, Major Schmeltz showed me a gravel road leading off the base. He said it led to a seasonal resort hotel! Every spring, it seemed, tourists came from Denmark by the thousands…mostly young adults. He told me they flew in via com-mercial airliner, stayed a few days to roam the hills covered with a deep green mossy lichen for a few brief weeks, then returned to their desultory existence in their homes in Denmark, resuscitated by a beautiful annual sojourn with Mother Nature. As if to punctuate his an-nouncement, a Boeing 727 landed and disgorged a few passengers, who were whisked away in a hotel van, and took off immediately.

Major Schmeltz seemed particularly proud of the building, which he offered to us if we wanted to stay overnight. Like the others, it was made of concrete slabs, but it bore a sign on the door which amused me. The sign said, simply, "The Arctic Motel!" We declined his offer and announced that we would spend the night at Sondestrom Air Base, about 250 miles north along the western shore of Greenland. It was a much larger base and could provide maintenance support for our C-130 airplane in case we needed it, I explained.

I took some mental notes of the size of the flat area which could possibly be used to park aircraft, as well as the storage capacity of the fuel tank. Finally, I observed that it must be fairly quiet and peaceful. Eigel's answer startled me. "Oh, yes, it is," he remarked. "That's what my wife likes most about it!"

"Your wife!" I asked. "Your wife lives here?"

"Oh, yes," he answered, smiling at my obvious astonishment. "We have a suite of rooms right here," he said, nodding in the direction of the Arctic Motel. "In fact," he added, "here she comes right now." He was looking across the fjord to the west as he said it. Turning, I looked across the fjord and saw, way out in the middle of the jagged, jumbled maze of ice floes, a small, dark, moving object. As I focused on it I realized it was a Land Rover, and it was weaving its way through the maze toward us. I was dumbfounded, and it must have shown, because Eigel sought to explain.

"She went across the fjord to that Eskimo village to shop, and now she's on her way home." I searched with my eyes and spotted a small cluster of low buildings, more like igloos, on the opposite side of the fjord at the foot of the mountains. What in the world, I asked myself, could she be shopping for in such a God-forsaken place…blubber? I also thought how dangerous it must be to run the risk of being swallowed up by a sudden opening in the ice…or a leopard seal or polar bear on the prowl!

"She won't be back for a while," he added, as I looked at my watch. We had to go on to Sondestrom quickly before it got dark. The weather there was worsening. We shook hands and, promising to stay in touch, then climbed aboard the airplane and departed. As the door closed behind me, I was struck by the incredible quiet of the place. There was not even a murmur of a breeze… just an eerie silence and all that rock and ice. I wondered how quiet it was at Narsarssuaq when the firn wind was blowing.

Because of the calm winds, we elected to take off in the opposite direction from which we landed…towards the fjord rather than the glacier, as it was much safer. The flight to Sondestrom Air Base took only an hour, and it was a far different environment there. Sondestrom, like Narsarssuaq, sat at the foot of glacier on a fjord. It was a fairly large base, serving as the support base for a squadron of ski-equipped C-130s that supplied our DEW line. They were the only means of logistic support for the defense early warning bases stretched across the northern perimeter of the North American continent, guarding against an airborne assault on the United States from Russia.

As a contrast to Narsarssuaq, Sondestrom was covered with snow, and visibility was restricted by falling snow. The surrounding mountains were not even visible. The base commander, Colonel Nathan Buford, U.S. Air Force, met us as we climbed out of our air-

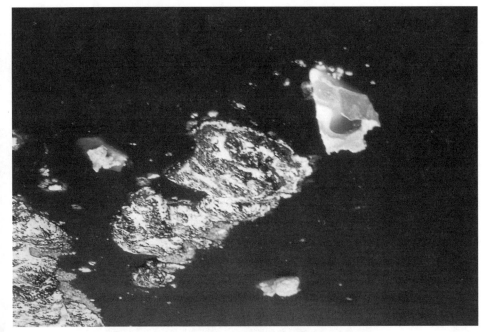

Iceberg at entrance to Narsarssuaq Fjord, May 1978. (Paul Gillcrist Collection)

Fjord at Narsarssuaq , May 1978. (Paul Gillcrist Collection)

plane. He was a colorful character. "Welcome to Sondestrom, Captain," he hailed me in a loud, cheerful voice.

As usual, I asked the same, unrefusable question I had asked at Narsarssuaq. "Colonel, would you mind giving me a tour of your base?" How could he refuse such a request? We climbed into his jeep, chaufferless, and took off across the tarmac. In the course of two hours we saw everything there was to see…mess halls, BOQs, enlisted barracks, communications facilities, the flight line, and, finally, the piece de resistance… Buford's Bluff.

We had stopped at a number of buildings to go inside. At each stop, the colonel got out, pulled out a retractable electrical cable, and plugged it into a readily available socket in much the same way that John Wayne would tie his horse to the hitching post. The idea was to keep the engine warm by supplying power to an electrical heating coil in the engine oil sump. I found myself wondering how many times he must have driven off without unplugging the cable.

At each stop something else caught my attention. The entire base had been built on permafrost. As a result, all the buildings (which were heated) were gradually settling down into the ground at the rate of several inches per year. You could almost tell how long a particular building had been standing by how far it had settled. But, Buford's Bluff…that was something else again!

It was a giant mass of rock rising out of the permafrost a mile or so to the southwest of the base to an elevation of about 3,000 feet. The jeep wound its way up a gravel road to a viewing point at the very top. The view from the top was truly grand, despite the reduction

Major Eigel Schueltz, Danish Air Force Base Commander, Narsarssuaq AB, Greenland, May 1978. (Paul Gillcrist Collection)

Narsarssuaq , May 1978. (Paul Gillcrist Collection)

in visibility. The colonel was obviously very proud of the view and of the base…his base! He pointed to a perimeter road and announced proudly, "That there is the longest road in Greenland…all seven miles of it!" In his anorak with the fur lined hood pulled tightly around his head, he looked like Scott of the Antarctic or some other famous explorer.

It was windy on top of Buford's Bluff. I was frozen…bone cold in my nomex flight suit, leather flight jacket and garrison cap. My teeth were chattering and my knees quivering. It was hard to articulate words as I responded to his question. "Well, what do you think of my base, Captain?" The inside of the jeep was unbelievably warm as we wended our way down the winding road.

It is strange that I remember very little about our evening at Sondestrom. Dinner at the Officers' Club was gracious, and I slept well in my BOQ bed. But I remember little of it. Next morning, at the crack of dawn, our *Hercules* rolled down the snow-covered runway en route to Norfolk via another operational TACAMO mission over the North Atlantic. This leg of the trip I spent largely in the back of the C-130, sitting at the keyboard of a secure teletype machine conversing with my number two at CinCLant Headquarters, Captain Detlow Marthinson, about routine office business.

I also typed out a trip report, spelling out just how much Marston matting would have to be shipped in to Narsarssuaq to construct an aircraft parking area. I also identified the need for a Marine Corps expeditionary aircraft arresting gear installation (MOREST), a number of supply trailers, Quonset huts, transportable fuel bladders, aircraft ground support equipment, and even an expeditionary radar approach facility. Twenty-four also seemed

Base Commander, Buford, Sondestrom AB, Greenland (Left), greets Capt. Gillcrist (Right), May 1978. (Paul Gillcrist Collection)

like the maximum amount of airplanes to provide an around-the-clock air defense capability to guard the "air bridge to Europe" without overwhelming the limited logistics pipeline that could be provided.

Bright and early the next Monday morning I stood in front of the same map on the floor of the CinCLant command center when the CinC walked in. He came over when I asked him to join me at the map, showing the southern tip of Greenland. I said, simply, "Twenty-four!"

He looked at me, a perplexed expression on his face. "Twenty-four what?" he asked.

"Twenty-four Phantoms," I responded, adding, "You can put 24 Phantoms at Narsarssuaq if you bring in the right support package." His expression now reflected understanding.

"How do you know?" he asked.

"Because I went there and paced it off myself." I responded proudly. He looked astounded.

"You went to Narsarssuaq? When? How?"

"Friday, in a TACAMO C-130," I responded, feeling very smug.

"Come to my office in 30 minutes, Paul. I want you to tell me all about it." He turned and walked out of the command center shaking, his head and muttering, "Amazing…simply amazing!"

Author's Footnote: Several days later another CinCLant TACAMO C-130 landed at Narsarssuaq. It only stayed on deck long enough to off-load a crate of Florida oranges for the base commander marked "Courtesy of Captain Gillcrist." A week later a post card arrived in the mail with a color photograph of Narsarssuaq taken from the air. It was from Major Eigel Schmeltz, Danish Air Force, thanking me for the oranges. The note on the card said he hoped we would stay in touch…we didn't !

Chapter 44:
Brigadoon

"Home is the sailor, home from the sea, and the hunter, home from the hills"

- Robert Louis Stevenson, *"Reunion"*

Even though the little Scottish village of Oban was far up inside the remote and rugged Firth of Lorent, it proved to be a memorable liberty port. Both Colyer and I savored that liberty port all the more because *Wasp* had just finished maneuvers in the Arctic Sea, and we had encountered more than our fair share of heavy weather. Though when I think of the tough time our escorts, the tin can sailors, had, I shouldn't complain.

It was a cold, blustery October day with a persistent force-five wind blowing in off the cold gray Atlantic when *Wasp* pulled into Oban. There was no dockside facility suitable for a ship the size of *Wasp*, so we anchored out in the Firth about a half mile from shore. Out there, the wind driven chop was sufficiently steep to question the use of the liberty launches.

The Firth of Lorent was as rugged as any Norwegian fjord. The craggy hills rose a thousand feet above the sea, helping to channel the wind and direct it against the little village of Oban as if in damp retribution. The land was pleasantly green, though, gentle on a weary sailor's eyes, and garnished with white sheep among the low, wind-pruned gorse and heather.

The little village itself could not be seen from where Wa*sp* lay at anchor because there was a headland jutting out into the Firth that hid the village from our view. The headland formed a snug inner harbor for Oban's small fishing fleet. By eleven a.m. that morning, all the ship's company who had been granted liberty were lined up in their best uniforms, anxious to go ashore.

Under normal conditions, the duty section would swing out the liberty launches and ferry us all ashore. This time, the Village of Oban sent its ancient little ferry to fetch its guests. That ferry was only about 120 feet long and 35 feet wide, small by any standard.

When Oban's ferry layed alongside, the liberty section scrambled aboard excitedly. The trip back to Oban went well until we rounded the headland and the little village came into view. Upon sighting the village, the entire liberty section moved in unison to the port side for a better view.

The ferry captain blanched as he felt the shift in the center of gravity. Then he stuck his head through the bridge hatch and roared with a thick scottish burr, " The f....ing boat's about to capsize, shift yer arses, and ye call yerselves sailors? Have ye lost yer senses, then?" The ferry boat continued slowly listing for a long moment before my shipmates came to their senses and trimmed the craft. If this incident had happened on the return trip, at night, and after a lively liberty, we would have capsized for sure.

That far north the weather felt like late November. Oban was about as far north as Whitehorse, Yukon Territory. It was a charming little village. In a way, it was like a modern day Brigadoon. The people weren't really out dancing in the streets as in the musical, but I vaguely recall Colyer doing a little soft-shoe dance on the way back to the liberty launch late that night.

The villagers themselves seemed innocent and carefree, because as the liberty section came ashore, the whole village stood in their open front doors, calling out to invite us into their homes for tea. Colyer and I declined all invitations.

Later on, upon reviewing our decision, I truly think that by that time in service, we felt as though we were of a lesser caste, and unworthy of their company. We had become too used to the nefarious crowds we were familiar with in past ports of call.

And we never approached the lassies; they were so shy and beautiful, innocent, red-cheeked and healthy. And so it was, in spite of the obvious fact that, "They were round in the counter and bluff in the bow," we changed our heading and made way for the nearest pub where we found friendly, ruddy faces. It was hardly compensation.

Actually, we were more hungry for real food than thirsty, so we first stopped at the tea shop for egg and bacon sandwiches. As our bill arrived, the waitress said "tupany ha." I could not understand the words or Highland brogue at first. After several repetitions we deciphered the speech. The waitress, a matronly woman with her hair in a bun, was politely saying, "You owe me two pennies and a half." Scotland was beautiful.

During our day of liberty, I decided to shop for a sheepskin vest, something to combat the chronic cold of duty on *Wasp*. Much to my surprise, there was no place in the village that handled vests. Next, I went in search of a yard of the clan hunting tartan. Today, I still wear a clan tie, made from that cloth, whenever I attend family weddings and funerals.

That single, short day of liberty in Oban was memorable, because it reminded us of byegone, innocent times and of life's simple pleasures, of friendly faces and familiar places—of home.

Chapter 45:
The Hubcap

"The best laid plans of mice and men, oftimes gang agley."

- Robert Burns:

As a lieutenant project test pilot at Patuxent River, MD, in 1959, I thought the next thing to God was the three-star Naval officer who occupied the office in the Pentagon labeled Deputy Chief of Naval Operations (Air Warfare), otherwise known as OP-05. Among other things, he controlled all the money spent at the Naval Air Test Center.

Vice Admiral Robert Pirie had the look of a man accustomed to power. I remembered him well from my days as a midshipman at the Naval Academy where he was the Commandant of Midshipmen. He was a strict disciplinarian and looked the part. He was known as "The Beard," and bore a close resemblance to Commander Whitehead of television ad fame. As the story went, he had a skin condition which did not permit shaving. I never believed it for a minute. For one thing, he kept the beard so impeccably trimmed that I knew he had to shave the edges of it frequently. But somehow it didn't matter, because he was a bright, energetic, and dedicated Naval officer...one of the better incumbents to occupy that office over the years.

Every year at budget review time, the "bean counters" in the Navy's comptroller's office examined a research-and-development line item call "Hydrodynamics Testing." This inquisition would ricochet down to Patuxent River, where the Navy's only hydrodynamics testing project was being conducted. The test vehicle was an old P5M flying boat with a very expensive single hydro ski mounted in its hull. The hydro ski was manually raised and lowered by a hand crank driving a chain drive. Of course, the raising and lowering always was done while dead in the water. As power was added the hull would slowly and ponderously rise up onto the ski until the entire weight of the huge flying boat was borne on that tiny ski. It was awesome to watch it skimming along on Chesapeake Bay or even the Patuxent River. The hydro ski was heavily instrumented to measure all sorts of data, from Reynolds number to stress loads.

The rate of testing was desultory at best…and I never understood why. I suspect that interest in hydro skis was low at the moment, but the policy from "The Beard's" office was to "keep it alive." This policy meant that every month or so one of the division test pilots with flying boat experience would haul the sea plane out of the hangar and take it flying…or rather, taxiing! The plane rarely ever flew. It just taxied around the Chesapeake Bay at high speed with the hydro ski extended.

On this particular spring day, the airplane was being prepped for flight…or more precisely, its semi-annual taxi test. The reason for the preparatory work was the extensive damage that had been done to the airplane the last time it taxied. The water had been a little too rough, and during a high speed turn on the hydro ski a wing tip had dug in and the seaplane did what was known as a "water loop"…a seaplane version of a ground loop! It was horrible to watch that huge airplane spinning like a top at 60 knots.

Several months of desultory repair was being wrapped up in time to accommodate a visit by "The Beard" for the expressed purpose of observing the tests from the seaplane itself. "The Beard" himself was going flying (or taxiing) with the test crew. My job was to see to the proper preparation of the old seaplane for such an auspicious visitor. As a precaution, I had asked my friend in Vice Admiral Pirie's office to keep me informed of his boss' progress on the trip down from Washington. He would be traveling with the admiral in a second car, and promised to call at least at the halfway point, in Waldorf. This would give me time to terminate the final checks being done by a civilian engineer on the seaplane's electrical systems and haul it out onto the parking ramp for the admiral's arrival. I even had our metalsmiths give the old seaplane a touch-up paint job!

The procedure for the test was to start up, taxi down the seaplane ramp into the water, crank down the hydro ski, and go roaring away down the Chesapeake Bay to collect God knows what kind of test data. I was sitting at my desk in the center bay, ground floor, of the Flight Test Division hangar when the Division Director, Captain Heber Badger, walked in. I immediately jumped up and asked him what I could do for him. Assuming that he would be interested in "The Beard's" progress, I told him they had passed Waldorf 10 minutes earlier and were expected at the main gate of the base in another 20 minutes.

No, that was not what had brought him to my office, he told me…dead serious. Then he dropped a hub cap onto my desk. "Paul, do you see where one of the three retainer clips has been broken off?" he asked. I said I saw that, confused at what this had to do with anything. I knew he owned a Volkswagen "Beetle," and this was off one of its wheels. "Here's the clip," he said handing me the small metal device. "Do you think one of your guys could braze it back on?"

Exactly at that moment there was a loud explosion in the north hangar bay as the whole building shook. A voice screamed "Fire. Fire in the hangar!" There were more explosions and more voices took up the cry, "Fire, Fire, Fire!" I pushed away from my desk and sprinted to the door leading into the hangar bay. A blast of heat struck me as I went through the door, and there I saw the P5M seaplane ablaze. Dense black smoke had already begun to descend from the ceiling. Within a minute I was doubled over to stay below the smoke level as I directed the sailors to get the hangar doors open and all of the multi-million dollar airplanes out.

A dozen blue jackets manhandled the huge rolling doors open, and others began pushing airplanes toward the doors. There wasn't time to hook up tow bars and attach them to tractors. It was either get them out in the next minute or two, or they would become part of an ever-increasing source of combustion. Several *Phantoms* and a *Vigilante* were already in motion. In the middle of the hangar was an old R4D we used for administrative transport purposes. "Get that thing out of here," I yelled at a group of sailors who seemed to be staring, transfixed at the exploding P5M. They started pushing it pretty fast. I yelled at one of them to jump in and ride the brakes so it could be stopped once outside without causing other damage to other things. He made a running dive for the rear door and missed, skidding on his stomach underneath the airplane. Another sailor tried and missed. The last I saw of the R4D, it was skittering crazily across the parking ramp outside the hangar, miraculously threading its way untouched among hundreds of parked cars.

A young sailor grabbed my arm and said he thought his buddy was inside the exploding fuselage of the P5M. With all of the magnesium in its construction, the seaplane was burning and exploding like a Fourth of July pyrotechnic device. I ran to the seaplane and climbed in through the rear fuselage door. I was feeling my way forward, since the airplane by now had been nearly filled with foam by some firefighter. It took quite a while and some scary moments before I felt my way blindly all the way to the cockpit. Climbing in between the two seats I felt with both hands for a body. There was none. Making my way aft, I felt in every conceivable place looking for the missing sailor. The seaplane was empty. When I finally climbed out I was a mess.

The hair had all been singed off my head, including my eyebrows. My green uniform blouse and trousers were all charred and torn, and my shoes were smoking. The fire sprinkler system was raining sooty water all over everything. By now the fire engines had arrived and a deluge of blackened water was pouring out the hangar door enclosure. A yeoman came up to me and told me that "The Beard" and his entourage were passing through the main gate when the tower of black smoke from the hangar became visible to them. A security patrol stopped them and told them there was a serious fire at their destination…the flight test division hangar. Vice Admiral Pirie directed the caravan to turn around and head back to Washington. He knew what was next and made the right decision to try to save the rest of his day.

An hour or so later the fire was finally declared out, and we assessed our damages. The only airplane lost was the P5M. Every other airplane had been saved without serious damage. There was fire damage to the hangar, including the roof, but it was all repairable. God bless the American blue jacket, I thought. When push came to shove, they always rose to the occasion.

It seems, as we reconstructed the chain of events leading to the disaster, that the P5M project officer had sent his test engineer to the airplane to run a routine systems check before "The Beard" arrived to fly it. The engineer sat in the pilot's seat with the airplane handbook open in his lap, and went through the system checkout procedures step by step. When he got to the weapons section, he read, "Pull jettison handle to ensure system continuity" or something like that. So he pulled the jettison handle without bothering to consider the possible consequences.

What he didn't know was that there was an auxiliary fuel tank suspended in the airplane's bomb bay on the rack normally reserved for torpedoes or bombs. The reserve fuel tank had been hung by his predecessor to allow greater fuel capacity for hydro-ski testing. When he pulled the jettison handle, the system did exactly what it was supposed to do…it jettisoned what was hanging on the bomb rack, in this case the auxiliary fuel tank.

The bladder-type fuel tank dropped to the floor of the hangar next to where an auxiliary power unit was operating, put-put-putting away on its small reciprocating engine. When the tank hit the hangar floor it burst open, spraying raw fuel all over the power unit, causing it to explode in a huge ball of fire.

I went into my office and sat down in my soggy green uniform, inspecting my exposed skin for burns. None were serious. There was a lot of singed hair on the back of my hands, but otherwise I was all right. I felt emotionally drained and physically exhausted.

I heard the door open behind me and spun my chair around to see Captain Badger standing there, the hubcap in his hand. "Before we were so rudely interrupted," he said, "do you think one of your guys could fix this for me?"

Chapter 46:
Sea Duty

"They think for 'emselves, an' they steal for 'emselves, and they never ask what's to do,"
- Soldier An' Sailor Too, Kipling

Towards the end of my time at Parris Island, Sgt. Jones, a poster-perfect, lean West Virginian and our senior drill instructor, explained the process of assigning recruits after boot camp. Sgt. Jones spoke of many areas of the Corps that we would be sent to. I particularly remember him speaking of two specific assignments.

The first was *Steward,* an assignment that placed the recruit in some senior officer's staff as a table waiter or coffee gofer. It was enough to make a Marine want to throw-up.

When, a week or so later, we sat and listened to the reading of the assignments, a black Marine that I respected got assigned as *steward.* I turned to see his humiliation and despair when he heard his assignment read for *steward.* He was a tough, resourceful guy who was a fighter, and maybe a little too confrontational. He and I had our differences, but I liked him and felt it was a shame that a quality Marine would be wasted. For the next three years, he would walk around in a little white jacket serving coffee and picking up underwear.

After the assignments were read, I walked over and told him how sorry I was. He sat with his head hanging and just shook his head from side to side. He never even looked up.

The week before the reading, Sgt. Jones also spoke of the second of the two assignments. "Now these are the real Marines, the Seagoing Marines, the best get sea duty," he said. Right then, I knew what I wanted. And so it was that as the seagoing Marines' names were read, my name was called, and I swelled with pride and relief.

Sgt. Jones never really explained what the duties of a seagoing Marine were, and it took me years to find out for myself. It turned out that we were capable of and eventually did just about every conceivable job. It was customary at that time to send all seagoing recruits to Portsmouth, VA, for additional training. Those of us who went there spent about two months running around learning little of any consequence, except that I learned never to act as spokesman again.

Contemplative moment—Don Colyer in the 5" gun tub on the U.S.S. Wasp, North Atlantic, March 1958. (Robert Gillcrist Collection)

It so happened that we all wanted to be assigned to the same ship. We were pals after enduring Parris Island and Camp Lejeune together, and got on well. The group asked me to act as spokesman and "Request mast," meaning the equivalent of an audience with the Pope.

My request was granted, and I went before the commanding Officer to make an impassioned plea for the group to stay together. The result was that the rest of the group was assigned to a new and prestigious ship, and I languished on extended mess duty while the world moved on.

And so I endured the mess hall at Portsmouth until I was injured and unable to work. Maybe I was lucky. The messboy who proceeded me went berserk one day while we were enjoying a lunch of bologna sandwiches and sardines. The way it happened was that as the messboy wandered among the tables throwing down platters of food, a sharp-eyed Marine noticed a mouse hopping along the mess hall wall.

Being a bunch of chronic wise guys, we all liked to needle the messboy, and this time was no different. "Hey, messboy, get that mouse out of here," ordered the sharp-eyed Marine. The messboy dutifully chased the mouse behind a fire extinguisher and slowly squashed it under his heel, to the sounds of squeals and eruptions of gas and fluids.

We all stopped eating for a moment to calm our stomachs, and in that pause the messboy's mind separated from his body. His eyes rolled up into his head and he leapt onto the table with a howl and bounded from table to table on across the mess hall like an orangutan, grunting and hurling food.

It was a good opportunity to spear a couple extra slices of bologna, and I made use of the distraction to build a second sandwich. Eventually they threw a net over him, dressed him in a straightjacket, and hopped the messboy away like a cottontail. We had to forego coffee that day, since there was no one left to serve. Sometimes you could tell when someone was about to go over the edge and sometimes it came as a surprise.

Since I was injured and wouldn't be able to scurry around the mess hall for weeks, my punishment ended and I was assigned to sea duty on *Wasp*. Incidentally, that was when Colyer and I became shipmates. When Colyer and I caught up with *Wasp*, it was tied up in South Boston Shipyard. The *Wasp's* Marine detachment were salty seasoned Pendelton Marines who had been together for years in the Pacific and Japan. They were a very tight detachment and did not take kindly to two green, smart-ass privates from Parris Island.

As a result, Colyer and I endured a lot of harassment and dirty details in the detachment until we went to Fort Devon to shoot for record. While at Fort Devon, Colyer and I shot better scores than the old salts. It was also at Fort Devon that the entire detachment engaged in some illegal activity, but only Colyer and I were caught. We ended up in the stockade there and took our licking without saying a word. After that incident and a couple of fights we were finally accepted.

Coincidentally, it was at that time that I went before a board of officers to apply for entrance to the Naval Academy Prep School. The board wanted to know why I spent so much time aboard, and before I could reply, Captain Weita, my CO, said that I was doing some special studies for him. *Semper Fidelis*. In truth, I was confined to the ship for the incident at Fort Devon, but the captain would never admit it to the swabbies.

After the Navy turned me down for prep school, the entire detachment called me lieutenant, much to the consternation of our real lieutenant. That moniker stayed with me until I left *Wasp*; the price of ambition, or was it arrogance?

The Marine quarters on board *Wasp* were spartan. The NCOs had a private compartment and the duty watch had a guard room. The rest of the area was filled with small, free standing lockers and a forest of steel pipes welded to deck and overhead. Attached to the pipes were racks of steel with a canvas piece and woven rope attaching it to the rack like a rectangular trampoline. These were the bunks. A thin pad served as the mattress, and a thinner olive drab wool blanket was our only cover.

At reveille, the 1MC would announce, "Heave out and trice up, make a clean sweepdown fore and aft." We would all get out of the trampolines and fold them up against the bulkheads and overhead, out of the way, until taps 14 hours later.

We were always cold. Boston in winter is so cold that in the Marine quarters at night I've watched from my bunk as a Marine awoke from the cold and sneaked to another Marine's bunk to silently steal his blanket. He then hopped back into his own bunk and curled up warm again to drift back to sleep. In time, his victim would begin to shiver and finally awaken to discover his blanket gone. This Marine would then steal another's blanket. I lay there watching this go on for hours one night, enjoying the pathos and artful language.

The detachment's duties were basically security, as is the case for most stations. We ran the brig, the naval version of Purgatory, as an extension of the security role. We also handled discipline every evening in the form of close order drill for all defaulters, in which one of us would march them about the hangar deck for an hour. Two Marines also acted as guards for the ship's captain and exec, something that I did for a while.

As part of the security role, the detachment guarded the nuclear weapons compartment. Those of us who stood watch there were required to wear a dosimeter, a small button-like device that measured our accumulation of radioactivity.

Once a year, the detachment would go off to some rifle range, and each of us would fire for record. The important thing was that you got to wear your score, so to speak, all year on your uniform. Within the Corps, marksmanship was important and a measure of the Marine, so an expert badge was worth striving for.

Since the detachment was trained as infantry, another duty was to organize and control the ship's landing party. Someone must have been reading *Horatio Hornblower*, because they thought we might need to put a landing party ashore some day, possibly to storm and occupy some obscure third world fortress. The idea was for the Marines to organize hundreds of sailors and incidentally arm them and form fire teams to go ashore and scale the escarpments.

When we formed up on the hangar deck to show the sailors what a machine gun or mortar was, the sailors who showed up were all the misfits and troublemakers. Nobody wanted to give up any of their good men, so we got the dregs. Fortunately, we never gave the landing party ammunition, or more to the point, we never went ashore on a mission.

Only once did we come close, and that was when Vice President Nixon and his wife Pat had their car overturned by a mob of Venezuelan rioters. On that occasion, President Eisenhower ordered us to head for Caracas. We actually did start to prep for a landing that time. It was a funny feeling, knowing that within about twelve hours, we would be hitting the beach for real.

Another detachment's duty was to fire a pair of 5-inch guns situated in an open gun tub on the after port side, just below the flight deck. The big guns were an enigma. They were really radar-controlled, I think. But, we worked them as though they were not. As I recall, it took four men to work a single 5-inch gun. My job was to pick up a 60 pound projectile from a rack and throw it into the breech. A man behind me threw a brass shell full of power into the breech, behind the projectile. The head gunner then pulled a lever, and a ram pushed the two parts up into the chamber and slammed the breech shut. Something unknown decided when the gun was on target and electrically fired the gun.

Things went reasonably well until one day when the guns were facing forward as the carrier cut through the sea at 40 knots. As the guns fired and I turned to snatch another projectile, the world lit up, and I felt incredibly hot in an instant. Turning in surprise, with a

60 pound high explosive shell in my arms, I was engulfed in flames. My pals and shipmates had all fled.

Apparently what had happened was that when the guns fired, the gas and flames were all pushed back down the barrel by the 40 knot breeze, and while passing through the gun, ignited the leftover powder. The whole mess flamed up in the gun tub. My mates reacted automatically and ran. I turned and was too late. Besides, what was I to do with the projectile in my arms? No permanent damage was done, and the projectile took the heat without exploding. I sported a dark tan for awhile and had to grow new eyebrows.

As I said, the guns were odd. They were supposed to track back and forth without touching the ship. The mechanism must have been worn, because the barrels would bang into the flight deck whenever we fired aft. To make matters worse, the forward gun barrel would swing in over the crew of the aft gun when firing aft. The muzzle blast from a barrel maybe five feet over our heads was enough the knock us down. With a projectile in my arms, that was not good. Why is it that all my life, I have seemed to get the shitty jobs?

Being responsible for the 5-inch guns had its own rewards, though. One gray drizzly day while Colyer and I were working on the gun, a whale surfaced alongside *Wasp*. It was a big bull. It probably saw *Wasp* as that Amazonian grayback cow of his fantasies and wanted to get laid. It never hurts to ask! There the both of us stood, leaning over the splinter shield, entranced. What a treat!

Wasp was like a small city. There were an infinite number of different jobs in that city. One day, Colyer and I were picked from a long list as two potential candidates and told to climb down into the void that exists between the steel outer hull and the inner hull of the ship and paint the entire void with a rust inhibiting paint.

Someone turned on an explosion-proof light, and we were handed buckets of some volatile paint, along with brushes. The hatch was dogged behind us, and we stood down there in the void, chatting and stroking. The place was cool, and nobody was on our ass. Not bad duty!

As time passed, the painted surface increased, and the vehicle in the paint displaced the rapidly disappearing oxygen. We began to feel like we were on one of our notorious 96 hour passes. The ones where you never actually sober up from the first night until you return to the ship four days later. You aren't drunk, actually, just maintaining an unusual level of alcohol in your body. We used to call it maintaining float.

Anyway, we slowly became intoxicated by the fumes and lack of oxygen. As we painted away, Colyer broke into song, and I harmonized with gusto, and the void created a steel echo chamber. We were having a grand time! Fortunately, the gunnery sergeant who was punishing us stopped by to see if we were goofing off. He stuck his head through the hatch, smelled the fumes, and found us in a soggy, paint-soaked heap, singing about a girl named Sue.

It took a squad of Marines to lift the two sticky drunks out of the void. It was the only time we were intoxicated while on duty. It was also the worst hangover Colyer and I ever experienced.

The passageways on a fighting ship are narrow and lined with steel ducts, pipes, junction boxes, valves, levers, racks, horns, and so on. The pipes lining the passageways on an aircraft carrier can contain diesel fuel, #2 fuel, #4 fuel, fresh water, salt water, aviation fuel, compressed air, hydraulic fluid, high pressure steam, low pressure steam, sewage, communication cables, electric power, (24v., 48v, 477v, 120v, 60hz, 400hz), and more.

And, on board Wasp, like any other incorporated entity, work and responsibility was distributed geographically. And so it was that the lieutenant of the detachment, Francis Kelly, assigned me to the task of identifying all the pipes in the Marine quarters. The job was to figure out what the pipes, conduits, and ducts contained, and also what direction the contents were flowing. After identifying all the pipe junction boxes and conduits, I was to stencil the information in a visible location for the damage control party in the event of an emergency.

With Colyer to help, we took out the plasticized drawings of the ship and began to decipher them. Remember, we were a couple of kids, not engineers. Believe it or not, in time we did a creditable job. It was a really interesting assignment. You can give a Marine any task you want, and he will do it. Whether or not he does it well is another question entirely.

On one pipe, we lied. All I can say is "The devil made us do it." It was obvious to Colyer and me that they should have chosen a naval engineer for the job. The notion astounded the two of us that grown men believe with the same absolute faith that an Irish priest places in the Holy Trinity, that our stenciled markings were correct. And so we devised a plan to test the limits of the crew's gullibility. We took a stanchion that looked like a pipe and identified it as "Top Secret," and gave it a direction of flow. Then we reported snappily to Lt. Kelly that we had completed the assignment. No one ever questioned this hoax!

Colyer got me in trouble often. And because we were punished as often as we were caught, we were given many assignments. In time, it became obvious to upper management that they could give the two of us any assignment with complete faith that it would be done quickly and well. We became so well known that when *Wasp* was unable to visit Port Au Prince, Haiti, due to mechanical failures, the captain decided to fly off a select group of five crew in an S2F to enjoy liberty in Jamaica.

The idea was that the 3000 mortals remaining on board would go on liberty vicariously. The captain must have been sneaking the medical brandy! Anyway, we got picked. Maybe the whole crew were sick of Colyer's and my mischief. And then when promotions came along, they actually promoted me! It was amazing.

The Corps is right in picking young men with a sense of immortality and absolutely no sense of responsibility. Those young men will do just about anything, if told to do so, and quite often in spite of being told not to.

Chapter 47:
Genesis

"And all I need is a tall ship, and a star to steer her by"
- Sea Fever, Masefield

It was one of those hazy July days in the mid 50s. The Korean War was over, and we were a peacetime Navy, finally. *Wasp* was plowing through endless dark blue oily swells in the mid-Atlantic, launching and recovering aircraft day and night, refining airmanship into an art form.

Colyer and I were working on the 5-inch guns, stopping periodically as was our custom to look out at the seemingly lifeless sea. Past experience had taught us that the ocean was really teeming with life. You just had to look in the right place at the right time to witness the life hidden below its surface. During one pause, we were rewarded by the sighting of a single-handed sailor as he emerged from the haze and sailed slowly by on a reciprocal course.

The sailboat was a small white sloop, maybe 30 feet in length, listing to a gentle breeze as it climbed the ocean swells, pitching and dipping with the regularity of a deep sleeper. The sailor was leaning back in the cockpit, one foot on the wheel, pipe clinched between mahogany jaws, relaxed and confident, as though unaware of the colossus nearby. He acted unconcerned, as though he was only sailing from his mooring to an adjacent dock, when in fact he was at the point of no return: 1,500 miles from the closest land.

And snugged down over white hair and at a jaunty angle, a crumpled, wide-brimmed canvas hat shaded his face. The jaunty angle of his hat and his pose seemed to say, "Who's the best sailor in the Atlantic?" And, "Which of us needs 3,000 hands to sail his vessel?" Oh, "And which of us has to suck up to an oiler every hundred miles or so?"

In a few short moments, that lone sailor disappeared into the heat haze as if into infinity and was gone forever, but the memory has kept me company for over 40 years. Colyer and I stood in the gun tub, leaning over the splinter shield, hip-shot, faded green fatigue caps snugged down, shading our eyes, mouths agape, thinking of the possibilities.

Where was he bound? It could be anywhere. All it took was the simple act of moving his helm to starboard or port to change his course to perhaps Trinidad, or to Tonga, Tenerif, or Tangier. That lone sailor did not have to answer to anyone but God—What unimaginable freedom!

Colyer was my shipmate during those years in the Marines. His given name was Pete, but he preferred to be called Don. He was fair haired, blue eyed, well built, good with his fists, and a natural salesman. When I first met Don I was puzzled by the crow's feet and squint that made his otherwise youthful face look older. Then Don explained about his family's love affair with sailing, and the years of squinting across the ocean in search of vagrant breezes while under sail.

The sighting of that single-hander made an indelible impression on two indentured young Marines with what seemed like a lifetime of service remaining to serve. It wasn't long after that impressive sighting that Don and I began to gnaw at the notion of buying an old sailboat after our discharge and sailing around the world. It was suddenly possible. We'd use our discharge pay to buy the boat and get jobs near the boatyard while we fitted the boat for ocean cruising. We'd sail to Pago Pago. If that old salt could do it, then we could surely do it!

Expanding on our notion occupied many a happy off duty hour sitting in the gun tub, supposing and planning, and brimming with youthful exuberance. The two of us talked

Don Colyer and Bob Gillcrist reunion at sea 37 years later, Long Island Sound, September 1997. (Robert Gillcrist Collection)

about navigation, provisions, weather, and a long list of other topics, things we would need to know: knowledge. As a direct result of the sighting of that single-hander, I approached Wasp's navigator and borrowed a book on navigation. After all, if we were going to sail around the world, then somebody had better learn some celestial navigation.

The navigation studies were tough sledding, but I'd stop by whenever I was stuck, which was often, and the navigation officer was kind enough to help me along. In addition to the navigation studies, we began reading anything that the ship's library had on single-handed sailors. Slocum's journey was literary oxygen! I even purchased a book that I still treasure, by Chapman, on seamanship and boat handling. That book sits on a shelf in my home, alongside *Heavy Weather Sailing*. And so, all those diverse studies occupied many of our midnight watch hours during the remainder of our time at sea.

Unwittingly, that single-handed sailor had given us a gift. The realization that the possibilities for human expression are endless. Anybody can make his mind up to sail around the world or write a book, or dream a dream. There aren't any limits or quotas. "It's the set of your sails and not the gales that bid you where you go."

It was the first time in my life that I was ever really motivated to study a difficult subject. For once, there was a tangible purpose for the studies. As I saw it, if I mastered my navigational studies, we'd make the next landfall. If not, we'd come a cropper. As a result of our new-found purpose, when I was up on the island or standing guard duty on the dock, I'd look over the bow, stern, breasting, and spring lines. The anchor watch now had some meaning, and I took the anchor watch seriously. I was becoming proprietary. Wasp was my ship.

Our education encompassed knots (in lines) and knots (nautical miles an hour), and nautical miles (6,000 feet, not the 5,280 foot miles we know). The topics were endless. What was the bottom like in a particular port? What about sea room, fetch, exposure, tide, and current?

Late one fall, *Wasp* docked at Quonset Point. While ashore on some errand, Colyer discovered that the recreation department had sail boats, and he took me for my first sail the next Saturday. With Don at the tiller, completely at ease and chatting away happily, we roamed Narraganset Bay all day, never once using the single oar that was provided. What a delight it was to actually harness the wind! And besides, we discovered that we didn't need a liberty pass. Nobody had thought of the idea of stealing away in a sailboat for a beer in some bar down the bay.

Weather observations became a daily routine, and they still are. Ancient weather lore, which took the form of proverbs and rhymes, held lyrical hints as to future weather. Just recently, I was reading a pilot book on the Turkish coast. The author gave substantial credence to the ancient Coptic Calendar: more lore.

Reading Chapmans, I learned to identify sloops and barks, cutters and brigantines, ketches, yawls, and schooners. On another level, there were dozens of entertaining sea chanteys and poems I absorbed like a sponge. And authors like Forester, O'Brien, and Reeman allowed me to sail vicariously, even in the depths of winter, to places as distant as Greenland

and Tarawa. That was how the love affair with the sea that my wife Ann and I have enjoyed all these years began. A chance meeting one hazy July day in the middle of the Atlantic.

And the seasons slowly changed as they must, and the days grew shorter as the summer of youth waned, and the autumn shades of maturity began to emerge. In August Colyer and I had been transferred from *Wasp* to the Brooklyn Navy Yard preparatory to our discharge.

After what seemed like a lifetime, my discharge date of October 10, 1958, finally arrived. The discharge process itself was disappointingly simple when compared to the personal commitment of time Colyer and I had made. There was no fanfare at all. Just the disbursement of some back pay. The seabag and the uniforms were mine to keep in case the Marine Corps decided to recall me to active duty, any time within the next six years.

It was late that warm and cloudy October morning before I cleared personnel. A free man at last. Outside in the cobbled barracks square, I stood indecisively, seabag over one shoulder, and a manila envelope containing my discharge in my other hand. My mind was a tangle of emotions. Should I find the work detail Colyer was on and say goodbye? Or should I just head out the shipyard gate? At that precise moment, Colyer came running out the barracks door. He knew! "You were going to duck out without saying goodbye, weren't you, you son of a bitch," Don shouted knowingly as he jogged across the barracks square.

Then, for a long moment Don and I stood there in the square, two lean, tan, tall young men with our lives ahead of us, holding that last handshake, grinning, and looking each other in the eye. We both knew that the old sailboat had been a dream. We would never sail to Pago Pago. Instead, The Prodigals would set course for home; to toil in the vineyards.

Don and I both knew that just outside that shipyard gate the damp and gritty pavements of life awaited us. We had each resolved privately to do what was expected, to go back to school, find a profession, a wife. It was time to assume our obligations. The understanding was unspoken; the adventure over. After an awkward silence we turned and headed in different directions. Colyer trudged back to the barracks to finish his enlistment. And with my seabag on my shoulder, I headed through another of life's gates. Behind me, Colyer called from the barracks steps, "Maybe in a couple of years."

Yeah, maybe in a couple of years.

Don Colyer and Bob Gillcrist reunion, Northport, NY, September 1997. (Robert Gillcrist Collection)

Chapter 48:
"A Wing and a Prayer"

"Halleluia, halleluia.
Throw a nickle on the grass;
Save a fighter pilot's ass.
Halleluia, halleluia.
Throw a nickle on the grass,
And you'll be saved."
- U.S. Air Force drinking song from the Korean War.

On the debit side, this story has all of the characteristics of a B-grade movie. On the plus side, it occurred to (and was related by) one of the most respected gentlemen in Naval Aviation; Rear Admiral E.L. "Whitey" Feightner, U.S.N. (Retired). It makes the story even more bizarre, because it is true… clearly stranger than fiction.

As it happened, Whitey, a post-command commander, was awaiting assignment as an air wing commander and flying a training flight in an A-4 out of Cecil Field, FL. The year was 1957. He received a radio call from Commander Jerry Miller, a member of CAG 4 staff, telling him to return and land immediately. Once on the ground, Whitey learned that he had a set of urgent orders to relieve the CAG on the *Forrestal,* currently deployed in the Mediterranean Sea. He was given 20 minutes to pack and get aboard the Admiral's airplane, which was scheduled to take him to Charleston Air Force Base where a C-121 transport airplane was waiting to take him to Naples. Upon his arrival at Naples, a carrier on board delivery airplane would take him directly to the carrier at sea. This was as high priority transportation as Whitey had ever encountered.

Whitey finally settled into his seat onboard the Air Force C-121 transport airplane after a hectic several hours of hurried preparation, and heaved a sigh of relief. The airplane roared down the runway at Charleston AFB headed for Naples, and ultimately the job of a lifetime. Certainly it was a happy moment for Whitey, because this was the best set of orders he could ever hope to get. He felt lucky…life just doesn't get any better than this, he thought. It was 1957, the Korean War was history, U.S. Navy carrier aviation was undergoing an unprecedented expansion, and Whitey felt the excitement of being a part of important developments in Naval history.

But fate intervened at this juncture. The airplane received a call from the tower ordering it to abort its takeoff and return to the passenger terminal. There two military policemen were waiting for him!

"Commander Feightner? Would you please come with me?" the young MP said. When Whitey asked why, he was told it was to serve as a courier for some very high priority Top Secret material that had just arrived and was enroute to a destination in Port Lyautey, North Africa. Whitey refused, explaining he had in his possession a legal set of orders to *Forrestal*. Apparently anticipating this reaction, the policeman whipped out an order authorizing him to commandeer any officer of any service for this courier run. The order specifically included any Naval officer enroute to a permanent change of duty post in the theater.

Whitey reluctantly accepted the courier duty...feeling as though he were being robbed of his choice duty by a very cruel and fickle finger of fate. But then, he thought, he would deliver this precious cargo and be off to *Forrestal* without too much delay after all.

The military policemen promised to retrieve his luggage and send it after him on another flight headed east the same day. They then marched Whitey to the biggest airplane he had ever seen...a C-124 *Globemaster*! He was put aboard, given a .45 cal. automatic pistol, and instructed to wear it on a web belt slung around his waist. His post was in an otherwise empty cargo space in the huge transport where a seat had been rigged for him next to a large pile of cargo hidden under a tarpaulin. This was, he was told, 10,000 pounds of Top Secret electronic materiel which he, Commander Whitey Feightner, was to deliver.

His mode of transportation on this particular day was one of the marvels of military aviation. The *Globemaster* was brand new and would eventually become the keystone of military cargo and passenger transportation. Powered by four Pratt & Whitney reciprocating engines and weighing more than 200,000 pounds empty, the airplane was able to span the Atlantic with more than 300 passengers with ease. The flight to Rabat, Morrocco, would be a long, 10 hour non-stop mission. There were no passengers and no other cargo...nothing but this Top Secret shipment, which was messing up his life...for the moment.

The flight took off about 8:30 p.m. This was a flight never intended to go well, Whitey thought, as he heard the starboard outboard engine throttle down to idle rather abruptly during takeoff roll. He later learned that this particular mission was a check flight for both the transport squadron commanding officer and his operations officer (pilot and copilot respectively). Furthermore, the check pilot, an Air Force captain, was going to retire after giving this check flight, the final mission of his career.

As a good check pilot would, the captain gave the lieutenant colonel a throttle chop (simulated loss of an engine) to see how he would handle it. The skipper didn't handle the simulated emergency well at all. At that point on the takeoff roll the correct action, since they were past the abort point, would have been to feather the idling propeller and continue on three engines. The lieutenant colonel didn't do this. Instead, he attempted to abort the take-off! As a consequence, the *Globemaster* rolled ignominiously off the end of the runway at Charleston and became bogged down in mud.

It took the crash and rescue crew almost four hours to tow the monster airplane back onto the runway, clean the mud off the main gear, and give it a thorough system check. The airplane was finally airborne at about 12:30 that evening.

Somewhere east of Charleston the plane commander figured out that they were going to need to make a crew rest stop at the Navy base at Bermuda. Why they didn't figure this out before takeoff is still a mystery to Whitey. I suspect that the crew had decided early-on that a night in Bermuda was not a half bad idea. So the airplane landed at NAS, Bermuda. The following day (crew rest expired at noon) they all went to the officers' club for brunch. Unfortunately, the only thing on the menu was Hungarian goulash. So, the crew feasted on that Eastern European delicacy while Whitey decided against it and settled on a ham omelet. As it turned out the omelet probably saved all of their lives!

The *Globemaster* lifted off the runway just before dusk, headed for Rabat, and Whitey was now looking forward to the end of his detour. This was the last leg of his courier duty flight…or so he thought. Just as the airplane was climbing through 2,000 feet a loud bang came from the number 3 engine (starboard inboard). Whitey heard the report and saw the engine being feathered as the propeller came to a dramatic stop. The airplane next circled Bermuda while the lieutenant colonel and the check pilot decided what to do about this new turn of events. The natural thing would have been for them to land and fix the engine. Unfortunately, this is not what happened. Bermuda didn't have the facilities to do much serious maintenance on the *Globemaster*. The check pilot finally observed that the loss of the engine provided a perfect opportunity for him to observe how the aircrew would handle a *bone fide* emergency. The two of them made the incredible decision to press on with the mission on three engines!

Certainly, the new airplane had the power and fuel to complete the flight on three engines. Nevertheless, Whitey felt a funny churning in the pit of his stomach when the giant airplane rolled out of its turn and headed east as the pilot added power. They were on their way, for better or worse. Whitey tried to settle down for some rest in his uncomfortable seat.

About three hours out of Bermuda, the crew chief shook Whitey from what was a fitful sleep (they were cruising at 9,000 feet, and it was freezing in the cargo compartment) and said, "Sir, the plane commander would like to see you up on the flight deck." He said there was a problem. The crew chief had made the understatement of the year! What had happened was that the check pilot, the Air Force captain, had come down with a case of food poisoning accompanied by severe stomach cramps. They had strapped him down in one of the crew bunks and the co-pilot, who was also suffering a milder case of food poisoning, was on the radio getting medical advice from home base. The lieutenant colonel described the check pilot's complexion as "blue" and said he was very worried about him. The suspected culprit was the Hungarian goulash.

The lieutenant colonel told Whitey that they were approaching a severe looking storm front and he had decided that he should try to get the number 3 engine started just in case. He further explained that he and the crew chief were going out into the huge wing to get the capricious engine started. He thought it prudent, since Whitey was an aviator, that the Navy pilot stand by in the cockpit while he was in the starboard wing. Whitey's assistance would be needed to start the wayward engine, and additionally, he would be a qualified pilot at the controls even though they were flying on automatic pilot.

Whitey's total multi-engine flying experience consisted of about 50 hours in a small, twin-engined Beechcraft C-45 and a few hours in another twin-engined R4D "Gooney Bird." Nothing in his total flying experience had prepared him for the "no notice" challenge presented by this four-engine monster on a black night in the weather 400 miles east of the Azores. The flight deck of the modern C-124 was an inexplicable array of throttles, control levers, instruments, switches, dials, needles, and knobs, the complexity of which boggled his mind. What did they think he was, a magician, he wondered?

Of course the first order of business, Whitey decided, was to get into the pilot's seat and figure out what all of the levers, dials, handles, and switches did. Nothing in his flying experience had prepared him for the formidable array of controls which surrounded him as he sat there, somewhat overwhelmed. This C-124 was a far cry from the single-engined, jet-powered carrier airplanes in which he had accumulated the bulk of his flying experience. His immediate concern was to keep the airplane from crashing into the water 9,000 feet below them. The crew chief told him as much as he knew about the cockpit controls. Next, Whitey concentrated on all of the dials, instruments, and needles…hundreds of them.

The colonel and the crew chief had been out in the wing about 45 minutes when the crew chief called Whitey on the intercom. He said they thought they had fixed the problem and were ready to start the engine. He reviewed the starting procedures with Whitey, whereupon they successfully started the engine. During this period Whitey sat in the pilot's seat and watched the approaching storm. They were just entering the edge of the storm when the turbulence started, and Whitey, not knowing how the monster airplane would perform on autopilot in heavy turbulence, decided to fly the airplane manually.

About 15 minutes elapsed, during which time Whitey became increasingly uneasy about the whereabouts of everyone. He was alone in the cockpit of the monster airplane, and aghast at the fact that the instrument panel seemed to be vibrating severely. It was dark, and the turbulence had kept him very busy trying to fly instruments.

"Hello, I'm lieutenant (junior grade) Robinson," the voice startled Whitey. He turned and saw an unfamiliar face. The newcomer explained that he was the navigator. He was a Navy Lieutenant (junior grade) on exchange duty with the Air Force. Then, he blithely announced something that chilled Whitey's blood. "The skipper's blind!" he said. "What do you mean, blind?" Whitey asked. Lieutenant Robinson explained that the lieutenant colonel had been overcome by carbon monoxide fumes while in the wing's engine nacelle compartment.

Despite the clearly placarded warning not to run the engine with personnel in the wing, the pilot had given the order to do just that, and remained crouched in the wing next to the engine nacelle while Whitey and the crew chief went through the starting procedure. When the lieutenant colonel collapsed, the crew chief managed to drag his body out of the wing and deposited him on a bunk in the lounge next to the check pilot and co-pilot. The crew chief was totally absorbed in trying to save the skipper's life. The colonel had regained consciousness! The medical personnel at Lajes were seriously concerned about the colonel's chances of surviving such a prolonged dose of carbon monoxide poisoning. The victims of the Hungarian goulash were also considered at risk.

While Whitey's mind was still trying to grasp the significance of what was unfolding, a voice came over the radio from Lajes.

"Air Force 27642, this is Lajes OpCon, we are aware of your problems and have launched a B-17 that will attempt to rendezvous with you in about 15 minutes. He is radar-equipped and will assist in getting you to Lajes." Shortly thereafter the B-17 pilot called to say that they were a mile in trail, had them in radar contact, and were prepared to escort them in to Lajes.

The first thing Whitey noticed about flying the *Globemaster* was the enormous amount of instrument panel vibration. The entire panel was shock-mounted, and each instrument seemed to jiggle back and forth almost two and a half inches. Whitey thought that there was something seriously wrong with one of the engines and suspected something catastrophic would occur at any moment. It made any kind of decent instrument scan impossible. When he later asked the crew chief about the vibration, he was told it was a natural phenomenon of the *Globemaster*.

There were other complicating factors; the principal one being weather. The ceiling and visibility at Lajes were below minimums, and there was a cross-wind of 25 knots 90 degrees to the runway heading, which was approaching the allowable limits for a C-124. For this reason, Lajes directed Whitey to continue on toward Lajes until they reached a clear area reported by another airplane about 50 miles west of the Azores. There he was told to circle until the weather improved enough to attempt a landing. This was forecast to occur about sun-up. Flying this monster airplane at altitude was one thing. Landing it was quite another. But, landing it under bad weather conditions at night and in extreme cross-wind conditions was yet another, much more serious problem.

Whitey followed the instructions that Lajes gave him and began circling in the clear area he found. The monitoring of the colonel's vital signs continued, with the medical people at Lajes becoming more and more concerned about his chances of survival. The combination of improving weather and the worsening of the colonel's condition caused Lajes to finally recommend to Whitey that they proceed inbound to Lajes to attempt a landing. Whitey asked the navigator to help put the still-ailing copilot into the right seat. He told the major that he would try to help him with the landing approach. The major sat there, apparently still feeling very sick, and told Whitey that "no way was he going to try to land the Goddamned airplane."

It was about this time that someone at Lajes began to wonder to whom they were talking. The voice on the other end of the line finally asked Whitey, "Who are you?" "I'm a Navy fighter pilot" was the reply. This could be one of the all time one-liners of Naval Aviation! The long, pregnant silence which followed that announcement caused Whitey to add, "And I'm a graduate of the Navy's Test Pilot School."

The episode ended with Whitey making the instrument approach and cross-wind landing aided by commentary only from a still groggy Air Force major. I suspect that the major was not nearly as groggy as he made himself out to be. The story has a happy ending. There, waiting for him at Rabat was *Forrestal*'s CAG with an A-3B to take him out to the ship!

Author's Footnote: The colonel ultimately regained his vision but remained permanently incapacitated and was retired on a medical disability. There is no record of what, if anything, happened to the major. No doubt, the Navy lieutenant (junior grade) went on to bigger and better things. But, there is one thing for certain. Both the lieutenant (jg) and the crew chief have doubtless regaled many an audience at military clubs all over the world with the totally improbable story of "that crazy Navy fighter pilot and the *Globemaster!*"

Chapter 49:
Friendly Fire

"Nothing is more exhilarating than to be fired at without effect"

\- Young Winston Churchill

Whenever I read of the public's outrage (spell it the media's outrage) over the "friendly fire" incidents in the Persian Gulf War, I want to throw up. To be sure, in a perfect world such things should not happen. Yes, if everybody did his job perfectly, such things wouldn't happen. And yes, they are sad events indeed for the families and loved ones who died in this "ignominious" way. All of those things are true. But, if one does an impersonal analysis of that war, he settles on the irrefutable fact that it was the safest major conflict in which this country has ever engaged.

Exchange ratio is a very callous measurement of a war...but it is also very absolute! By anyone's measure, the Persian Gulf War was the most one-sided major conflict in the history of the world. The exchange ration in human lives ranged from 1000:1 on the low side to probably three times that figure (or 3000:1). By comparison, the numbers for World Wars I and II were somewhere around 3:1! Nonetheless, the expression has a bad sound to it. No one likes it...especially when he has been on the receiving end of friendly fire.

Of course, the reason for friendly fire incidents can always be traced to friendly failure...of procedures, equipment, communications, or some combination of the three. Two events come to mind; two very personal events from which I luckily emerged unscathed...which highlight the unpleasantness of friendly fire.

The first occurred on 29 March 1967 over the Do San Peninsula, North Vietnam. The event was a two-carrier strike against two major targets in the Hanoi-Haiphong area. The other carrier's aircraft struck a power plant near Hanoi, while our carrier struck the airfield of Kien Anh near Haiphong. Our operation was a 16 plane strike...the first attack of the war against a North Vietnamese airfield. Eight A-4s dropped bombs on the airfield. Four other A-4s acted as anti-SAM forces, called Iron Hand. Four F-8s under my lead acted as fighter escorts. During the two to three minutes of the actual strike there were 22 SAM calls, the

Paul Gillcrist "manning up" Topgun F-5F at NAS Miramar, August 1979. (Paul Gillcrist Collection)

strike leader, our CAG, "Dutch" Netherland, was shot down, an A-6 from the other carrier nearly hit me with a Shrike missile, and an F-4 from the other carrier came within a nano-second of firing a *Sidewinder* at me.

I can forgive the A-6 crew for the *Shrike* near miss (less than 100 feet). They obviously never even saw me. But, I cannot forgive the F-4 crew, because they aimed the missile at me, and it would certainly have gotten me. Their error was lousy target recognition. If it hadn't been for my sharp eyed wingman, George Hise, the *Sidewinder* would have taken me out. If I was lucky I would probably have spent some time in the Hanoi Hilton. As it turned out, George saw the F-4 approaching firing range, called it out to me, and told me to break right. I executed the hardest high g barrel roll I have ever done. The maneuver was calculated to place me behind my attacker...which it did, perfectly. I recall being in a cold fury as I sat behind the F-4, which was now in a full afterburner climb. My *Sidewinder* tone sounded in my headphones, telling me it was seeing the airplane's tailpipe. My finger curled around the trigger, and I almost squeezed it. Thank God I did not!

The last friendly fire incident occurred 13 years later when I was well into my tour of duty as the fighter wing commander at Miramar. I had been put in charge of a classified program which involved exposing operational tactical air crews from both the Air Force and the Navy to actual enemy equipment that had been acquired by various means. When I briefed my boss, Vice Admiral "Dutch" Schoultz, about the program, he expressed an interest in seeing it in operation...first hand.

It took a few weeks to set it all up, and on the appointed day I flew a Topgun F-5F to NAS North Island to pick him up. His aide and I went through the business of strapping him into the rear seat and showing him how all of the switches worked. Then I climbed in the front seat and lit the engine off. I could see Dutch's aide saying a silent prayer for our safety. I do not believe the aide had as much faith in my aeronautical ability as his boss apparently did. In saying goodbye, the aide reminded me of a little known fact of which I was unaware. "You know, of course, admiral," he said confidentially, "an F-5 has never flown before with five stars in it!

We took off and went to the prearranged rendezvous, and I showed Dutch how his tactical aircrews were getting this most important training. From what he said to me over the intercom, I concluded that up to this point he was most impressed. The scenario involved our observing a U.S. Marine Corps F-4 engage the project vehicle in a one-versus-one engagement from a position of advantage. The vehicle was cruising straight and level at an altitude of 15,000 feet, and the F-4 attacked it from a right "perch" one mile abeam and 5,000 feet above. I should point out that, by sheer coincidence, both the project vehicle and our airplane were small and colored silver. We were on the opposite side in a left perch about 1.5 miles abeam and 5,000 feet above...watching! I explained all of this to Dutch over the intercom, and we watched with great interest as the *Phantom* called "rolling in."

The scenario also included the project vehicle holding his course and speed until the attacking *Phantom* reached *Sidewinder* firing range, at which point the F-4 aircrew would call Fox Two. Then, and only then, was the project vehicle allowed to maneuver as necessary to shoot down his attacker if he could. Standard air combat maneuvering rules applied from then as to minimum altitudes, minimum distance between the two dog fighters, and other considerations. I recall having a funny feeling, as the *Phantom* rolled into the attack, that all was not going to go well for us. But it was a passing feeling which I ignored.

As the *Phantom* descended toward the small silver colored airplane, it accelerated in full afterburner to 600 knots, and I found myself anticipating what the project vehicle's counter move would shortly be. Then, I noticed something odd. The *Phantom* had bottomed out of his descending run and was now crossing behind the project vehicle and toward us. He passed well into the *Sidewinder* firing envelope, but did not call "Fox Two." I thought that was curious. Then it dawned on me what was unfolding before our eyes.

The *Phantom* aircrew had lost sight of the project vehicle, and had spotted us instead. We were a small, silver-colored airplane! Incredibly, the Marine fighter was arcing up towards us, still in full afterburner and 600 knots. What I did next was pure instinct. I called out to Dutch over the intercom, "Oh s—t, those idiots are making a run on us. Then I slammed both throttles all the way to full afterburner, booted right rudder, and started a defensive break turn into them. In retrospect, it was a silly thing to do. We were slow and never would be able to counter a *Sidewinder* shot from where we were. But I did it anyway, just as we heard the radio transmission I was dreading.

"Simulate Fox Two," the voice said in a triumphant tone. I decided it would be pointless to continue this into a dog fight and called the attacked on the radio, putting as much acid into my voice as I could.

"Root Canal Four Four (not his real call sign, which I cannot remember), this is Topgun One. You are making a run on the wrong airplane!" There was a long, three or four second silence, during which the *Phantom's* afterburners winked out and the airplane broke off the run. Then came the only thing which seemed appropriate.

"Oops!"

After all, the intrepid Marine aircrew had just accidentally shot down (simulated) Commander, Naval Forces, U.S. Pacific Fleet and Commander, Fighter Airborne Early Warning Wings, Pacific, all with a single *Sidewinder*!

As briefed, we landed at the local air facility, but the offending Marine aircraft did not. They suddenly developed an unexplained "aircraft malfunction" which dictated their bingoing to their base at MCAS El Toro. I understood their need to make themselves scarce. During the debriefing, the air was tense and seemed to crackle with static electricity until Dutch defused the situation with one of his famous one-liners, after which we all broke up in uncontrolled laughter. "Well," he exclaimed with a wry smile, "for the first time I appreciate the full meaning of the expression 'the fog of war.'"

Of course, news of the giant f*aux pas* ran through the fleet like wildfire, and the errant Marine aircrew were treated like pariah for having brought great discredit upon the Marine Corps. Thereafter, there was a tendency for Miramar aircrews to refer to MCAS El Toro as "Mudville." It seemed like a perfect excerpt from that classic poem, "Casey At The Bat":

"There will be no joy in Mudville,
Mighty Casey has struck out!"

Gillcrist and Schoultz in a Topgun F-5F over San Diego, May 1980. (Paul Gillcrist Collection)

PART IV:
Women in Naval Aviation

"Life is either daring adventure or it is nothing."

- Helen Keller

I spoke to the graduating class of the U.S. Air Force command and staff college during the 1997 "Gathering of Eagles" celebration at Maxwell Air Force Base. During the question and answer phase someone asked, "When will the Tailhook scandal end for the Navy?"

My answer was, "Perhaps, never." By way of explanation I asked them, "Is the Watergate scandal over?" I even suggested that the word tailhook might appear in a revised edition of the Webster Dictionary as a new word in our lexicon signifying something pejorative, such as an abandonment of the concepts of "special trust and confidence"…words which appear in all of our officer commissions. A small group of Naval officers violated the special trust and confidence invested in them by the American people. The U.S. Navy may never be the same.

But, I warned the gathering that the Navy was not the only military service in the spotlight. Witness the feeding frenzy in the Army over the Aberdeen scandal and the Air Force General whose name had been proposed as the next Chairman of the Joint Chiefs of Staff. We are approaching the next millenium. Over 52 percent of the voters in this country are women. The pool from which the armed forces draw their human resources is becoming increasingly populated with qualified women.

Women in this country think they should have a legitimate shot at anything. Who are we to say they should not? This is a new world, I warned the 600 members of the graduating class…*GET WITH IT!*

Chapter 50:
The Human Blowtorch

"Fire has become the decisive argument."

- Ferdinand Foch: "Principles of War" 1920

We sat there ogling her (and not very subtly), as soon as she entered the room. She was really something to look at…a pert, petite brunette with a face like the map of Ireland and large, quizzical brown eyes. But she walked with authority, spoke with authority, and ignored the lecherous expressions on the faces in her audience. She was clearly in charge and, just as clearly, didn't seem to care what we thought.

We were a class of about thirty young fleet pilots from various naval air stations up and down the west coast, and we were gathered for our initial fleet annual aviation physiology training at Naval Air Station, Alameda, just outside of Oakland, California.

The year was 1954, and naval aviation was in the process of transitioning from propeller driven carrier airplanes to jet-propelled machines. One of the natural offshoots of such a dramatic change was the venue in which carrier pilots were soon to find themselves…high altitude and high speed flight. These two new aspects of carrier aviation introduced us to two new pieces of equipment…each a matter of life and death. They were oxygen masks and ejection seats.

Lieutenant Nancy Murtagh's job was to see to it that we survived the transition. Her responsibilities were truly impressive. The aviation physiology department at Alameda was an enormous assortment of facilities. Her ejection seat training program included a tall structure, like a railing sticking almost straight up into the air four or five stories. At the bottom of the rail was an ejection seat. After several hours of escape system lectures she would strap each of us into the seat and have us reach up and yank down hard on the face curtain firing mechanism. A reduced explosive charge would go off with a loud bang, and the seat (with pilots attached) would roar up the rail to simulate a real firing. Then the seat would be gently ratcheted down by safety personnel, and we would climb out…better prepared for an ejection than we had been a few minutes earlier. Upon completion of the course of instruction each of us would be given a wallet-sized card certifying that we had indeed completed ejection seat training...signed by Lt. N.M. Murtagh. Across the top of the card was printed in bold letters the acronym: O.M.I.A.S.S. It stood for some contrived name which I have long since forgotten. But, every Pacific Fleet carrier pilot carried in his wallet a signed Oh My Ass card...and never forgot the winsome young lady who gave it to him.

Ejection seat and low pressure training were the principle thrusts of the aviation physiology training program at Alameda. But they also taught water survival, Dilbert Dunker ditching, helicopter rescue, life raft procedures, night vision, and a host of other, related training. It was a large responsibility for a Lieutenant. But, Lieutenant Murtagh was more than just an aviation physiologist. She was the first woman aviation physiologist in the Navy. A engineering graduate from the University of California, she went through a rigorous training regimen at Pensacola, FL, and was ordered directly to Alameda, which possessed one of the largest and newest set of facilities in the Navy. It was a feather in her cap to be assigned to Alameda.

The most complicated set of training equipment at her facility was the low pressure chamber. Housed in a separate building filled with pumps, generators, gaseous oxygen storage tanks, and other heavy equipment was the "chamber," a large steel tank with windows, a hatch, and a control station. A dozen students could be put in the chamber at individual seats. The air would be pumped out slowly to simulate the effects to which Navy carrier pilots would be subjected on a flight to 45,000 feet. On the way to altitude, the chamber would be stopped at 30,000 feet long enough for a few volunteers to take off their oxygen masks and to demonstrate the effects of hypoxia (insufficient oxygen) and anoxia (lack of oxygen). The volunteers would be asked to do relatively simple assignments like taking a deck of cards and dropping them individually through four slots by suit. After eight or ten cards the average volunteer would start making mistakes. He would mix up the suits, then he would giggle and start laughing. Usually, the instructor inside the chamber would stop the demonstration by then. Occasionally, however, it would get too far, and the volunteer would pass out or go into convulsions. The instructor would slap on the oxygen mask, and the stricken volunteer would wake up with a start and a sheepish grin.

A rubber surgical glove would be suspended from the top of the chamber, its top tied off securely. As the pressure in the chamber dropped during the climb, the glove would begin to expand. The idea was to give a graphic example of what would happen to captured gas in the intestines. It was very graphic! By the time the chamber reached 45,000 feet the surgical glove had ballooned to the size of a basketball. Jet pilot training taught that the gas must be relieved to prevent painful intestinal distention. The obvious solution, our petite instructor explained, was flatus. We all thought that was hilarious, until some of us began to feel a little discomfort. Then we saw some of us leaning over to one side to ease out a little gas (unobtrusively). Of course, the oxygen system was called "diluter demand," and mixed oxygen with ambient air. The ambient air became pretty fetid inside the chamber, especially if many of the students had been to the Mexican Village the previous evening for dinner. In all, the chamber run took a few hours and was the *piece de resistance* of the three day training session. By the end of the three days we all had a very thorough idea of the hazards of carrier aviation, and especially high altitude flight.

But, the high point of the three day training session occurred in the first five minutes of the first lecture on the first day. Lieutenant Murtagh strode in purposefully and asked for a show of hands by anybody who smoked. Nearly all of us raised our hands. Then she asked for another show of hands for anyone who smoked in the cockpit. There were a few hands…but not many. We all suspected there was a "hook" in the question…and many of the older members of our group had been brought up in propeller-driven fighters.

Well, she explained, with the coming of jet aviation, airplanes were going to altitudes where oxygen masks would have to be worn from take-off to landing. Oxygen and smoking constituted a serious hazard. Therefore, smoking in the cockpit of a modern jet fighter was absolutely forbidden. I'm sure she saw the glimmer of disbelief in the expressions on many of our faces. As she made the last statement, she turned on her heel and walked over to a bank of oxygen bottles on the opposite side of the room. Her back was turned to us, and we couldn't see precisely what she was doing.

What she was really doing was taking in a huge lung full of pure oxygen from a tube attached to one of the bottles…but we didn't know that! She closed the valve and, turning, crossed the room in a few strides, holding the lung full of air as she fished in her pocket for a cigarette lighter. Then she stopped a few feet from the front row, lit the lighter, and held it about a foot in front of her mouth. We watched this with detached curiosity.

Then she exhausted all of her oxygen-laden breath in a gush into the cigarette lighter flame. The was a loud WHOOSHING sound, and a sheet of flame six feet long streaked from the lighter towards the students, passing over the heads of the first two rows of us (I was in the third row). All of us instinctively lurched backwards, causing the folding chairs to topple like a row of dominoes. For a few minutes there was chaos in the room as we all scrambled back to our feet and back into our seats. Lieutenant Murtagh flicked off the lighter, put it back into her pocket, and waited a pregnant ten seconds for all of us to quiet down. Then she said, calmly and quietly, the most important eight words in aviation physiology that I have ever heard: "THAT'S WHY YOU DON'T SMOKE IN THE COCKPIT!" What a presentation!

Author's Note: Two years later I married Lieutenant Murtagh. The Navy's loss was my gain…BIG TIME…BOTH WAYS!

Chapter 51:
"Juice"

*"Madam, there is nothing so dreadful as a great victory—
excepting a great defeat.*

- Duke of Wellington

Lucy Young is one of the most talented pilots I have ever known. Presently a captain in the Naval Reserves, Lucy (call sign "Juice") is a fully rated airline captain, but because of seniority is flying as a First Officer of a Boeing 767 for USAir. I first met her when, as Commander, Fighter Airborne Early Warning Wings, Pacific, I visited her parent squadron, Fleet Composite Squadron ONE at NAS Barber's Point, Hawaii. That was 1979, and she was a starry-eyed young Naval Aviator, eager to prove her mettle against the strong current of male sentiment opposing women in Naval Aviation. Lucy was one of three female aviators in the wing.

Lucy was born 9 September 1954 and raised in Roxbury, CT. She attended high school in Washington, CT, and won an ROTC scholarship to Purdue University, where she graduated in 1976 with a biology degree. In October she went to Pensacola to begin Naval Aviation flight training.

As did most of her female peers acquired by the Navy in those years, she came with spectacular credentials. She was a top-notch student in high school and college, an exceptional athlete, and a student-body leader who achieved incredibly high scores in the battery of aptitude tests the Navy asked her to take. After receiving her commission she was assigned, for a short period, to VA-42 at NAS Oceana, VA. Then she was ordered to the Training Command, and proceeded to set records for performance wherever she went. Her high scores in basic training won her a selection to jet transition in the TA-4 Skyhawk at Kingsville, TX, where she checked out in the TA-4 jet trainer. She proceeded to excel in the TA-4 until the point where male students began what is called Air Combat Maneuvering (ACM). Since females were not permitted at that time to be assigned to combat units, her training regimen bypassed ACM and carrier qualifications, and she proceeded to low-level and tactical formation training in the TA-4.

As usual, she excelled, and was subsequently considered ready for assignment to a fleet support squadron. Her orders were cut, assigning her to Fleet Composite Squadron One (VC-1), permanently located at NAS, Barber's Point, Hawaii, on the island of Oahu, not far from Pearl Harbor. VC-1 was known as the "Blue Alii" (a Hawaiian expression for chief). It was the main fleet support squadron for the 3rd *Fleet*, which was located at Pearl Harbor. VC-1 operated a mix of airplanes ranging in variety from a dozen TA-4s to six helicopters, to a single C-118 (four-engine reciprocating transport airplane), considered the personal transportation for the Commander-in-Chief, U.S. Pacific Fleet.

Lieutenant (junior grade) Lucy Young had been sent to VC-1 to fly the A-4 in support of fleet operations. Her airplane was used to simulate high-performance enemy airplanes, air-to-surface missiles, and surface-to-surface missiles, as well as to act as radar targets for the fleet's guided missile ships. For reasons which she never explained to me she acquired the call sign, "Juice."

As did most of the women in Naval Aviation in that period, Juice aspired to be the first woman to do something out of the ordinary, something unusual, something spectacular. The first opportunity came during a major Air Force exercise that occurred in the Hawaiian Islands in 1980. This story did not come from my initial interviews with Juice. Rather, it came from Commander, 3rd *Fleet*, Vice Admiral Kinnaird McKee, during a courtesy call I made with him at his headquarters on Oahu. He had been briefed on the incident by one of his staff officers. Even as a submariner, he could clearly see the irony of one of his youngest aviators, a female, flying a TA-4 *Skyhawk*, kicking the ass of a seasoned Air National Guard combat veteran flying a frontline F-4 *Phantom* II.

Lieutenant (jg) "Juice" Young, VC-1 NAS Barbers Point, Hawaii, May 1980. (Lucy Young Collection)

It seems that Juice was assigned to participate in the exercise to serve as an "enemy aircraft" intruding into the air space over the target area near the island of Kahoolawe. In accordance with the restrictions placed upon her by the fact that she had never received "air combat maneuvering" training, she was restricted from dog fighting with any of the other participants in the exercise. Her mission was to fly over the target area and simulate an attack on any of the "Blue" (friendly) ground units she saw in the area.

Juice was well aware of the deathless aerial combat maxim, "Speed is life!" Accordingly, she appeared over the target area in her little *Skyhawk* at about 5,000 feet above the terrain and clicking off better than 450 knots...about as fast as anyone could get the machine to go at that altitude. A few miles west of the target, she spotted a Blue target combat air patrol "maintaining air superiority" over the combat zone. The rules of engagement governing the exercise did not permit Juice from doing anything more in air combat maneuvering than a defensive turn against any attacking airplane...such as one of the F4C *Phantom* IIs she had just spotted. It was clear to Juice that the enemy had not yet spotted her. Her eyesight was legendary in VC-1. She usually acquired visual contact with opponents well before they ever saw her. Naturally, Juice attacked!

Converting some of her kinetic energy, she climbed toward a position behind the section of *Phantoms* from which she could execute a successful guns attack. Neither of the Hawaii Air National Guard aircrews saw her until it was too late. By this time, she was six o'clock high and about a mile behind the *Phantoms* in a gentle descent with her throttle "firewalled."

The wingman spotted the attacker and called frantically to his section leader that they had a bogey at six o'clock high. He then directed the section leader to break left, hard. Only then did our combat-hardened fighter pilot spot the tiny A-4 behind him. He did the right thing. He slammed both throttles into full afterburner and yanked the *Phantom* into a shuddering seven g left turn. Anticipating this move, Juice executed a perfect "high yo-yo" that placed her several thousand feet above the *Phantom* and again at six o'clock. The little Skyhawk topped out of the yo-yo maneuver with practically no airspeed and in an inverted attitude. Looking through the top of her canopy at the *Phantom* below her, Juice eased all of the back stick pressure, neutralized rudders and ailerons, and floated for a few seconds...long enough for her to see what the *Phantom* pilot was going to do. Then she tweaked the ailerons, eased slightly back on the stick, tapped just a touch of right rudder and started down for the kill. It was a perfectly executed yo-yo, and as she dropped like a stone, the Phantom dumped the nose of his airplane over and tried to "bug out." But, it was too late for that.

Juice had too much of an overtake speed advantage, and slid in about 300 feet behind the *Phantom*, adjusting the controls to hold her gunsight pipper on the *Phantom*'s cockpit for the requisite three seconds. Then she did the thing that was to make her famous forever. Juice keyed the radio microphone button on her throttle and called, "This is Atlas 41, guns, guns, guns."

Had the "rules of engagement," as specified in the exercise operations order, been strictly adhered to, the following would have happened: the *Phantom* aircrew should have looked behind them and acknowledged that they had indeed been "killed." They then should have taken themselves out of the exercise by exiting the area using the speed, altitude, and route specified in the exercise's "kill removal" procedure.

Juice should have continued her mission, looking for other targets. The exercise judges would have awarded Juice a bone fide kill.

But this is not what happened. When the *Phantom* pilot heard the "guns, guns, guns" call, he did several things almost simultaneously. He shouted an obscenity to his RIO, slammed both throttles into full afterburner, kicked full left rudder as hard as he could, and hauled back on the stick in a eight g break maneuver. The combination of left yaw caused by the rudder application, low speed, and the high angle of attack induced by eight gs caused a compressor stall in the left engine. Since both the pilot and RIO were straining their neck muscles to look behind them, neither noticed the left engine fire warning light come on and the exhaust gas temperature gauge needle begin its inexorable climb to (and past) the red line. A combustion turbine blade failed under the combination of tensile and thermal stress, and the engine literally exploded.

The pilot of the stricken *Phantom* declared an emergency, set up a precautionary approach to the nearest runway at Hickam Air Force Base, and, trailing black smoke from his left tailpipe, shut down the other engine on the duty runway after rolling to an ignominious stop. There, surrounded by crash and rescue with their rotating beacons winking, the aircrew abandoned their airplane.

The pilot, in his official statement (written immediately after evacuating the airplane), stated that, "Everything was fine until I heard the female voice calling, 'guns, guns, guns.' After that I don't know what came over me." It was vintage Lucy Young!

Juice's second opportunity for fame came not long after this incident when a message came through VC-1's maintenance control office, directing the squadron to deliver one of their TA-4J airplanes to the overhaul and repair facility at NAS Pensacola for rework. For most squadrons such a message would be treated as routine, and a pilot would be directed to fly the airplane to Pensacola. But for VC-1, stationed in Hawaii, it was a little more complicated. The distance from NAS Barber's Point to NAS Alameda (the nearest naval air station in the continental United States) was over 2,500 nautical miles...over twice the normal ferry range for a TA-4J. The squadron immediately checked the TransPac schedule for the next eastbound U.S. Marine Corps flight traveling from Iwakuni, Japan, to the United States and requested a "slot" from the Marines. Two days later a message came back offering a slot in an eastbound TransPac flight which was scheduled to come by in three weeks. Juice heard about this opportunity and went immediately to the skipper, Commander Robert "Bull" Curtis, to plead with him to fly the mission. He turned down her request because the squadron had a standing policy of assigning such TransPac missions to "second tour" (more senior and more experienced) aviators. After all, he reasoned, the mission required flying the 2,500-mile leg over water with at least two inflight refuelings from a Marine Corps KC-130 aerial tanker. Then, after landing at NAS Miramar, the pilot would have to fly to Pensacola, FL, requiring at least one fuel stop en route. No, it was not a routine mission by any stretch of the imagination. Could Juice accomplish the mission safely? Of course she could. The real question was whether he should assign the mission to her or to a more experienced pilot...given the many hazards inherent in the mission.

Undaunted, Juice persisted until Bull Curtis finally caved in and agreed to her flying the mission, but only with the stipulation that he fly in the rear seat. Bull Curtis' solution falls into the category of King Solomon's choice. No pilot likes to fly in the back seat of anything. This guy was a real leader!

The Marines arrived, inbound from Iwakuni, and landed with a great deal of fanfare to stay overnight for a well-deserved crew rest. On the following day, all participants gathered in a large conference room to brief for the final leg of the TransPac. There were several aircrews, including four *Phantom* crews, two USMC A-4M pilots, and, of course, crew members from the Marine aerial refueling squadron. There were a total of 12 airplanes involved in the complex evolution. Safety was paramount!

The aircrew of the sole Navy airplane were there too...and the presence of a comely young female pilot did not go unnoticed by the exuberant young Marine aviators gathered in the conference room. It also became apparent that the senior pilot of the entire flight of receiving airplanes was Bull Curtis. Therefore, it was determined that the TA-4J would be the first airplane to receive fuel at the three pre-determined refueling points. These three points were laid out on a chart showing the vast expanse of the Pacific Ocean lying between Hawaii and Southern California. The first refueling point was called the "point of no return." This was a point about 250 miles east of Oahu, beyond which the airplanes in the flight with the shortest range could not return to Hawaii unaccompanied. This, of course, was determined by the four *Phantoms* in the flight. It was important to test the ability of the *Phantoms* to accept fuel from one of the tankers. If any airplane in the flight could not do so, for any reason, it would be ordered to detach and return to Kaneohe or Barbers Point. The second refueling point was about half way between Oahu and Miramar. This point was determined by the ability of the A-4s to complete the flight without further refueling. The third refueling point was approximately 500 miles west of Miramar. This final point was determined by the ability of the *Phantoms* to complete the flight without further tanking assistance.

Tanking procedures were briefed *ad nauseum*, including safety procedures, as well as emergency procedures. Finally, an aircrewman from one of the C-130 "Duckbutt" radar monitor planes briefed how he was going to give radar coverage and vectoring to the flight leader, who happened to be the colonel leading the flight of four KC-130 tankers. It was a long and tedious briefing. When it was over, the participants streamed out of the room and headed for their airplanes...happy to be out of the briefing stage and into the actual flight.

Bull Curtis and Juice Young headed for their sedan that would take them to their airplane. A launch coordinating officer would ensure that all of the participant airplanes in the flight were launched on schedule...first the Duckbutt airplane two hours early, then the tankers, 30 minutes early, then, finally, all of the recipient airplanes at zero hour, in one large, seven plane formation.

On 16 November 1980 the airplanes made a running rendezvous and headed out on course. At a point about 230 miles east of Oahu, while cruisng at an altitude of 30,000 feet, one of the *Phantoms* called out a large radar contact thirty miles ahead. It was the tanker group, and they were right on schedule. The flight leader throttled back a little and commenced a gradual descent to 25,000 feet, 5,000 feet above the tanker's altitude. He then called the tanker leader and told him he had them in visual contact, was rendezvousing with him, and asked him to head out on course. The tanker leader put his four tankers into a right hand echelon and ordered them to stream their tanker stores. It was a beautiful sight. Each of the huge *Hercules* HC-130 airplanes had a single refueling basket streaming from each wing. Bull Curtis' airplane was assigned the left wing store on the lead tanker in the formation...the first airplane to tank.

The radio traffic up to this point had been crisp, professional, and brief. This was the way it should be. Juice detached from her position in the formation and maneuvered her *Skyhawk* into the start position 20 feet aft of the aerial refueling basket. She was doing the last-minute things one does prior to tanking...she flipped the helmet visor down, trimmed out the slip stream effects from the tanker's left wing, adjusted her seat upward an inch or so to a comfortable position for tanking, and turned off some of her electronic equipment as a fire hazard reduction measure. Just as she was settling into a comfortable position, she had the random thought about the beauty of the moment. There was a clear blue sky. The vast Pacific Ocean stretched beneath them was a gorgeous azure blue. A sense of adventure was shared by all of the aircrews as they started into this incredibly complicated evolution. Each of the aircrewmen knew the next few minutes had to reflect their very best flying...their lives literally depended upon it!

Juice was about to add throttle to advance the 10 feet or so that separated her airplane from the basket floating deceptively in front of her. Her in-flight refueling probe, which extended out from a point on the right of the fuselage nose, was poised much as a knight's lance prior to the first joust. Then her reverie was interrupted by an unidentified voice which boomed out of nowhere into her headphones.

"Now, young lady," the voice began in a voice like a chaplain's in the confessional. "The name of the game is to poke that long pointy thing in front of you into that little hole in the basket...just in case you didn't know!"

Bull Curtis was horrified upon hearing this gesture at suggestive humor from one of the Marines in the formation. It was certainly not the kind of thing which would be expected to increase Juice's confidence prior to a delicate flying operation. After all, he opined, they were 250 miles east of Oahu, and if this snide double *entendre* flustered Juice enough to cause her to be unable to engage the basket with her probe, they would have to turn back to Barber's Point. To his utter astonishment he felt the power come on, and the little *Skyhawk* jumped forward, the tip of the in-flight refueling probe knifing directly into the center of the basket with a solid "chunk," which could be felt in the airplane's airframe. Simultaneously, he heard Juice's voice coming back in a sharp rejoinder.

"No sweat! I always wondered why you guys seem to have so much trouble with it!"

Obviously everyone in the formation had been watching their every move, especially the owner of the anonymous voice. Now he was quiet...thoroughly chastised by a very confident young woman. Now they were all quiet. Bull Curtis recalled to me that voice communications throughout the rest of the tanking evolutions were exceptionally subdued.

Juice became legendary during the remainder of her stay in Hawaii. She went from there to her next tour of duty at Kingsville, TX, where she became the first female instructor to "carrier qualify" in the *Skyhawk*. Although her squadron and wing commander graded her in the top of their large group of youngster instructors, Lucy was doomed by the system. The Navy was still not assigning women to command of fleet (combat) squadrons. The very best she could hope for would be command of a fleet support ("special mission") squadron.

It was simply not enough! She made the hard decision to leave the Navy to accept an attractive offer to fly for the Federal Aviation Administration, and later, the airlines. She transferred to the Naval Reserves and, typically, continued to advance. She is now a captain in the reserves, and the first woman to serve on the board of directors of the Tailhook Association. Each time I meet her at a convention I feel the same sense of regret.

Juice was one of the best!

Author's Note: It somehow seems improper to write a story about Juice without mentioning her running mate and cohort, "Rookie." An equally talented Naval Officer and aviatrix, Rookie specifically asked me not to write about her...so I will not mention her name. But she arrived at VC-1 at the same time Juice came, and the two went through flight training together. They were an unforgettable pair of female pilots, who both hit the glass ceiling at the same time and left the Navy for careers in the airline business. As a passenger, I would feel comforted to find that either of them were piloting the airplane I was riding in!

Lieutenant (jg) "Juice" Young in T-A4F over the Big Island, Hawaii, May 1980. (Lucy Young Collection)

Chapter 52:
"Jugs"

"It ain't over 'til it's over!"

- Yogi Berra

I hesitated to use this title at first because of its obvious sexual overtone, but decided at last to press on because it aptly reflected the state of the United States Navy regarding women in aviation, for better or worse. There were three women pilots in the Fighter Airborne Early Warning Wing when I arrived…"Juice," "Rookie," and "Jugs." They were all unforgettable…but for different reasons. Juice agreed to let me write about her with the stipulation that I first show the piece to her. Rookie declined my request, so I have honored our agreement. I never found Jugs, and so have omitted her last name…but I believe she deserves mention. By the way, the year was 1979, and all three pilots did extremely well.

I first heard the call sign Jugs when I was flying an F-14 in the off-shore operating area. I didn't give the name a second thought, primarily because I never heard her respond; and therefore, didn't know Jugs was a woman.

Call signs can sometimes be bestowed by one's peers and somehow stick…despite all efforts to obliterate, ignore, or even resort to fisticuffs to prevent their further use. I think Jugs' call sign was bestowed despite her objections. At the time I didn't see any harm in it. When I was a youngster in my first squadron, one of my peers developed the call sign "Wedge." Despite all of his efforts to the contrary, the name kept appearing on the squadron flight schedule until he finally gave up trying to get the schedules officer to stop printing it (Wedge, it was often explained by his peers, was "the simplest tool known to man"). We all resorted to calling him Wedge…so Wedge he was until he left the squadron. The same went for Jugs I suspect.

She was a tall, handsome blonde with a slightly prominent nose and, as the reader might suspect, she was well-endowed in the upper torso. She was also bright, outgoing, and aggressive. She flew the A-4 *Skyhawk*…and flew it well.

She entertained thoughts of moving upward in tactical aviation by hook or by crook, and even button-holed me at a cocktail party with a request to fly the F-8 *Crusader*, which happened to be the airplane assigned to the photo reconnaissance fleet replacement squadron at Miramar. Had I agreed, she would have been the first woman to fly the airplane. I didn't have to approve or disapprove because the request never came to me in writing. To this day I am not sure whether I would have approved. As were most of her female peers, Jugs was interested in becoming the first woman to do something unusual in Naval Aviation. As it turned out, she got her wish…although it wasn't exactly what she had in mind.

The event of note occurred one evening when I had been in the job about three months. Just as I was about to leave the office, the telephone rang to inform me that there had been a rather serious taxi accident at the fuel pits between an A-4 *Skyhawk* and an F-14 *Tomcat*. I jumped into my sedan and drove to the fuel pits to see for myself. En route, I recall being irritated because taxi accidents are usually the result of personnel error. Since pilot error accidents usually reflect poor supervision, I felt that this accident could reflect badly on the command.

When I reached the fuel pits, the crash and rescue crew had already separated the two airplanes, since both airplanes' engines had been running at the time of impact. The danger of fire justified getting the two aircraft away from one another on the taxiway. The F-14 aircrew had already left the scene, but the A-4 pilot was still there being attended to by medical personnel in an ambulance. I got out of my sedan and walked over to the back of the ambulance, genuinely concerned for the welfare of the pilot. She was standing there with the assistance of a hospital corpsman, holding an ice pack to her face.

It was dark, but I was nonetheless able to recognize the pilot. It was Jugs, and she was a sight to behold. Her eyes were red from weeping, and blood had been streaming down her face and all over the front of her flight suit from a bloody nose. For the moment I decided to leave her to the corpsman and went over to survey the damage. What I saw shocked me. The back end of the F-14 looked like it had been hit from behind by a freight train. I instantly knew that the damage to the F-14 alone would be enough to constitute a "major aircraft accident." The sight of the mangled fighter made me sick. Next, I examined the A-4. It looked as though it had flown into the side of a concrete abutment. The first six feet of the nose section was crushed like an accordion.

I turned to the crash crew for an eyewitness account. Most landings at Miramar are made on Runway 24 Right…the long one. There is a high-speed taxiway parallel to the runway that landing airplanes use after turning off the duty runway. At the point where the high speed taxiway intersects the beginning of the aircraft parking mat, there is a circular fuel pit where airplanes can refuel with their engines running. It is a way of simplifying the turn-around of airplanes. The F-14 was sitting in this fuel pit, refueling with one of its engines running, when it was struck from behind by Jugs' airplane. It seems that a crash truck happened to be following Jugs as she taxied back toward her hangar after landing. They had seen the whole thing.

"How fast was she taxiing?" I asked them. They looked a little sheepish and told me that it wasn't very fast.

"God damn it. How fast?" I persisted.

"Oh, not more than 30 miles an hour, I'd say," the driver said. I instinctively knew that he was fibbing a little to keep the pilot out of too much trouble.

It is worth explaining to the reader that for most tactical airplanes as much as 40 percent of their weight on takeoff is fuel. The residual thrust of their engines at idle power is usually enough to permit slow taxiing. However, after landing, when they are several tons lighter (fuel used up), the airplane will accelerate at idle power. Since it is bad procedure to ride the brakes of an airplane, especially after a landing, most pilots allow a taxiing airplane to accelerate to a good speed on a long straight taxiway, then slow it down with a few strong brake applications before allowing the speed to build up again. The process is repeated as necessary until they reach their ramp area and are parked. The question of speed was only part of the problem, as I saw it. One of the corpsmen from the ambulance came over to where we were talking. I turned and asked him, "How did she get hurt?"

"Her face struck the instrument panel when she hit the F-14," he answered.

"Didn't her oxygen mask protect her face?" I pursued. He had an odd expression on his face.

"No, Sir," he responded, looking as though he were walking on egg shells.

"How come?" I asked, beginning to fear what I knew what his answer was going to be. "Wasn't her shoulder harness locked?"

"Well, sir," the man answered sheepishly. "She was already unstrapped and had unhooked the mask!"

I nearly exploded. "What?"

"She told me she had unstrapped and was already shutting various systems down in the cockpit, when she looked up and saw the F-14 right in front of her," the young man said almost apologetically. All I could do was shake my head and walk away.

There is an old maxim in aviation: "The flight isn't over until you are chocked and shut the engine down." How true! Complacency had set in, and Jugs was so sure of herself that she thought she could speed up the remainder of the mission by starting the shut down process while she was still taxiing (probably too fast) at night on a busy airfield. Now I was really ticked off!

I walked back over to Jugs. The flow of blood from her battered nose seemed to have been stanched. I knew it would be hurtful to jump all over her at this moment...but I was really angry.

"Well, Lieutenant, you wanted to be the first woman pilot to do something spectacular, and you have. You are the first female Navy pilot to cause a major aircraft accident. Congratulations!"

I turned and walked away fuming. She burst into tears!

Chapter 53:
The Magic Button

"When you get to a man in the case,
They're like as a row of pins.
For the Colonel's Lady and Judy O'Grady,
Are sisters under the skin."

- Rudyard Kipling: "The Ladies"

I knew the moment she stepped out of the hangar door and started toward me that she was a female. It was the gait! Every other observable aspect of her appearance masked her gender. From the cloth helmet with goggles, her blue denim work shirt and trousers, down to the rough flight line work boots, she was dressed like any other sailor in Fighter Squadron 124. But she walked like a female of the species. She did not undulate, however. Her stride was purposeful and businesslike, and it told me one more very important thing—she knew what she was about!

I was furious! Having been sitting in that cockpit of the F-14 with the engines running for a full 15 minutes and still unable to taxi out for takeoff, I was angry and frustrated at such a system that could confound a reasonably intelligent adult...like me! After several weeks of study and ground school, I was about to go out on my first F-14 flight, and the Goddamn wing-sweep system was acting up...or was it me?

One of the things all Navy pilots must do before taxiing out to take off is to assure themselves as well as the ground personnel that the aircraft was ready for safe flight. This meant that after starting engines, I was required to check out all systems. It was done in a standard sequence with the airplane captain by a series of hand signals, directing the pilot to do certain things with the cockpit controls. The proper range and movement of all flight controls was one of those things. Finally, we got to the most complicated of all the airplane's systems, the wing sweep.

Just before engine shut down on the previous flight, the pilot disconnected the wing sweep system, went into the mechanical mode, and put the wings into what is called "oversweep," which enables the parking of the airplane in a smaller space. It sweeps the wing tips all the way back to 68 degrees and puts the wing tips over the horizontal stabilators. So, the first thing the pilot has to do after starting engines is reset the wing sweep system by re-engaging (stowing) the mechanical wing sweep lever. This, of course, is done after determining that there is adequate hydraulic pressure on the system. The next step is to see if the wing sweep system worked in the manual hydro-mechanical mode. Once this is determined, the wing sweep system is checked out in the automatic mode, the one in which most of the flight will be made. When the automatic mode is selected, all of the red and amber flight control system lights turn green…meaning ready for flight.

That was my problem. I couldn't get the red and amber lights to turn green. The automatic system wouldn't engage. There was a strained conversation going on between me and the radar intercept officer (RIO) in the back seat. Neither of us could figure out what I was doing wrong. I even made a few obscene comments to myself in my own oxygen mask. "Friggin' electrons!" In desperation, the RIO must have made some hand signal to the plane captain standing to our left, who was still trying to give me hand signals. Somehow the word of my aeronautical incompetence must have been passed on to the people in the troubleshooter's office in the hangar (probably by one of their hand-held radios). That was when the young lady came out of the hangar and started towards us.

When she reached a position a few feet to the left of the airplane's nose she stopped, looked directly at me, and held up a radio plug-in cable in her hand. The RIO informed me she was going to go up into the nose wheel well and plug into the airplane's intercom system so she could talk to me. She was holding up the cable to get my confirmation that I understood. I grimly nodded my head, and she disappeared under the fuselage for a minute. The RIO reminded me to switch my radio control to Intercom so I could talk to her. She reappeared and looked directly at me. I could barely make out a pair of dark eyes through the tinted goggles. I thought I saw thinly disguised amusement…and it irritated me even more.

"Well, Admiral, what seems to be the trouble?" a very pleasant female voice asked.

"I can't get the Goddamned wing sweep to go into automatic" I rasped, my voice thick with anger. She then asked me several questions about what I had done and what I was seeing in the cockpit on the instrument panel and the port console. Her questions had the effect of further irritating me, and I knew why. Basically, I suspected that I must have done something wrong…and the thought embarrassed me. After all, I reminded myself; this little slip of a girl probably joined the Navy fresh out of high school, had been to basic, then advanced electronic technicians' school, and now, as a new Second Class Petty Officer, was about to show the admiral how ignorant he was about the F-14 flight control systems.

"Admiral," she said, as cool and calm as though she were talking to a child, "reach down with your left hand and find the circuit-breaker panel just outboard of your left knee." I did so and nodded. I felt it, but couldn't see it because my left leg obscured a view of it. "Now, count forward with your fingers to the fourth row of circuit breakers." I did so and nodded.

"Now, Admiral, count down with your fingers to the fifth circuit breaker from the top." I did so and nodded again. "Okay," she continued as though she were speaking to an infant, "Now, pull the circuit-breaker out, but keep your hand on it." I did so and nodded again, becoming angrier as each second ticked away. What the hell kind of nonsense is this, I asked myself?

"Now, Admiral, reach over with your right hand and push in on the Master Reset button on the instrument panel." I did and nodded. "Now, sir, holding the Master Reset button in, push the circuit-breaker back in." I did so, and it was as though she had waved a magic wand! All of the red and amber warning lights in the cockpit instantly turned a beautiful green. I was absolutely stunned!

This little slip of a girl had just made my day! Before I could stop myself, an oath escaped my lips. "Well, I'll be Goddamned!!" She smiled and said, "I'm going to disconnect now, Admiral. Have a nice flight." With that, she ducked out of sight into the nose wheel well and reappeared a moment later with her headset cable in her hand. She turned without another glance and walked back toward the hangar, leaving me in shocked admiration.

We gave the plane captain the signal to pull the chocks and taxied out for our flight. I don't recall ever seeing her again. All I could think of saying to the RIO as we taxied away from the VF-124 line was. "Damn. The Navy got its money's worth when we signed her up!"

Chapter 54:
The First Team

"There is nothing like a dame. Nothing in the world!"

- Rogers and Hammerstein: "South Pacific"

Lieutenant Commander Frank "Beak" Brown and I were flying an F-14 on a night air intercept training mission in the off-shore operating area west of San Diego. I don't remember any details of the mission, but the way it ended has stayed with me in startling clarity. As we had briefed, Frank called and checked out with our Navy radar controller before leaving the operating area. We were told to shift to a certain radio frequency and to call San Diego Approach Control, our air route traffic control center, for clearance to Miramar. The center cleared us to the initial approach fix for a radar-controlled approach to Miramar. The fix was located over the Laguna Mountains, about 20 miles east of the naval air station. When we arrived at the fix, we were cleared to shift to another radio frequency and check in with the radar approach control center for Miramar, where a Navy radar controller would take us from there. When we checked in, we were greeted by a very competent sounding female voice.

"Hoppy 465, you are cleared for a radar-controlled approach to Navy Miramar. Turn left to two six zero. Descend to four thousand feet. Call passing twelve." We acknowledged the instructions and called leaving Flight Level 200 for 4,000 feet. She rogered our transmission and was now officially in control of our destinies until we were turned over to the final controller. As we descended through 12,000 feet, Frank called and so informed her. She rogered our transmission and told us to shift to a new radio frequency and check in with our final controller. As Frank was dialing in the new frequency, I mentioned to him on the intercom that the woman sounded "pretty sharp" to me. He agreed…very young, but sharp.

"Miramar Approach, this is Hoppy 465, level 4,000, over," Frank transmitted. To my surprise, another female voice came up on the line…this one just as crisp and professional as the other.

"Roger, 465, this is your final controller. Do not respond to further transmissions…"
What followed was a series of directives from our final controller, telling us we were slightly
above glide slope or giving us minute course corrections to a heading other than the 240,
which was the runway heading in order to correct for winds. I followed the directions, even
though the weather was good enough for me to make out the runway lights in the distance.
The directions were unbelievably accurate, finite, anticipatory, and precise.

We touched down on centerline with a centered ball (optical landing system), and she
told us to shift to tower frequency on roll-out. Then, I did something I rarely ever do. I
complimented her.

"Approach from Hoppy 465, that was the finest GCA (ground controlled approach)
I've had in years. Thank you." Without waiting for a response, we shifted to tower frequency, because the end of the 12,000 foot runway was coming up fast. There wasn't time
for further niceties. Frank checked in on tower frequency.

"Miramar Tower, this is Hoppy 465. GCA roll-out, over." The end of the runway was
now only 2,000 feet ahead of us, and our speed was well under control. By now, I wasn't
surprised that the voice which came up on the radio was female.

"Roger, 465. Call ground control when clear of the runway. Out." As I turned off at the
end of the runway, Frank shifted radio frequencies and checked in with Miramar Ground
Control.

"Miramar Ground, Hoppy 465, clear of the active, over." Sure enough, a female voice
responded, and directed us to return to our line via the high-speed parallel taxiway. Frank's
voice came up on the intercom.

"Jesus, Gator, the whole Goddamn bunch is female."

After we filled out the yellow sheet at VF-124 maintenance control, Frank accompanied me to the parking lot, where we parted company, got into our separate cars, and headed
home. My house was on the base. His was about a 20-minute drive down the highway. It
was now past ten o'clock, and it had been a long day. I was tired and looking forward to a
nice sleep.

Pulling out of the parking lot, I began to reflect on the events of the last 30 minutes and,
on a whim, turned my car toward the tower building. I parked in front in the space reserved
for ComFitAEWWingPac and walked in, still dressed in my flight suit. The Operations
Duty Officer recognized me as I told him I was going up to the tower. He grabbed for the
telephone as I entered the stairwell leading up to the tower. It was three flights of stairs to
the door marked TOWER PERSONNEL ONLY. I opened it and went up another flight of
stairs to a steel door equipped with a cipher lock. By now my bad right knee was giving me
fits. I knocked on the steel door and waited a few seconds until it was opened from the
inside. It was totally dark inside, but I could make out the silhouette of a female sailor.

"Good evening, Admiral," she said, and then led the way up a short, steep steel ladder
one more level to the tower enclosure. This steep ladder was really tough on my knee. By
the time I got to the top, I was ready to sit down. The tower supervisor met me at the top of
the ladder and introduced herself as First Class Petty Officer So and So. She offered me one

of those high supervisor's chairs, into which I settled with a clear sigh of relief. Then she put a mug of steaming coffee into my hand and proceeded to introduce all of the tower duty personnel. She was obviously very proud of her team. She told me it was the only all-female watch team at Miramar.

The control room was a circular space surrounded by glass windows. Below the level of the glass was a series of six telecommunications stations. Sitting at each was a person with a radio headset and attached lip microphone, much like those worn by telephone operators. The room, especially from my perspective on the supervisor's chair, provided a panoramic view of the surrounding area. It was almost totally dark. The only illumination came from the consoles of the telecommunications panels at each station. Sitting at each station was a person speaking at regular intervals into the microphones. One of the operators was the regular tower operator...the one to whom we spoke during our landing roll-out. Next to her was the ground control operator...the one to whom we spoke after we turned off the duty runway. Next to her was an operator whose job was to monitor the conversations between the GCA controller and the aircrews making GCA landings on Runway 24 Right. Next was the person whose job was to monitor the field carrier landing pattern (FCLP) being carried out on Runway 24 Left (the short runway). Next in line was an operator whose job was to transmit directly to the crash and rescue personnel in the event of an emergency. There was a station dedicated to monitoring all aircraft departures from Miramar.

Finally, there was a station dedicated to monitoring all of the radar approach control (RAPCON) transmissions between the Federal Aviation Agency facilities and aircraft.

It was a typical clear weather weekday night at Miramar. Regular visual flight rules traffic (VFR) was coming in from the entry point at Atlas and entering the landing pattern for Runway 24 Right at 1,200 feet. The traffic would arrive in flights of up to four airplanes every 15 minutes or so at the time I was observing in the tower. This left-hand traffic pattern was on top of the left-hand FCLP pattern, which was being flown at 600 feet. The FCLP pattern contained six F-14s that were shooting simulated carrier landings on the left runway every 40 or 50 seconds. GCA radar-controlled approaches would come in from the push-over point seven miles east, and were normally single airplane flights. In between landings on Runway 24 Right were the routine training flights departing the field. They would leave in groups of two to four airplanes whenever the tower operator could fit them in between other landings.

As I sat there in my chair in the darkness sipping my coffee, I marveled at how smoothly all of these disparate flight operations were being coordinated by this group of talented air controllers. The tower supervisor must have sensed my interest, because she took the time to point out to me other aspects of interest in the flight operations. Each of her operators was speaking in muted tones...clearly audible, but muted so as not to create chaos. They were directing traffic in an intensely stressful environment, but they were doing it so professionally that it looked easy.

I remembered giving a presentation to a group of San Diego city officials one evening. I had read them a startling statistic. There were more flight operations going on at Miramar on any given day than at John F. Kennedy International Airport in New York. In fact, it was the busiest airport in the United States. The year was 1979.

Finally, I left the tower to its competent operators and made my way home. I realized that I had been in the tower for over an hour. The time was pushing midnight. As I walked in the door at my quarters, I made the cryptic comment to my wife, "You will never guess where I've been for the last hour!"

Those kids were truly "the first team!"

Epilogue:
A Deck Too Far

" It's all over."

- Mrs. Arleigh Burke to her husband on the occasion of his
retirement as Chief of Naval Operations.

Each of us, the three authors, searched his military career for exemplars of specific events which would give the reader an idea, as a closing vignette, of the rich panoply of characters who have made the U.S. Navy and Marine Corps such unique organizations. Of course, we admit to searching for a story which would be entertaining. We further admit to looking for the humorous aspects of military life. Hopefully, many of our stories served both purposes.

But, there was always the hope, in our recounting of events, that there was a moral to be told. Unfortunately, as we each re-read one another's contributions, we came to realize that we weren't that lucky. Some of the vignettes had a moral, many did not. However, we did agree that the work we were jointly doing contained a constant element, usually not articulated, but often emerging subliminally, containing the following haunting thought. There was at least one point in each of our separate careers where we failed to do the right thing...or failed to do the right thing well enough. Sometimes the consequences of our failure were comical, sometimes they were serious...but always there were consequences...and always there was accountability.

So, we agreed to settle on one of the vignettes to be used in the epilogue that seemed to say it all about not doing a job well enough. This is the one we chose:

"The saints are the sinners who keep on trying"
- Robert Louis Stevenson

A Deck Too Far

Have you ever done something that did not work out right or that maybe you were a little ashamed of? Something that surfaces every once in a while in idle moments, and makes you uncomfortable? A young woman treated badly in the heat of the moment, a promise not kept, a failure to produce when all were dependent on you?

Well, one of my failures has to do with the chaplain's organ. It still bothers me after 40 years!

Wasp had been assigned a new chaplain, and we Marines called him Padre. He was so young, and brimmed with faith, hope, and charity! Padre had come aboard our city state filled with great expectations of caring for his nautical flock.

Perhaps a more fitting analogy would be to say that Padre came aboard *Wasp* as a fisher of men, and took his seat in the fighting chair of pastoral pursuits. Or that Padre found himself surrounded by circling barracuda. Or even that it was evident to Padre that to land a single trophy out of that shipload of sinners was going to require extraordinary skill.

The biggest lure in Padre's tackle box of divine props was the new organ, sort of like musical chum, something that he could spread on the palpable fumes of stale beer and vomit permeating the ship's heads on any Sunday morning in port. Something that *just might* draw in those groggy trophies that he had been told of all through Divinity School, a fisher of men as it were.

There came a day when Padre asked Lt. Francis X. Kelly, USMC, for help in moving his organ. Lt. Kelly suggested that the chaplain speak to that good Irish-Catholic fellow in the detachment, popularly known as Lieutenant. And that was how I became responsible for organizing the moving of Padre's brand new organ.

The organ was his pride and joy, as well as a major prop in his traveling road show. Why he picked on me, a private in the marine detachment, is unclear. Somehow, Padre concluded that since I was a catholic, I would see to it that his organ would be moved in some mystical manner without so much as a scratch. Oh ye of too much faith.

The organ, a rich, glossy, golden-oak instrument, had arrived on the dock alongside *Wasp* a few weeks before the cruise, and was left on the hangar deck for Sunday services until *Wasp* went to sea. Padre had been warned that the hangar deck space would become precious once *Wasp* was underway and had recovered its aircraft, so he decided it was time to move his operations to the library in the bowels of the ship, many decks below the hangar deck.

As soon as I got my assignment to move the new organ, I went in search of volunteers to help. And where better to find volunteers than in the Marine detachment, my shipmates? All of the marines were volunteers; something we frequently reminded each other of when the going got bad. "We did volunteer, remember," we said jokingly.

Looking back, perhaps I was too eager for volunteers. When Sly, Trout, Davis, and Fawcett agreed to help, I should have become suspicious. They were all Southern Baptist or Klansmen—good 'ol boys. Now, good 'ol boys are really good 'ol boys. I like them. They just have to be approached gingerly, kind of like an old, overripe stick of gelignite.

Everybody has his own preconceived ideas about the diverse groupings in the United States. And being a Yankee and a New York cityslicker to boot, put me on precarious ground when working with good 'ol boys. But, I've found that once they see you can shoot better, spit farther, drink harder and chase women faster than they can, they do a group re-evaluation on you and ease up a little.

So, I can't say that my volunteers did it on purpose. The job was just too big for us. The organ was too heavy, the knife-edged steel hatches too small, and the ship's ladders too steep. In short, the library was a deck too far. The damage we did to the organ was not catastrophic, it was slow and insidious, greeting the panting movers at every turn and hatchway. With honest forethought we had wrapped the organ with blankets and rope for protection, but the knife-edges of the steel hatches cut through the blankets like shears through a sheep's wool coat.

The veneer of the organ, when we finally stumbled through the library hatch, breathless, looked like a seagull's wing feathers after being run over by a hundred cars. No doubt Padre feels some discomfort of his own to this very day, because when I hesitantly untied the rope and pulled off the blankets, Padre's first words were "Holy shit." Not the sort of thing a chaplain would want a bunch of impressionable young Baptists to hear.

And so, when that day arrives when I step up to the Pearly Gates to report in, "another Marine reporting, sir, I've served my time in Hell," I can imagine St. Peter frowning and replying, "That may well be, Private, but back on *Wasp*, you really screwed up the chaplain's organ."

Glossary

"amateur night" -The evening of payday in the Navy when all the young sailors went ashore in hopes of falling in love with a pretty woman. Older sailors would generally go ashore later after the young sailors struck out and were out of money. In the alternative, one could follow the sage advice given to a friend of mine by a wise old chief, "Go ugly early."

Asshole - Nautical and civilian usage differs. The nautical definition is the kink which can form in a line or hose. Civilians use the term to describe people like Donald Trump and Barbra Striesand

"bend on" - Attaching a line to another line on a ship. We would also use the term to describe getting dressed, "Man, when we get to Hong Kong I'm gonna' bend on my blues and hit the beach!"

"black shoe"- Used to describe the Navy's surface community people. Submariners simply wore oil soaked shoes. Aviators used to wear brown suede type half boots. They now wear boots, I believe. The term is a bit of a pejorative when used by either aviators or submariners.

blue water - Coastal waters are anything but blue. Deep water is a beautiful, deep blue. Deep water is associated with being "at sea," in other words, blue water cruising is being in the middle of the ocean.

"Bock Sheep" - the order given by a sailor on liberty to the cab driver when he wants to be taken back to the ship.

Bollard - A vertical, cylindrical steel device, bell shaped at the top which is mounted on the edges of piers for ships to drop their lines around when they tie up.

bolter - a missed carrier arrested landing attempt during which the airplane becomes airborne and must make another landing attempt.

"Bravo Zulu" - Naval message code for congratulations.

bridle slap - impact of the catapult launching bridle (a heavy steel cable device) on an airplane at the end of a catapult stroke.

Brow - Civilians call them "gangways." On a sub it is an aluminum walkway placed from the pier to the deck, with a railing on one side. It is bolted to the deck underway. If someone gets around to it a canvass banner with the boat's name is hung from the railing.

bubblehead - Describes all submariners with a blend of admiration, affection, and of course, pejorative. See "Sewer pipe sailors."

Captain's Mast - The first step in the military justice system. When a sailor seriously violates the rules he is formally brought before the captain where all the facts are revealed and he is either punished or let off. There is no essential difference between this procedure and that in the 18th century Navy except the rules are now different and the punishment is damn sure different!

cat hook - the hook-shaped device on the catapult bridle which attaches to the airplane at the keel pin.

cat shot - the catapult stroke during which an airplane is launched from an aircraft carrier.

Chow - Nautical expression for food or a shipboard meal.

cleat - any device aboard ship which can be used for attaching lines (usually used for mooring).

"cold iron" - expression for a ship shutting down its boilers (going "cold iron"). When this happens (usually alongside a pier equipped with connections for such amenities as steam, electricity, sewage, water and communications) it means the ship is totally dependent upon shore power.

commissioning pennant - A thin flag longer in the fly than the hoist. Has 7 stars declining in size in a blue field followed by a red and white stripe ending in a swallow tail. Every Navy ship from the day of commissioning flies this pennant over the ensign.

Condition "Zebra" - the highest state of combat readiness on a ship which is normally set during "General Quarters" and during which all "Zebra" fittings are shut and must not be opened.

"crab" - Japanese bar girl talk for cab.

"crub" - Japanese bar girl talk for club.

Dago - short for San Diego.

ditty bag - A small, white cotton, draw string bag issued in boot camp to keep razors and toothpaste. They are thrown out after boot camp but the term remains to describe any container used aboard ship for personal odds and ends.

Dogs - Heavy steel fingers on all water tight doors and hatches which grab the opposing frames and form a strong seal so as to withstand water pressure from either side. They are operated by a crank - this is called "Dogging down the hatch."

donkey dick - the extension bar used on an aircraft hydraulic jack for leverage in raising the airplane…it received its name because it bears a remote resemblance to an equine phallus.

engine order telegraph - a pedestal on the bridge of a ship on which are mounted the engine throttles. Each throttle is a signaling device for each screw indicating the power required by the OD. The signals are answered in the engineering spaces where power is actually applied.

Ensign - The U. S. flag. The "jack" (union jack) was at the bow, in port only, and was only the blue field of the ensign.

EOD - explosive, ordnance, demolition, the division of the ship's weapons department responsible for disabling explosive devices.

eye splice - a loop at the bitter end of a ships wire or rope through which a line can be threaded.

"fart sack" - a mattress cover. A sheet sewn into a bag which is slipped over a thin, foam mattress found on each bunk. After sleeping on one side for a week or two it is flipped over for a bonus of another week or two depending on the level of festidiousness of the particular sailor.

General Quarters - the maximum condition of combat readiness which is rung over the ship's 1MC public address system when the ship goes into battle…a loud and distinct klaxon sound.

Gimbal - Two concentric rings attached by two axis at 90 degrees from one another. Gimbals are used to keep the compass level at all times. They are also used by civilians in power boats to keep their gin and tonics from spilling.

grab ass - mischievous behavior by a sailor while on duty which is counterproductive or even hazardous, also call "skylarking" or "clutchbutt."

"hash marks" - Another example of dual definitions. They are diagonal strips on the lower left sleeve of the enlisted uniform, each stripe representing four years service. The other refers to soil stains at the rear of skivvies, sometimes used as a measure of just how harrowing or scary a shipboard evolution might have been.

Heavie - A long coil of cotton line used in mooring a ship. It has a knot on one end called a "monkey's fist" with a chunk of lead inside. A sailor on the boat throws the line on to the pier (called "stretching") he then "bends" the end of the heavie on to the boat's mooring line which is then pulled to the pier by yard workers.

hernia bar - a long steel bar with two right angle bends in it. The end screws into the nose and tail of a bomb. It is used by aircraft carrier ordnancemen to transport small bombs

hook skip - the bouncing motion of an aircraft arresting hook when it makes contact with the flight deck during a landing attempt.

hook slap - the impact of an airplane's arresting hook when it strikes the flight deck "round down."

hold back fitting - the small, throw away metal device which attaches an airplane to the holdback cable. It breaks during the initial motion of a catapult shot. The catapult crewmen can be seen throwing the broken fitting over the side after a catapult shot.

Horsecock - An anatomically vulgar term for cold cuts - specifically bologna and salami. The actual words "bologna" and "salami" are never spoken in the Navy, but they do appear on ship's menus.

hull number - Once all Navy ships had big white numbers on them for easy identification for us and, unavoidably, the enemy. It appears that the practice has been changed for some subs. They **have** a number, it just isn't plastered all over the sail anymore.

"Jarhead" - slang for a U.S. Marine.

knot - a nautical measure of speed equaling one nautical mile (6,080 feet) per hour. This distance (rather than 5,280 feet) was established since it is equal to one minute of longitude measured at the equator.

"knockers up" - the tactical call from the strike leader telling his flight to turn on their armament master and deceptive electronic countermeasures switches (usually given when approaching enemy territory.

Leave - also "shore leave" meaning permission to leave the ship for an extended period (in excess of 72 hours).

Liberty - permission to leave the ship for the pursuit of pleasure for less than 72 hours.

Locker - In its purest form, it is a metal box with a door and a lock. However, it is often not a tangible thing, but only a place in the Navy. In the Navy everything has a "locker." The chief's quarters on a sub was "The Goat Locker." We even had a locker for emotions, "did you hear about Shorty Freeman throwing a smoke grenade into that bar where the UDT guys hung out in St. Thomas?" "Christ, how stupid can you get? If they caught him, they'd put his humming bird ass in "THE HURT LOCKER."

lose the bubble - submarine jargon for losing situational awareness. It is associated with the pitch and roll indicators (similar to a carpenter's level) in early submarines. If the bubble disappeared from view it signified a serious and unusual roll attitude.

marlin spike - a long, wooden tapered device used by a boatswain's mate for splicing rope or line.

mess cook - Considered the absolute worst and lowest of Navy jobs. It is always temporary unless the sailor is unbelievably unlucky, or a cronic screw up. The job is doing the dishes and peeling potatoes. In heavy seas the job actually exceeds "worst of Navy jobs."

mode one - one of three automatic carrier landing modes, involving a fully automatic carrier arrested landing

number 10 can - The Navy gets most beans, vegetables, soups and the like in cans about the size of a half gallon. Empties were used for all kinds of things, including seasickness. It is also an expression of "quantity" as in, "Hey Wally, how much M.E.K. do you want?" "Oh, a #10 can would do," or, "I was so hungry last night at the Bar Atomic that I had about a #10 can full of yaki soba."

Olongapo (Po City) - a small town filled with camp followers located outside the main gate at Naval Air Station, Cubi Point in the Philippines.

O'Rourke - Calling for Ens. O'Rourke. The sound made when throwing up either due to excessive indulgence on liberty or rough weather OR a combination of the two.

over rotate - to raise the nose of an airplane excessively on take-off or during a catapult shot.

over shoot - to fly past or cross over the extended centerline of an airfield or an aircraft carrier during a landing approach.

pad eye - a small depression in the flight deck of an aircraft crossed by two steel bars…used in tying down aircraft.

piddle pack - a small plastic bag issued to aviators of single-seat aircraft on long flights to collect urine.

"pogey bait" - slang for candy…used in bribing young ladies encountered while on liberty.

quarter deck - the roped off area on the main deck on a naval ship adjacent to where the brow is attached. In port the Officer of the Day (OOD) is stationed here. Ceremonial honors are rendered here for arriving dignitaries.

Quarters - The Navy's version of the commercial world's "morning meeting." Heads were counted, announcements were made, that day's orders were read and work assignments were handed down. This was only done in port on a sub, never at sea. It was always very informal, at least on *Barbero*. Bacon sandwiches were not uncommon.

rack - One of many terms for a bed frame in the Navy either on ship or ashore.

relief tube - small device in single seat carrier aircraft used for jettisoning urine.

running lights - Ships' night time lights, GREEN for starboard and RED for port. They permit other ships to identify the general direction of a ship at night which otherwise can't be seen. Sailors also use the term for human eyes as in, "I hit that f--king bosuns mate right between the runnin' lights last night with an Asahi bottle."

Sack - Another expression for a bed.

salt - Really an old expression used to describe someone who's been in the Navy a long time and who knows his way around - "knows the ropes." It is literal since his hats and clothing have obviously suffered the ravages of salt spray. Everything a salt owns, which is metal, is a bit green, and his khakis are all slightly lighter than everybody elses.

scuttle butt - A water barrel on old ships analogous to the modern day water cooler in an office where rumors were exchanged. (see "the word")

sea bag - Issued on the first day of boot camp to carry all the musty smelling, ill fitting uniforms you were just issued, along, of course, with your brand new, fully stocked ditty bag. Seabag was also used when describing a fellow sailor's IQ or mental state; "Hey, Gillcrist, did you get a load of that new engineman? The guy ain't got a full seabag!" Invariably someone would correct him and say, "Oh no, he's got a full seabag, it just ain't stowed right."

short timer - someone who has a limited amount of time remaining in his enlistment.

skinny - the latest rumor, the scuttlbutt, the scoop, nearly always wrong...see "the Word."

skivvies - white cotton under shorts.

skylarking - another word for "grab ass."

snipes - Enginemen and electricians who never make it topside. They were always oily and pale as hell. When they did get topside, they squinted terribly as though they had done time in "solitary."

"SOS" - creamed chipped beef on toast, a regular Navy breakfast item. Stands for "S—t on a shingle."

spud locker - the area on the main deck of a ship farthest aft where potatoes used to be stored. Also means the read end of the flight deck of an aircraft carrier into which a landing airplane can crash if it is a little low.

squared away -ship shape - everything clean, in order and in its proper place. Used to describe personal appearance.

stern shot - a rear view of a pretty woman.

submarine shower - a classic oxymoron. Since submariners did not take showers at sea, we would go topside and air out holding your arms aloft while the fresh air blew past your arm pits - in the windward sleeve and out the lee.

21 thread - manila line about 3/8 inch in diameter with almost an infinite number of uses.

the word - carries a much higher authenticity than "the skinny," "the scoop," and "scuttlebutt," no doubt attributable to its biblical origins. "The word" usually comes from much farther up the chain than, say, the guy sitting across from you eating "SOS" at breakfast. He might ask,"Hey, Suarez, what's the skinny on liberty when we hit Okinawa?." If you asked the Exec the same question you would say, "Hey, Mister Watkins, what's the word on liberty when we hit Okinawa?"

"three sheets to the wind" - an old, old nautical expression meaning very drunk. Synonyms are: shitfaced, wasted, hammered, snot flying drunk, fallin' down drunk etc.

three wire - the target arresting wire on an aircraft carrier.

"tits up" - nautical slang for broken or out of commission. Used to describe the condition of aeronautical equipment, also called "tango uniform," and refers to a dead animal lying on its back.

torpedo juice - alcohol used in torpedoes which occasionally has been stolen and consumed by seamen for "medicinal purposes."

trap - a successful carrier arrested landing attempt.

trice - verb meaning to tie up and therefore out of the way, usually used in describing how bunks are tied up against the bulkhead to get them out of the way. Morning wake up announcement made over the IMC is, "Reveille, reveille, reveille. Heave out and trice up."

"two block" - as close as you're going to get. When using a block and tackle you really can't draw two objects any closer together than the length of the two hooks and two wooden blocks. The expression is used all the time aboard when a sailor is either up against an object he can't move or a situation he can't alter.

under rotate - failure to raise the nose of an airplane high enough after take-off or a catapult shot. In the latter case the result is flying into the water.

waterways - the deck level area under the labyrinth of pipes and valves covering the insides of the pressure hull. It has a lip next to the passageways so the dripped oil and water don't pose a hazard to walking. The fact is that the hazard is a moot point since the waterways are kept spotlessly clean and always freshly painted

yardbird - civilian shipyard worker...usually used in a pejorative sense indicating someone who is not motivated by anything but his lunch hour, coffee breaks, and quitting time.

Zebra fittings (Zulu fitting) - hatches, access panels and escape hatches which must be dogged down during General Quarters for watertight security. All are identified by a Zebra marking.

1MC - the ship's general public address system used to broadcast General Quarters and administrative announcements during the day.